June 1998



Yvonne + Herman –

It was a pleasure working with you + we hope you enjoy your Brewster experience!

Please Come Again!

Shannon Whitehead
Group Tour - Co-ordinator.

# The BREWSTER STORY

WSTER BROS TRANS CO., LTD
GUIDES & OUTFITTERS.
RRIAGES. SADDLE PONIES.

# The

# BREWSTER STORY

## from pack train . . .

Distributed by
EJH Literary Enterprises, Ltd.
Box 2074
Banff, Alberta T0L 0C0
Canada

First printing, 1981

Designed by Jon Whyte
Printed and bound in Canada

Published by
Brewster Transport Company, Limited

# to tour bus

For my son, Geoffrey,
who had his moments too

by E. J. Hart

# Preface

In an area so young as Western Canada there are few instances where a company can boast of a history extending back almost ninety years. Even more rare is one whose very name conjures up in the mind of many of those who hear it an image of a particular geographic region. However, the name Brewster fits both moulds — a company whose roots reach back to the days of mountain travel by pack train in the early eighteen-nineties and which is synonomous with the Canadian Rockies. These factors alone would make it worthy of an historical treatise, but there are also additional reasons why its story is of interest.

My particular fascination with the story began as a result of research on an earlier book, *Diamond Hitch*, which recounted the exploits of the pioneer outfitters and guides of Banff and Jasper. Jim and Bill Brewster were among this group, but what set them apart was their willingness and ability to move beyond it into other areas of transportation and tourist service as the times changed. Although this aspect was not covered in *Diamond Hitch*, I hoped to be able to follow it up at some future date. In 1976 Jack Hayes, then president and general manager of Brewster Transport, asked me if I would be interested in writing the company's history. After happily accepting his offer I began making my way through the myriad of papers the company had so fortuitously kept over the years and interviewing those who had been associated with it.

As the complete story emerged several other factors became apparent. One was that in recounting the history of Brewster Transport and its predecessor companies, I was essentially writing the history of tourism in the Canadian Rockies. So involved was the company in all aspects of tourism — transportation, merchandising, entertainment, accommodation — that its story more-or-less encompassed the development of this key industry. Even more exciting was the realization that the characters of the story were among the most interesting and colourful ever to inhabit the region. They were an independent, innovative and frequently tough group of individuals who, sometimes against seemingly insurmountable odds, kept the company afloat. Particularly striking was Jim Brewster, leading me to structure the story around his life to a great degree.

There are many people who deserve my heartfelt thanks for their help on this project. First of all, to Jack Hayes for making it possible and for his patience in answering my persistent questions through numerous interviews. Also to other employees of Brewster Transport who always lent their assistance when requested, particularly Dave Morrison and Bill Hope. To all the people who kindly took the time to provide interviews, I also wish to express my appreciation. Two in particular, Pat Brewster and Dell Brewster, require special recognition for the numerous occasions on which they allowed me to impose on their time. A special thanks to Ferg Lothian, Parks Canada historian, who was tireless in his search for information for me. Finally, to Jon Whyte for his excellent editing abilities and his assistance with the design of the book and to Ed Cavell and Robin Armour for their work on the photographs.

Because of the nature of a company history it was often necessary to quote figures. In several instances I chose to round them off to the nearest hundred or thousand depending on the circumstances. As the history of the company spans a long period of time the reader should keep in mind that a dollar was many times more valuable at the turn of the century than it is today.

John Brewster

# Prologue

One warm summer evening in 1892, W. L. Mathews, manager of the CPR's Banff Springs Hotel, mounted his horse and headed down the road to the town, crossed the steel bridge over the Bow River and proceeded up the dusty main street of Banff. Riding past the town's few stores and several scattered residences, he turned to the left and entered the yard of a sturdily constructed log house. Mathews was tired after a long day of catering to the needs and whims of the wealthy international clientele the wonders of the "Canadian Pacific Rockies" were attracting in ever-increasing numbers. Whenever the pressure of business began to weigh on him, he visited his friend John Brewster whose dairy, small but thriving, provided for the needs of the hotel as well as those of the townspeople.

After greeting John, his wife Bella, and their four active young sons, Bill, Jim, Fred and George, Mathews was escorted to the parlour where he was offered a chair and some refreshment. Within minutes he was relaxing and began to relate to his host the trials of his day. Particularly bothersome had been his failure to secure a guide for an important English couple, ardent anglers who wished to pit their skills against the wary trout rumoured to inhabit the numerous lakes in the vicinity. Normally Mathews would have called on Tom Wilson, his regular guide, to take on the chore but the summer was proving exceptionally busy and he was engaged elsewhere.

With the hope he had overlooked someone, Mathews asked Brewster if he knew anyone capable of escorting his guests to one of the more remote lakes. Brewster's answer, seemingly insignificant at the time, was laden with historic consequence. It set in motion a chain of events that would lead his family into diverse aspects of transportation and tourist service in the mountains for more than seventy years. These would range from pack trains, to horse-drawn vehicles to the first motorized transportation in the park. It sowed the seed for the transportation giant that would eventually span the Canadian Rockies right up to present times — the Brewster Transport Company.

Jim Brewster, the teenage guide

# I: The Teenage Guides

The Brewsters of Banff had their roots in sturdy Church of Ireland stock from Irvinestown, County Fermanagh. During the 1830s William A. Brewster was the manager of a rambling 900 acre estate owned by the Irvine family. The Irvines were wealthy landed gentry with a long history in the area, their acquisition of the estate and its huge house, which employed some forty servants, going back to 1613. Brewster's position carried great responsibility for he had to oversee the care of the crops and livestock as well as the carriages and other equipment. But, like many young Irishmen of his day, he was keenly interested in the stories filtering back from North America circulated by the relatives of those who had already emigrated.

One of the Irvine children, James, had trained as a minister in the Church of Ireland and about 1838 left for Canada on missionary work. William Brewster had been quite close to James Irvine and, when the latter wrote to him about Canada's possibilities, he decided to go, a decision made easier since Ireland was in the grip of one of its frequent famines. In 1841 William arrived at Kingston on the shore of Lake Ontario and within a short time was successful in acquiring a farm near Joyceville, across the Rideau Canal. Soon afterward Sarah Jane Irvine came from Ireland, ostensibly to vist her brother, but during her visit she saw a lot of William Brewster and then one day inexplicably disappeared. She and William had slipped across the United States border and were married at Port Vincent, New York.

The couple settled down on the farm and by dint of hard labour and good management soon acquired a second farm in the same area. Quickly William established himself as one of the leading men of the community and seems to have become involved in the politics of Upper Canada. He became a good friend of John A. Macdonald's and through this association he later acquired the contract for the Barfield Toll Bridge over the Rideau Canal. In addition he successfully bid on a munitions hauling contract with the British Army and was likely involved in a variety of other local businesses as well.

**Irvine Castle, Fermanagh, Ireland**

William and Sarah Jane's marriage was abundantly blessed with children, four girls followed by four boys. John, the eldest of the boys, born on March 6, 1852, had a mind of his own. At the age of fourteen he left for school one day and disappeared for two years. He had a passion for the sailing vessels that plied the Great Lakes and spent this period working on them.

On returning home at age sixteen, John's father told him he had three options: he could leave and never come back, continue his education, or learn a trade. Choosing the last option, he spent the next four years apprenticing as a blacksmith at the wage of $8 per month. It was hard work for starvation pay, but when he completed his term he was prepared to meet the future with a certificate and the muscles to go with it.

Within a short time John had acquired a farm of his own near Joyceville, probably through his father's assistance. Despite his years of training he decided not to do any commercial blacksmithing, although he frequently did veterinary work, the knowledge of which he had gained during his blacksmith training. About 1879 he married a local girl, Isabella Thompson, and on July 15, 1880 they had their first child, a boy named after his grandfather, William Alexander Brewster. On February 4, 1882 a second son was born and named after an uncle, James Irvine Brewster.

In spite of John Brewster's rather good station in life in Ontario, in 1881 he decided to try his luck in the west. Reports of seemingly limitless opportunities provided by the push of the Canadian Pacific Railway into the heart of the Canadian prairies were undoubtedly attractive and the personal experiences of one of his brothers already in the west reinforced them. James Brewster was in the Qu'Appelle district by the late 1870s and his other brothers, William and George, headed for Winnipeg soon afterward. Whatever the motivation, John left his family on the farm and proceeded to Winnipeg where, because of his husky build, he immediately found work stacking wet, heavy lumber at $1.75 for a ten-hour day. Other opportunities soon presented themselves and in late 1881 he became one of the first three drivers on the newly created Winnipeg Street Railway system. He apparently returned home for a short period after this, but by 1883 was back in Winnipeg.

Fortunately, during the course of his blacksmith training John had picked up some knowledge of the boiler-making trade which enabled him to land the position of foreman for a crew being sent to install a boiler in a boat at Medicine Hat. He and his men were deposited with the boiler at Swift Current, the end of steel, and then had to haul it the remainder of the way with a four horse team. The boat, christened "The Marquis," being built at Medicine Hat, would make the run to Coalbanks (Lethbridge) to take on coal for the steam locomotives of the CPR. After the boiler was installed John helped in the onerous chore of lining and teaming the steamer up the South Saskatchewan and Oldman Rivers to Coalbanks and then accompanied her back down on the maiden voyage.

After returning to Winnipeg, John decided to move his family out from Ontario and it arrived during the winter of 1883-84. Employment in Winnipeg was becoming increasingly scarce and he had to put his wits to work to find means of support. He struck on the idea of hauling fish from Lake Winnipeg to the town where they would find a ready market. After purchasing a team of horses and building a sleigh, he put his plan into action and his involvement in the "whitefish trade" proved successful enough to keep him at it for several winters.

Nevertheless, because of the precarious economic situation of the time, John was always on the watch for other good prospects. In 1886 he found one in a letter from his brother Bill. William Brewster, trained as a wheelwright and cabinetmaker, was hired by the Dominion Government's Department of the Interior in 1886 to do some specialized work. The Department, responsible for the newly created hot springs reservation in the Rocky Mountains near the CPR station of Banff, had decided to make the springs more attractive for tourists, upgrading the already popular Cave and Basin springs by erecting masonry walls around the pools and constructing bath houses in a rustic "Swiss style." Bill was hired to do the rather difficult carpentry on the bath houses and accompanying caretaker's residence.

On his arrival at Banff, Bill had detrained at Siding 29, or "Old Banff," in the shadow of Cascade Mountain, but surveys were already underway for a new townsite along the Bow River across from the Cave and Basin. Plans were also afoot for the CPR's large hotel adjacent to the new townsite above the confluence of the Bow and Spray Rivers. Obviously the area was on the verge of an era of expansion. Bill noted in his letter that there didn't appear to be a cow between Calgary and Revelstoke and suggested that if John started a dairy he might do quite well.

The suggestion was all that John needed. By October, 1886 he was in Banff to look the situation over for himself. Prospects for the dairy seemed favourable, although it was going to take some time to set up. In the meantime he was able to secure some blacksmithing work with the government over the winter of 1886-87. At the same time he began building a log home near what eventually would be the corner of Banff Avenue and Moose Street (Lot 3, Block 17). The location was outside the surveyed limits of the townsite at this time and not until July 1, 1892, after the survey had been extended, was he granted a lease.

By the spring of 1887 work on the house and an accompanying barn had progressed and he began to acquire cows for the dairy. Most of these came from around Morleyville where a recent acquaintance, Andrew Sibbald, put him in touch with a few people who had animals for sale. Once operations began, his first customers were the hundred-odd people who had decided to make their home in the new town of Banff. But by the summer of 1888 the Banff Springs Hotel had opened and, as he had hoped, became his largest customer.

The dairy on its feet, John brought his family out to their new home in the winter of 1887-88. During the four years they had lived in Winnipeg three more children had been born, Frederick Archibald on December 18, 1883, George Osborne on July 20, 1887 and a daughter Evelyn who died as an infant. With few regrets Bella Brewster and her four boys left Winnipeg by train and arrived at the boxcar depot of "Old Banff" on March 17, 1888. It was St. Patrick's Day, an auspicious occasion for an Irish family to begin a new life.

The wisdom of John's decision to settle in Banff quickly became apparent. By the early 1890s the town was growing rapidly with new hotels and businesses to look after the needs of the visitors coming to "take the waters" at the famous hot springs and to enjoy the mountain scenery. Their number rose dramatically, 7250 being registered at the various hotels in 1891 compared with only 3000 three years earlier. As a result, Brewster's dairy herd had to grow and new pasture lands had to be found.

A bill given Royal assent on June 23, 1887 extended the original hot springs reservation of ten square miles, set aside in 1885, to 260 square miles, creating Canada's first national park, Rocky Mountains Park. George Stewart, the first park superintendent, was initially left pretty much on his own to make decisions affecting the running of the park. However, in November, 1889 a set of regulations was enacted that, among other things, provided for the pasturing of animals. The superintendent could permit the holder of a lot or lots to pasture a cow or horse thereon provided there were not more than two such animals per lot. In Brewster's case an exception had to be made since both the town and the CPR depended on him as a source of supply. About this time he also began to rent pasture lands from the government, paying $100 a year for the privilege by 1898. In addition he entered into an agreement with the CPR to pasture animals on some of the land they owned along their right-of-way near the town, particularly in the vicinity of the Vermilion Lakes.

The growing herd also meant that John needed assistance for his milking and delivery chores, jobs which to a large degree fell to the lot of his sons Bill and Jim. During the summer tourist season the lads arose at 3 a.m. to milk approximately twenty cows each and then make the early morning delivery to the Banff Springs Hotel. When the hotel was closed and only the needs of the townspeople had to be furnished, part of the herd was taken to winter near Kananaskis. John was then able to handle the remainder of the herd, allowing his sons to see to their education.

**Bella Brewster with her sons Bill, Jim, George and Fred in Winnipeg**

Both Bill and Jim had begun their schooling in the Winnipeg Protestant school system, evidently performing quite well. Jim on one occasion received an honour card awarded for "Good Conduct, Industry and Regular Attendance." After the move to Banff both attended the town's first school classes held in part of the superintendent's office during the summer of 1888. These classes were soon shifted to a large walled tent which first occupied a site on the north-west corner of Wolf Street and Banff Avenue and later the north-east corner of Wolf and Beaver Streets. As the eldest in attendance, Bill was given the

William Twin

responsibility of fireman, stocking the stove with a good supply of wood each evening and returning early each morning to stoke up the dying embers. Bill also spent part of the summer of 1891 going to the McDougall school at the Morley Indian Agency, staying with his uncle James Brewster who was working on the Mount Royal Ranch across the Ghost River from the settlement.

By the fall of 1891 the boys' attendance at school had become somewhat spotty. For example, the record showed that they were present from August 14th through September 25th but then for the rest of the term were "kept out to work at home." This was mainly due to the increased workload at the dairy but was also at least partially attributable to the fact that they took every opportunity available to slip away with William Twin, a Stoney Indian, to explore the mysteries of the surrounding mountains.

William, a member of the Wildman family of Stoneys, was known as Twin because he had a twin brother, Joshua. Having received some instruction at the McDougall mission, he could speak some English. He was extremely knowledgable about the mountains, particularly the Kootenay Plains area, where he often wintered with a few other Stoneys, and the southern watershed of the Bow River, his usual hunting territory. When development began in the Lake Louise area in the early eighteen-nineties he put his knowledge to good use, aiding Willoughby Astley, manager of the Lake Louise Chalet, in building some of the first trails in the vicinity. A striking man in appearance, he was described by mountaineer Walter Wilcox who found him making a trail to Lake Agnes when he visited the lake in 1894: "William was a fine looking Indian. He came nearer to a realization of the ideal Indian features such as one sees on coins, or in allegorical figures, than almost any savage I have ever seen."

William first appeared at the dairy about 1888, at which time John hired him to help take off a hay crop on a small field between the first and second Vermilion Lakes. Thereafter he returned every summer to help with the hay and quickly became a good friend of the family. Much of his time was spent with the young Brewster boys recounting his hunting experiences in the mountains before the white man, relating Indian tales and lore and teaching them the rudiments of Stoney and Cree. By 1891 he was teaching Bill and Jim how to hunt mountain sheep, goat, bear and other varieties of big game to be found in the area. He also began to take them on horseback trips to some of the trout-rich hidden mountain lakes. On one such expedition Jim probably became the first white man to visit Mystic Lake when he was only nine years old.

Thus it was that when W. L. Mathews mentioned the problem of a guide for his fishing party on that summer evening in 1892, John Brewster was able to offer a suggestion. Bill and Jim, although only twelve and ten years old respectively, had already gained a great deal of mountain experience from William Twin. William himself was also available, and, if Mathews were willing, he and the two boys could take the party to some trout-producing waters. Mathews, aware of the boys' maturity despite their young years, agreed that it was worth a try.

Little is known of the trip's details — only that the party, escorted to Sawback Lake, found it teeming with fish. The English couple, undoubtedly pleased with the results, mentioned their satisfaction to Mathews and so he began to call on the boys to perform similar services for other clients that summer. Neither Bill nor Jim had the means to finance the horses and equipment necessary to handle such requests, but their father agreed to let them use some of his horses and bought them a few pack saddles and a bit of camping gear.

Although at first the two were keen to put their new-found independence to work, their attention soon began to wander to other boyhood pursuits and work at the dairy took up most of their available time. Then early in the fall of 1892 John was approached by Mrs. R. G. Brett, whose son Harry had been sent off to St. John's College in Winnipeg. He had written home to say he was lonely and wondered if his friend Bill Brewster could come down to join him. John agreed and sent both Bill and Jim to the college as boarding students that fall. They remained until February, 1893 when an outbreak of scarlet fever closed the school and the boys were sent home. When the danger had passed it was too late to return and they continued their education in the schoolhouse that had been built on Banff Avenue.

After returning from Winnipeg, Bill began to spend much of his time away from home, mainly at a ranch which his father was developing near Lacombe. On September 25, 1891 John had purchased a quarter section of land* with house and stables from a Harry Anderson of the Blind River district for $100. He soon began to keep both horses and cattle at the site and found it necessary to register a brand, an algebra x ($x$) † alloted on March 30, 1892. The ranch buildings and stock required someone present at all times and young Bill shouldered much of the responsibility. He spent the better part of 1894 there, but returned to Banff to attend school in 1895. By 1896 he was back at the ranch and spent most of the next two years looking after its development.

Eventually tiring of the rather isolated life, Bill left the ranch to go to Golden for the winter of 1897-98 at the invitation of his uncle Jim. James I. Brewster had purchased the Russell House Hotel at Golden but, because of his easy-going nature, he was having trouble with his bartenders dipping their hands into the cash. He asked Bill to tend bar for him and see if he could help straighten out the problem. Bill accepted and soon found that he had bitten off a big chunk of responsibility. Golden, the headquarters of the CPR's tie and bridge timber cutting operations, had seven big lumber camps in its vicinity. Consequently the Russell House bar was a rough-and-ready place and the seventeen year old Bill soon showed several battle scars from the brawls which frequently erupted. When he left in the spring of 1898 he was quite a bit wiser and a lot tougher.

By the summer of 1898 the Klondike Gold Rush was underway and Bill proceeded to Edmonton where he met two Montana cowboys who suggested taking a bunch of horses to sell up in the gold fields. With the money he had saved from his bartending, Bill bought some horses and the three set off northward on the Klondike trail. After laying over in the Swan Hills country for a time due to bad weather they went on to the Peace River which they followed upstream to its source at the head of the Liard River. Here they intended on wintering, but as the cold weather approached they had second thoughts and decided to return. Fortunately Bill traded off the horses for a considerable number of beaver, mink and marten pelts which eventually fetched a good price in Edmonton.

While Bill was off on his various exploits after 1893, his brother Jim spent his time much closer to home. His attendance at school was still hit-or-miss but essentially he continued to go until April, 1897 when he left for good. During this period his winters were spent helping his father with the continually expanding dairy. By

*SW¼, Sec. 6, Tp. 40, R. 26, W. 4

†The brand was apparently meant to be back to back horseshoes but was mistaken for an algebra x by the registrar.

**The Brewster family at the Brewster Dairy, 1898. Left to right — Jim, Fred, Bill, Jack, John, George, Pat, Pearl and Bella**

1896 John found that there was no longer sufficient space for expansion on the four lots he was now occupying on the Banff Avenue site but an agreement with the CPR allowed him to move his headquarters to some of the land they had let him use for grazing purposes. In the summer of 1896 the log house on Banff Avenue was dismantled and moved to the new location on Whiskey Creek along the access to the old CPR tote road, just across the tracks from the Banff station. Immediately after the move, John and Bella's last child, Forrest Oliver (Pat), was born on September 20, 1896 joining his four brothers born before the family came to Banff and two children born in the interim, Pearl on July 25, 1889 and Jack Walker in May, 1893.

While most of Jim's activities continued to revolve around working at the dairy, he spent a part of his summers as a stableboy and guide for the CPR at the Lake Louise Chalet. Beginning in 1894 the CPR's advertising campaign attracted numerous tourist-explorers, scientists and mountaineers from the United States and abroad anxious to discover the mysteries and to ascend the peaks of the Canadian Rockies. Few experienced guides were available, which probably accounts for Jim's employment despite his tender years. Unfortunately, his first client proved to be an irascible old Irish colonel named Robert O'Hara who wished to be guided to the lake which would eventually bear his name. O'Hara had been told of the existence of this lake by J. J. McArthur, a Dominion Land Surveyor, who had glimpsed it from the top of a mountain along the railway line while performing his photo-topographical surveys. Jim brashly assured the Colonel he could guide him to it, but while proceeding up Cataract Brook he became lost in a maze of fallen timber. O'Hara was furious and thereafter used one of the men working for outfitter Tom Wilson to aid him in his explorations. In later life the incident would make Jim the butt of many a good natured jibe by Wilson.

Undoubtedly he performed other guiding activities for the CPR in the Lake Louise area after 1894, but it was not until the summer of 1898 that another of these was recorded. On that occasion Rest F. Curtis and Professor Charles E. Fay, members of the Appalachian Mountain Club of Boston, decided to make the first traverse of Abbot Pass from Lake Louise to Lake O'Hara. Jim, suggested by the CPR, acted as both porter and guide and performed much more competently than he had with O'Hara. After the party reached Lake O'Hara and his patrons wished to return back to the railroad via Cataract Brook, Jim proved his value by discovering a route when the trail petered out and then led the way back and forth across the stream on fallen logs when heavy timber blocked their progress. When camp was made for the night Curtis and Fay had to gather wood for the fire "while Jim slept the sleep of the just and the young," but on the whole they were well satisfied with his services. Curtis summed up their thoughts by stating "we think we discovered in him the raw material of an excellent guide." The accuracy of his assessment was to be proved in the years immediately ahead.

Jim near Abbot Pass, 1898

Jim's home at the Brewster Dairy. Left to right (front) — Jim, George, Pearl, Lade, Phil Moore; (rear) — Fern, Bella

# II: A Second Try

While Bill and Jim were engaged in their own particular pursuits between 1892 and 1898, interesting developments had been taking place on the tourist scene in Rocky Mountains Park. Most of the tourists arriving at this time were from the wealthy, leisured classes and wished to have their days filled with interesting pastimes while they enjoyed their visit to the mountains. Apart from bathing in the hot springs and shopping in Banff's several curio stores, they usually chose to take short drives or rides in the vicinity of Banff in order to enjoy the magnificent scenery. Carriage roads to the Upper Hot Springs and the Cave and Basin had been constructed in 1886 and by late 1887 one nine-and-a-half miles in length had been opened to Devil's Lake (Lake Minnewanka). Other pleasant drives followed: the Loop at the base of Mount Rundle in 1889, an extension of Cave Avenue to Sundance Canyon in 1892, an extension of Buffalo Street to the Hoodoos and then on to Anthracite in 1893, and a road from the station toward Vermilion Lakes connecting with the old CPR tote road in 1894. For those who preferred saddle horses, a few bridle trails were constructed around Banff, such as the path to the summit of Tunnel Mountain cleared in 1890. At Lake Louise the CPR cooperated in building trails to points of interest near the Chalet in 1894.

At Banff several small livery stables developed in the early nineties to handle the sightseeing requests of tourists. Added to these in 1893 was a more substantial livery business as the CPR recognized it needed its own livery services to serve the desires of patrons at the Banff Springs Hotel. A contract was let to W. L. Mathews, Colonel James Walker of Calgary and Major John Stewart of Ottawa who set up the CPR Transfer Company and built a substantial stable along the road between the hotel and the town.

The nineties also saw the appearance of the new type of tourist — mountaineers and tourist-explorers who wished to visit and examine the remotest parts of the Rockies and to climb some of the numerous unconquered peaks. Walter D. Wilcox and his friends from Yale University started the trend with their climbs and explorations in the Lake Louise region. From there they and others, particularly those associated with the Appalachian Mountain Club (Boston) and The Alpine Club (London), pushed the frontiers south to Mount Assiniboine and north to the Columbia Icefield by 1898. Likewise Banff became known as a headquarters from which to begin big game hunting and fishing trips, and increasing numbers of wealthy sportsmen arrived annually to pursue their prey.

These factors meant that the outfitting and guiding professions became very attractive as the decade progressed. The main benefactor proved to be Tom Wilson, a native of Barrie, Ontario who had come west as a NWMP constable in 1880 and had then packed for CPR surveys through the mountains from 1881 to 1883. His knowledge of the mountains was second to no one's and as early as 1887 the CPR was asking him to escort some of its patrons on hunting and fishing trips. By 1893 he had established an active outfitting and guiding business at Banff with corrals and headquarters on the south-east corner of Banff Avenue and Buffalo Street. Soon he received permission to advertise himself as "Guide to the CPR" and, as he held a virtual monopoly his business expanded rapidly, requiring numerous guides, packers and cooks, rough-and-ready individuals who could handle horses and meet the wilderness on its own terms. Most of the famous early outfitters and guides who eventually plied their trade along the CPR line, such as Bill Peyto, Jim Simpson, Fred Stephens and Bob Campbell, received their training working for Wilson. They only exceptions among the pioneer outfitters and guides were the Brewsters.

After returning from his unsuccessful but not unprofitable attempt to reach the Klondike, Bill played hockey for Edmonton's Thistle Club for the winter of 1898-99. The following spring he returned to his father's dairy and found his brother Jim at loose ends, much like himself. By this time the dairy herd had grown to almost 100 animals and their father had hired several men to help with the milking and deliveries, a development which lessened the importance of the boys' help. In fact both Bill and Jim had reached the age where they had to decide what they wished to do with their lives. Neither had any formal training in a trade, and their education, good as far as it went, did not go too far.

In spite of their limitations both brothers could spot an opportunity quickly, a trait they had inherited from their father which would often stand them in good stead in future years. In the spring of 1899 opportunity seemed to lie in the direction of outfitting and guiding, more so since they already had some experience in this line of work. But the situation had changed since their first short-lived venture of 1892. To be successful they had to emulate Wilson and employ bold but trustworthy men to handle their parties and maintain a sizeable string of saddle and pack horses and good equipment to make their clients' trips as enjoyable as possible. It would require time and money. Of the first they had plenty, but of the second almost none.

Again their father stepped in and offered his assistance. If the boys promised to stick with it this time and if they agreed to let some of their younger brothers in on the business if it proved successful he would stake them. They agreed and in the summer of 1899 acquired from the Stoney Indians some of the necessary saddle and pack horses, branding them with their newly registered pronghorn brand.* At the same time they built a pack shed at their father's dairy to serve as a headquarters. In May, 1900 they launched their enterprise under the name of "W. & J. Brewster, Guides and Packers" with posters placed around town and an advertisement in the recently initiated Banff newspaper, *The National Park Gazette*, reading

Tourists Attention

W. & J. Brewster Guides and Packers Complete Camping and Packing Outfits And Experienced Guides Furnished To Any Part Of The Mountains On Short Notice At Reasonable Rates.

The "experienced guides" were, of course, themselves, with William Twin lending his assistance from time to time.

*In later years the company brand was referred to as the "elkhorn brand" but records show it was meant to represent the horn of an antelope.

# Camping, Fishing, Hunting and Alpine Climbing

## In the HEART OF THE CANADIAN ROCKY MOUNTAINS

W. & J. BREWSTER

EXPERIENCED GUIDES AND PACKERS

Good Horses Complete Outfits
Indian Hunters if Desired
Reasonable Rates Correspondence Solicited

Address W. & J. BREWSTER
NATIONAL PARK, BANFF,
ALBERTA, CANADA

The season proved to be pretty much a failure, except for a few small fishing and hunting parties. Wilson's well-developed service and highly skilled employees skimmed the cream off the tourist crop. His reputation had spread so rapidly among the alpine and sporting fraternities of Great Britain and the United States that parties arriving in Banff insisted on his services. Their trips were the kind that produced revenue since they lasted anywhere from two weeks to a month and demanded large amounts of horses, equipment and manpower. The regulations of 1889 allowed an outfitter to charge $3 a day for a guide and $3 a day for a saddle horse, but he was free to negotiate the cost of other supplies, foodstuffs and services with his client. The Brewster boys' clientele tended to be those who Wilson felt would not be profitable to handle.

Despite their problems the brothers remained undaunted, realizing at the outset that breaking into the business was not going to be easy. But they quickly found they enjoyed the lifestyle that the profession entailed. Life on the trial was not easy: escorting a party through the wilderness required long hours of hard work rounding up horses, packing, making and breaking camp, cooking, clearing trail, piloting intransigent horses across dangerous rivers, through downed timber and over high passes. But it allowed them to experience the moods and beauties of the mountains they both loved, and to be paid to participate in their passions of hunting and fishing. Equally appealing was the town life of the trailmen as, generally speaking, they tended to be a pretty wild and woolly bunch. Regulations forbade barrooms and saloons in the park, but bootleg whiskey was easy to obtain, and all night carouses were common wherever packers and guides gathered. Both brothers, happily fitting into this mould, began to establish lasting reputations for living the "high life." Jim, in particular, soon became one of those colourful individuals of whom legends are made, but with it came a love for the bottle that would plague him for the rest of his life. Bill, no slouch when it came to drinking, was more noted for his eye for the ladies.

Because of the meagre returns of the 1900 season, other sources of income would be needed to support them while they got on their feet. Both played hockey for the winter, Bill with a Revelstoke team and Jim at Lacombe. Then in May, 1901 Bill fortunately obtained the position of forest ranger and game guardian for Rocky Mountains Park. The regulations of 1889 prohibited the shooting, capturing or killing of wild animals in the park and the taking of fish by any means other than rod and reel. Limited manpower at Superintendent Stewart's disposal weakened the enforcement of the regulations, but he hoped hiring a game guardian would remedy the situation. But there proved a far more pressing problem to deal with in the frequent, destructive forest fires that burned virtually unchecked along the CPR line, caused mainly by the sparks thrown off by coal burning locomotives. Bill's primary job was to inspect the locomotives as they passed through Banff, ensuring they had the proper spark screens to prevent such occurrences. In addition, he had to clear some fire breaks to prevent the spread of fires that did break out, and on occasion accompanied the chief inspector of timber and forestry on inspection tours. For these duties he received a salary of $50 per month, but still had some time to devote to guiding.

**Bill and a lady friend**

While Bill's time in 1901 was split between official and business activities, Jim devoted all of

Jim (right) with a pack train party at the Brewster Dairy

his time to developing their outfitting operations. More horses would be needed if they were to compete with Wilson so in July he and his brother Fred left for Fort Macleod where they purchased twenty-five head. Driving the animals to Banff took a week and they immediately put them to work handling the few parties that W. & J. Brewster had been able to book.

The company's first venture into the contract packing business developed that summer as well. Contract packing involved bidding on a contract to haul supplies and equipment for either government development work or for some company engaged in resource exploitation, usually mining. Early parks legislation allowed mining and logging within the park boundary. Both had flourished, the Eau Claire and Bow River Lumber Company cutting on several timber berths along the Spray River, and the Canadian Anthracite Coal Company establishing coal mines at Anthracite in 1886. Several other small mining developments were attempted during the eighteen-nineties, both in the park and in its immediate vicinity, and contract packing soon became commonplace. The contract packer had to calculate carefully how many pack horses he would need to haul the goods — which, in addition to foodstuffs, might include drills and bits, tools, stoves and dangerous explosives — how long a round trip to the development site would take, and how many trips would be needed. If his bid were accepted he could very well find himself out of pocket if he misfigured.

Fortunately W. & J. Brewster made a profit from its first contract. Sam Wigmore, a group of Calgary businessmen and Dr. R. G. Brett of Banff had an interest in a mine known as the Jubilee property along the upper headwaters of the Cascade River north of Banff. During the summer of 1901 the group brought in a mining expert from Ottawa to evaluate the prospect and it afterwards proceeded with some development work. The company won the bid for the packing contract and Jim spent much of the summer on the long trail between Banff and the mine.

Despite their profitable initial entry into the contract packing business, the 1901 season proved only slightly more successful than the previous one. They lured few parties away from Wilson and unless they attracted more tourists interested in taking longer trips their business seemed doomed to failure. There was little the brothers could do to change the situation. But their luck held good. The CPR, for the first of many times, came to their rescue.

Because of the CPR's key position in the development and the proper promotion of Western Canada, individuals and organizations often approached the railway for its support of their projects advertising the area and its attractions. Among the groups which frequently called on the railway were the various sportsmen's clubs in the United States which requested its help in finding representatives for the annual spring Sportsman's Show held in Madison Square Garden. In the fall of 1901 the railway's western officials had to find representatives from the game district on the eastern slopes of the Canadian Rockies and asked Bill and Jim if they would be interested, offering to pay their travelling expenses to and from New York. Their father agreed to cover living expenses while they were there, allowing the boys to accept the invitation. Immediately they set out to fulfill the requirements for their display, which was to depict the sporting possibilities of the district by means of the choicest specimens of game to be found within it. Throughout the fall and early winter they constantly hunted for both big and small game and put together a fine collection of heads and hides of grizzly and black bear, bighorn sheep, mountain goat, cougar, caribou, moose, elk, deer, lynx and beaver, and added to it an assortment of Indian beadwork, buckskin shirts, belts, knives and moccasins which they felt would interest those attending the exhibition. At the end of January, 1902 the boys departed on the train for the east with their game collection and other useful items, including a tepee of the type used for shelter when out on the trail. In New York they set up the tepee and other pieces of camp outfit as the centerpiece of their imaginative display, which attempted to depict a sportsman's camp in the mountain wilds.

Meanwhile crowds of sportsmen began to flood into Madison Square Garden to see what the show had to offer. Among them were two classmates at Princeton University from prominent American families, Philip Augustus Moore and Frederick Byram Hussey. Moore's grandfather and granduncle had started Old Crow Whiskey Distilleries and had made a large fortune from it. As one wag put it, the first generation made the whiskey and, unfortunately, the next one drank it, substantially depleting the company's coffers. Nonetheless there was still plenty of money in the family and Moore benefited from an excellent education. Although slight of build he was an accomplished athlete, his credits including tying for the United States intercollegiate pole vaulting championship in 1901 and winning the gymnastic championship on the parallel bars in 1902. Hussey's grandfather, Dr. Curtis Grubb Hussey, had been a pioneer developer of copper claims in the Lake Superior region and in 1849-50 had founded Pittsburg Copper and Brass Rolling Mills, the first manufacturer of sheet copper and brass in the United States. Beginning in 1859 he also became interested in producing steel and eventually headed Hussey, Howe and Company, the nation's first producer of crucible steel in large quantities. Fred's father, also named Curtis, eventually became involved in the management of these companies but unfortunately met a premature death in 1884. However, as in Moore's case, there was ample money in the family and Fred too was well educated. At Princeton he was drawn into friendship with Moore because of their shared love for athletics and the outdoors, his particular forte being baseball.

Both Moore and Hussey had some previous experience with outfitters, Moore having visited a dude ranch in Wyoming and Hussey having hunted big game in the western United States. Accordingly they were quickly drawn to the Brewster exhibit, which was proving to be the highlight of the outfitting displays at the show.

Phil Moore and Fred Hussey

There they found the Brewster brothers handing out literature and drawing those interested into conversation. Jim, already beginning to polish his gift for smooth talk into a well-developed repertoire, was proving particularly adept at this. Along with his slightly bow-legged stance and his colourful western garb of buckskin shirt and grizzly bear chaps, he sounded and looked very much like a "western original" and was bound to attract attention. Already the Brewsters had several important parties lined up for the coming season and after talking with them Moore and Hussey determined that they must be among them. Since they were both due to graduate from Princeton that fall they decided on trying to convince their families to make a trip their graduation present.

Returning to Banff, Bill and Jim began to prepare for the parties they had booked. As they had also been able to line up more packing contracts, they immediately had to increase the company's manpower. Obviously the place to look was among the ranks of Wilson's corps of well-seasoned guides and packers and they acquired two men from this source. The more experienced was Tom Lusk, a former Texas cowhand who had begun guiding for Wilson in 1896 and had a reputation for having as good a knowledge of horses as any man on his crew. The other was Frank Wellman, a curly red-haired nineteen year old lad from Ontario who had begun packing for Wilson at the age of fourteen in 1897.

With the manpower situation temporarily solved, they expected the 1902 season might provide the breakthrough they so desperately needed. The year turned out better than they had dared hope with numerous fishing and hunting parties, a result of the Sportman's Show appearance. The T. S. McIntyre party of Dayton, Ohio they guided to the virgin game country on the headwaters of the Athabasca River. Another, ultimately more important party consisted of Hussey and Moore, who had graduated and received their requested reward. Jim personally conducted them on a successful hunting trip and cemented the friendship that had blossomed in New York.

Contract packing also proved fairly lucrative that year. Early in September, W. & J. Brewster began packing provisions and tools to a camp of fourteen "prospectors" on the Cascade River about ten miles from town. Rumours as to what they were looking for and who was financing them were rampant in Banff, but, as in the case of most contract packing for resource developers, the brothers had to keep close-lipped. Ultimately it came out that the interested party was the Natural Resources Department of the CPR and that it was looking for coal — the beginning of development at what subsequently became Bankhead Mines.

A second contract, secured with the government, involved the building of a meteorological observatory at the top of Sulphur Mountain. The four mile switchbacked bridle trail up the mountain, built in 1902, represented an altitude gain of some 3000 feet, requiring difficult work for both horses and packers. The lumber and tools, unwieldy to pack, frequently needed adjusting as the horses ascended the steep incline. In addition, heavy loads of sand and water were required to mix cement at the summit. On the other hand, numerous trips had to be made over an extended period of time, resulting in an excellent pay-day for the company at the completion of the contract.

Their feet finally on the ground, Bill and Jim again made the trip to New York early in 1903. Further success attended their efforts and they lined up numerous parties for the coming season. Arriving home in early May, they immediately set out to hire additional help, being fortunate to find three young men who would prove valuable for many years to come. They were Fred "Tabby" Tabuteau, a recent immigrant from Ireland who had worked for Wilson; Bill Potts, the son of a partner in the Alberta Hotel at Banff who had spent some time cowpunching on his grandparents' ranch near Morley; and George Harrison, a native of Sibley, Iowa who had come to Canada in 1900 and had worked on a ranch near Cochrane. All three had considerable experience with horses, and they soon had plenty to handle. In the middle of May, seventy-five head, brought into town from their winter range, were quickly alloted to the various parties waiting to go out on the trail. Among these parties were two bound for the renowned bear hunting country to the north of Donald, B.C., one headed by William Buckhout of New York and the other by G. O. Shields, editor of the popular outdoors magazine *Recreation*. A third party which soon followed them to the area was composed of Hussey and Moore, who had been so pleased the previous year that they had decided to return to enjoy the excellent hunting as well as the companionship of the Brewsters.

During the course of building up their business over the period from 1901 to 1903, Bill and Jim also began to enhance their personal reputations as concerned and responsible citizens of the growing town of Banff. Jim had married in the fall of 1901. His wife was Tressa (Lade) Bagley, who had come from Iowa in 1893 with her parents and five brothers and sisters to land purchased from the Hudson's Bay Company, about a mile-and-a-half east of Lacombe. She probably met Jim soon after, during one of his visits to his father's ranch in the same district. Subsequently her sister Sylvia (Tead) had married William Froste, the station agent at Lacombe, and about 1896 he was transferred to the CPR station at Banff. Lade Bagley had come to Banff to live with her sister, attending school as a classmate of Jim's during his last year of formal education in 1897. After their marriage Jim's new station in life brought with it certain responsibilities and these were further augmented when the couple was blessed with their only child, Fern Pearl Brewster, on August 20, 1902. She was born in the new two-storey frame home which Jim had constructed adjacent to his father's log house at the dairy.

Even previous to Jim's marriage the brothers were already well-known and respected in the community. The sons of one of Banff's leading citizens, they were also two of the town's best athletes. Both were accomplished hockey players and they frequently upheld the local colours as members of Banff's baseball team. Their skills also went beyond these two fields; during the annual Victoria Day sports event in 1901 they virtually swept the field. Jim placed first in the single scull boat race, the 100 yard dash, the standing high jump, the running long jump and the hop, step and jump, and Bill exhibited his superior horsemanship by winning the quarter mile pony race.

Starting in 1902 the brothers began to participate in another favourite local activity that would bring them even more prominence: acquiring leases to develop for commercial purposes. The foremost practitioner of this art was

**Lade Brewster**

Dr. Robert G. Brett who had begun his successful medical and business career in Banff in 1886 with the building of "The Sanitarium," a combined hotel and hospital located at the south end of Banff Avenue. To this property Dr. Brett had added numerous other leases on which he eventually constructed a drug store, a blacksmith shop, the Grand View Villa Hotel at the Upper Hot Springs, the Brett Block and several residences, all of which provided substantial revenues. The lesson was not lost on the young Brewsters who resolved to do their best to follow where Brett had led. On December 1, 1902 Bill secured the lease on Lot 16, Block 1 (131 Banff Avenue), and on May 1, 1903 Jim acquired the lease on Lot 15, Block 1 (129 Banff Avenue).

In the heart of Banff's business district, these two valuable pieces of property provided an opportunity for the brothers to engage in commercial development, but they lacked the funds to take advantage of the opportunity. The slim returns from W. & J. Brewster paid their own expenses, leaving a bit to plough back into new equipment and horses, but that was all. However, in 1904 funds came available from an unexpected source that would allow them to develop both these properties and several others as well.

Brewster Brothers' "hotel bus" at the Banff station

# III: Partners and Partings

In 1897 developments began on the CPR livery scene that would play a key part in W. & J. Brewster's future. Colonel James Walker and his partners decided to divest themselves of the CPR Transfer Company, selling it to the CPR itself for $3000. The livery stable was thereafter run as a part of the Banff Springs Hotel, and the outfitting business was, of course, turned over to Tom Wilson. But in 1902 the CPR's recently created Hotel Department, wishing to have securely contracted services at its disposal, set about formalizing some of its rather informal transportation arrangements.

The first to be approached was Wilson who had extended his outfitting operations to Lake Louise and Field to handle patrons at the Lake Louise Chalet and Mount Stephen House. In addition he had begun a livery service at Laggan (Lake Louise Station) and Field to transport passengers and baggage to the Lake Louise Chalet and to the new Emerald Lake Chalet being developed by the CPR. With this foothold, Wilson was the obvious choice to continue on, and in 1902 he signed a contract which stipulated that he would operate his livery business to the satisfaction of the company and "would keep on hand at the said points a sufficient number of Democrat waggons with adjustable covers and other buggies, conveyances, vehicles, harness, saddles, pack saddles and work horses as may be necessary for the use and accommodation of the Company's passengers or guests . . . ." In return the CPR agreed to collect fares on his behalf amounting to $4 for one or two persons taken on a return trip to Emerald Lake, 50¢ per person taken from Laggan to the Lake Louise Chalet or vice versa, $2 per day for each saddle or pack horse and $2 per day for each packer.

After Wilson contracted at Field and Laggan, the outfitting business at Banff became much more competitive. The chief benefactors proved to be W. & J. Brewster and Bill Peyto who, after working many years for Wilson, had set up an outfitting business of his own in 1901. Eventually, though, the Hotel Department decided that while it desired to keep the livery service at Banff in its own hands, it should contract outfitting services. Early in 1904 the concession was awarded to W. & J. Brewster.

Why Bill and Jim and not Bill Peyto obtained the coveted appointment as Guides and Packers to the Canadian Pacific Railway Company" is not known with certainty. Peyto, reputed to be the most competent and colourful guide in the area, possessed a loyal and influential clientele of mountaineers and hunters. On the other hand, Bill and Jim were well known to the local railway officials through their early association with John Brewster's dairy, their initial guiding endeavours and their later involvement in the Sportsman's Show. Their politics was also another factor in their favour.

The CPR was acutely aware of the political winds of the time and for the preceding eight years the federal party in power had been the Liberals under the strong leadership of Sir Wilfrid Laurier. No more loyal and vociferous supporters of the Liberals were to be found in Western Canada than among the members of the Brewster clan. The family had been strong Conservatives due to the friendship of William Brewster and Sir John A. Macdonald and the acquiring of the Barfield toll bridge concession through it. But when John Brewster and his brothers, then living in Winnipeg, failed to acquire some property they desired after running afoul of some government-appointed land agents, they switched their loyalties to the Liberals, hoping to secure the agents' ouster. Irishmen took their politics seriously and, after his arrival in Banff, John became deeply involved in supporting the Liberals on the local scene. Unhappily the representative in the Legislative Assembly of the North West Territories for the district of Banff was Dr. Brett, a powerful Conservative.

Brett had first been elected to the Assembly in June, 1888 and was re-elected in 1891 and 1894. Although John respected his abilities, when it came to politics the latter did everything in his power to try to unseat the popular doctor. But Brett's high profile in the constituency and his astute political acumen made him a formida-

**Phil Moore and Bill (in centre rig) at the Banff Livery, 1904**

ble opponent. All John's efforts on behalf of the Liberals came to naught. In the 1898 election the Liberals finally put forward a particularly strong candidate in the person of Arthur Sifton, brother of Clifford Sifton, Minister of the Interior. John worked hard on Sifton's campaign and, to their future benefit, so did Bill and Jim. Sifton won the seat by six votes, but Brett contested the result and a judicial recount gave him the seat by two votes, although the matter did not end there. A by-election held in June, 1899 again gave Sifton the majority and he remained Banff representative until 1903 when he was appointed Chief Justice of the Supreme Court of the North West Territories. In 1909 he became the second premier of the Province of Alberta. Bill and Jim had made a wise decision in lending him their support.

Whether it was politics or other factors which lay behind the brothers' acquisition of the CPR outfitting concession, it was unquestionably a landmark in the company's history. With it came the secure base upon which they could expand and diversify their interests and it helped to attract the capital which allowed them to. The capital came from Philip Moore and Fred Hussey, who were looking for interesting investments now that they had graduated. They did not intend to become actively involved in the company but hoped to spend some time in the Rockies with the Brewsters and felt that the outfitting concession made the company's success more likely. The partnership, formalized early in 1904, took the name of Brewster Brothers. To it Bill and Jim contributed the assets of W. & J. Brewster and their Banff Avenue lots, while Moore and Hussey each put in approximately $25,000 in cash.

After the formation of the new company, the partners' first objective was to develop the Banff Avenue properties. As soon as weather conditions permitted, construction began on a livery stable at 129 Banff Avenue, a small, inexpensive frame building, the total cost of construction and the horses and rigs to stock it amounting to $5000. It began business early in May, 1904 under the name of Banff Livery and, because of its central location, immediately proved popular. At the end of May, Brewster Brothers, with "commendable enterprise," as the local press put it, began running a twice daily return stage between Banff and the rapidly developing new mining town of Bankhead. Another innovative step taken in late June at the livery was the installation of a telephone with a direct connection to the CPR station.

On putting the new livery service into operation, the company had to comply with several government regulations regarding licence fees and tariffs. According to the amended regulations of 1890, livery stable licence fees were $10 per annum for each vehicle drawn by two or more horses and $6 per annum for vehicles drawn by one horse. In addition, all drivers of public vehicles had to be licensed at the rate of $1 per annum. Rates for the hire of carriages and other vehicles varied depending on the destination or the time. Some examples: 50¢ per passenger from the Banff station to any hotel or boarding house within a radius of one-and-a-half miles; $2 per passenger from any point within one mile of the Banff bridge to Lake Minnewanka; $1 per hour for the first hour and 25¢ per hour subsequently for any vehicle drawn by two horses and carrying not more than four persons. Rates for the cartage of freight or general merchandise were subject to agreement between carrier and customer.

While Bill and Moore looked after the initial stages of development at Banff Livery, Jim and Hussey left in the latter part of May for a bear hunt on the Columbia River. From Golden where a canoe awaited them, they boated downstream to the Big Bend region where the country provided excellent habitat for their quarry. After a successful month's hunt which earned them a bag of four black bears, one cinammon and two grizzlies, they returned to Banff in mid-June to begin the season's outfitting activities. A major trip had been planned for early July, the party to be composed of Dr. Stearns, a patent medicine manufacturer from Detroit, Hussey, Moore, and Halsey Williams, a Princeton classmate. Their destination was the confluence of the Miette and Athabasca Rivers where plenty of game was known to exist, country which had not been reached directly from Banff before.

**Jim watching Phil Moore perform gymnastics during Yellowhead trip, 1904**

Early in July, Bill Potts went ahead with eighteen pack horses through Wilcox Pass, down the Sunwapta to its junction with the Athabasca, then on to Athabasca Falls where he awaited the rest of the party. They soon joined him, Jim guiding, assisted by packers George Harrison, Fred Tabuteau and Bob Logan, and cook Sid Collins. Gaining the mouth of the Miette, they established a permanent camp to serve as their base for the next two months while they hunted and explored the area. At the end of July, Jim and Hussey returned to help two of their men, Frank Wellman and Bert Sibbald, with a large party being taken to the Ice River district. Returning to the Miette in mid-September they awaited the arrival of Bill Brewster and Sibbald to bring Dr. Stearns and the game they had gathered back to Banff. Then in early October the remainder of the party pushed on westward through Yellowhead Pass to Tête Jaune Cache, up the McLennan River and over to the headwaters of the Canoe River, down the Canoe to its confluence with the Columbia at the Big Bend and then up the Columbia to Donald. There they caught a train for Banff just as the winter began, and Moore and Hussey continued on to the eastern United States.

Jim's and Hussey's amazing travels that summer and fall kept them away from the business at Banff for most of the busiest season. The same situation occurred the following spring when they were once again absent when an important development took place on the CPR front.

The winter of 1904-05 was spent planning further expansion of Brewster Brothers' activities. The major undertakings were to be a store constructed on Lot 16 beside Banff Livery and an opera house to be built on Lot 24, Block 10 (302 Lynx Street) which the partnership had recently acquired. Hoping they could compete with the other major merchandisers of Banff, the partners decided to build the store on a large scale. The design called for a two-storey frame structure with the lower floor devoted to general merchandise such as groceries, hardware, dry goods and clothing while the upstairs would serve as the business offices for Brewster Brothers. The completed building was expected to cost in the neighbourhood of $25,000. The idea behind the opera house was two-fold — to provide a meeting place for the local Masonic Order, of which both Jim and Bill were active members, and to serve the need in the community for a place to hold dances, theatrical productions and other entertainments. Calgary contracter D. G. Gunn designed a two-storey frame structure to serve the dual purpose.

Work was virtually completed on the store and was progressing rapidly on the opera house when Moore and Hussey returned from the east early in April, 1905. Construction also soon began on several other smaller structures which the partners had decided to build on additional leases they had acquired. One of these was a small two-storey building erected immediately behind the store on Lot 23, Block 1 (132 Bear Street) intended to be the future home of the Brewster Bakery. To the Brewster guides, packers and cooks who bunked on the upper floor when in off the trail it quickly became know as 'The Birdcage,' one of the wildest and most notorious establishments in town. Another building was a blacksmith shop on Lot 2, Block 7 (204 Banff Avenue). Bill and Jim had purchased the lease on this lot for Brewster Brothers from L. R. Cartmell in April, 1905, but government regulations stipulated that a transfer could not be made to a company unless it was incorporated and had the power to hold land. Brewster Brothers as originally constituted was a simple partnership and it was not until July, upon proper legal incorporation, that the transfer was formally completed. This had not deterred the construction of the blacksmith shop as it was in operation before the lease had actually been transferred.

Despite the attention which these building activities and the organization of new business enterprises demanded, Jim and Fred again departed for a spring bear hunt in the latter part of May. As in the previous year, they went by train to Golden where they rendezvoused with the rest of the party, which included Harry Radford of New York and Walter Steinhoff and C. Hatch of Golden. The men headed downstream to Kinbasket Lake and then up what they referred to as the Middle River (Kinbasket River) toward its source in what they termed the Seton Glacier (Clemenceau Glacier). On the upper reaches of the river they hunted on the exposed southern slopes which were already clear of snow and were beginning to sprout wild celery, a delicacy to hungry grizzly bears. The party secured a few good bears, but one particularly large specimen Jim spotted he set his sights on bagging. Although he was an excellent bear hunter, later reported to have taken 162 grizzlies in his lifetime, this one came very close to evening the score:

> We downed some fine specimens, but there was one big fellow foraging around in an open space that I much coveted. He generally came out toward evening. So I went after him as the day was waning. Straight up the mountain side — I must tell you that with the falling temperature the air flies downward and the game can't smell the hunter. After a tough climb, partly concealed by some brush, I came out at the point where I thought the old boy would be. He wasn't in sight, so I took up a position under a tree and waited. Unfortunately, a light cross current of air betrayed me when I came abreast of him, and my scent hit him square in the nostrils. Or else he may have heard me. At all events, I observed, about seventy-five yards away, something was moving in the bush. Also I

heard the heavy cough and the snapping of teeth, unmistakable evidence that a mad grizzly was coming out to make a fight for his pasture. All bears have bad vision; small eyes like pigs. When he broke through the brush, stood up on his hind feet and began to squint like an old man sensing something he couldn't locate, I put the bead of my rifle on the spot under his left arm, just over the heart, and fired. He didn't drop, although I heard the slug sock him. When a grizzly don't fall, look out. He located me from the direction of the echo and without a second of delay charged on all fours. I didn't dare take the time for another shot. If I missed — good night! So, dropping my rifle, a handicap for swift tree climbing, I started upward like a squirrel. Before I got out of danger he had arrived and ripped my left calf open with a swipe of his paw. But I kept on until I was twenty feet aloft in the branches.

. . . In a few minutes after I got out of range darkness fell. Below, in a rage that was hideous, my captor began to dig at the roots of the tree, which he shook repeatedly to test its solidarity. Round and round the base he clawed, shoveled, snorted and coughed his rage. I had no means of knowing how he was getting along with his work, but he certainly kept at it until I observed that the arc of the swaying perch was widening perceptibly. I was scared to death. . . . About 2 A.M. the grizzly made one last heroic attempt to shake me down and finish me up. But my unstable retreat resisted the onslaught. Soon thereafter I heard him lumbering away into the brush, as though disgusted with the whole enterprise. His departure encouraged me to climb down after daybreak. I found all the lateral roots of the tree exposed and some of them actually broken off at the base of the trunk. Had it not been for the strength of one of the larger tap roots, which resisted the onslaught, young Mr. Brewster would not be here in Banff telling you what happened up a certain tree in the region of the Middle River, 1905.

Despite missing his grizzly, Jim did bag a prize white-tailed deer on the trip which stood at the top of world records for many years.

**Jim and New York stockbroker Stuart Wing with hunting trophies**

While Jim was saving his hide from a grizzly, Bill was involved in intricate negotiations on behalf of Brewster Brothers. As mentioned, the CPR had taken over operation of its own livery service at Banff in 1897 and had decided to retain control when granting the outfitting concession to Brewster Brothers in 1904. It had gradually built up its equipment, mainly using democrats and carriages for sightseeing and enclosed Concord coaches, known as 'hotel buses,' for transporting guests between the station

**The CPR's new tally-ho at the Banff Springs Hotel**

and the Banff Springs Hotel. In the summer of 1903 the company proudly took delivery of its first tally-ho, or "English drag," a convertible multiple-seated carriage capable of transporting ten to twelve passengers. This vehicle, drawn by a four horse team and fitted out with a driver, a footman and a bugler, all attired in suitable livery, was used primarily on the sightseeing tour to Lake Minnewanka.

In spite of its advancements in the livery service field, by the spring of 1905 the CPR's management decided to contract it out at Banff as at Laggan and Field. The recently appointed manager-in-chief of hotels for the company was Hayter Reed, a man of wide experience who had served on the North West Territories Council and as Commissioner of Indian Affairs for Manitoba and the North West Territories. He quickly determined that Brewster Brothers were the best qualified livery people to handle the contract and that it would be wise, as experience with Wilson had shown, to have the livery and outfitting services in the same hands. Consequently, in early June he contracted Bill and made him a proposition that contained eight major points:

1. That Brewster Brothers would take over the whole CPR livery service and plant based upon a valuation to be made by two competent persons, one appointed by each interested party, and that in the event of an agreement being incapable of being reached by these two persons a third person would be appointed whose decision would be binding.
2. That for 1905 $1500 would be paid for the privilege but that the charge would increase proportionately to the increase in business done on renewal of the contract.

3. That the contract be for one year, renewable by mutual consent.
4. That once the transfer took place, payment would be made to the CPR immediately.
5. That two teams with wagons and harness together with their drivers would be supplied by Brewster Brothers for the exclusive use of the hotel and that a third team with carriage would be supplied as well with the driver's wages to be paid by the hotel.
6. That the hotel would have full control of the charges for the livery service and that where a dispute arose with a guest over these charges the manager of the hotel would be the sole arbiter. Further that the business was generally to be subject to the CPR's control and direction and that if the requirements were not met it would be at liberty to cancel the agreement on one month's notice.
7. That Brewster Brothers would have permission to use the barns and other buildings connected with the livery service owned by the CPR with the hotel to pay the insurance on these buildings.
8. That all the foregoing would be provided that a proper arrangement could be made for the transfer of the teamsters in connection with the plant so that no breach of faith would take place on the part of the hotel.

Unstated in the terms offered with the agreement was the right to be the sole solicitor of conveyance in the Banff Springs Hotel and on the station platform.

When Bill received the offer he was in a quandary. Jim and Hussey were incommunicado and Phil Moore was beginning to suffer from a bout of malaria that would keep him hospitalized for much of the summer. The problem he faced was that because of the large capital outlay required to build the store, opera house, blacksmith shop and other buildings, the company could not put up the money to purchase the CPR livery plant. Nonetheless, Bill was not about to let the opportunity slip without doing everything in his power to prevent it. A series of discussions was held with Reed and they finally agreed upon an arrangement. The CPR would hand over the management of the livery immediately but it would only loan the plant until such time as the evaluated price was paid.

Returning from their hunting trip in the middle of June, Jim and Hussey were amazed by Bill's coup. They gave the agreement their sanction and proceeded immediately to evaluate the CPR's horses and equipment. The partners requested that their evaluation be done by Dr. Brett, who was familiar with livery equipment because he owned a good deal of his own. Reed accepted his evaluation of the hotel's stock, harness and saddlery but found he had provided a figure of $140 less than the hotel's on the vehicles. Being in no mood to quibble over such a small sum, he suggested they split the difference. The total came to $8001; $3775 for forty-three horses, $3175 for carriages, tally-hos and wagons, $914 for harness and $137 for sundry items. After they reached an understanding that Brewster Brothers would employ the livery manager and teamsters to the end of the current season, the CPR livery passed into the company's hands on June 24, 1905.

Brewster Brothers' numerous important accomplishments in a period of just over a year paled in significance when compared with the acquisition of the CPR livery contract. The company could probably have gone on to become a successful medium-sized business without this contract, but with it much more became possible. It provided the key for the company to move beyond local outfitting and merchandising to become a broadly based mountain transportation corporation with diverse other associated interests.

All this was in the future in June, 1905 and it is unlikely any of the partners visualized the contract's ultimate importance. At the time their attention was turned towards paying off the CPR as quickly as possible. Fortunately the year 1905 proved to be a good one in which to begin the new livery service as tourists flocked to Banff in unprecedented numbers. A large Boston based travel agency, Raymond-Whitcomb Touring Company, had begun to offer tours to the Canadian Rockies and when the first group arrived early in July, Brewster Brothers were hard pressed to keep up with the demand. The Banff *Crag and Canyon* reported that "Visitors poured into Banff in a steady stream yesterday, 162 going up to the big hotel. So heavy was the traffic that No. 96 came in in three sections. . . . Every one of Brewster Bros. rigs was engaged yesterday afternoon for the service of this large party."

At the same time both Brewster Brothers Store and the Banff Opera House gradually began to show their worth. Although the finishing touches were not applied to the store until mid-June, business had begun as soon as possible. By the end of April, Arthur Saddington, who had come out from England in the early nineties to join his uncles George and William Fear, had been hired as manager and was ready to open the doors. Business developed slowly at first but once the tourists began arriving it picked up considerably. The same was true at the opera house which, although not quite complete, opened on June 1st with a performance by Dale's English Opera Singers at which only thirty people were in attendance. However, initial resistance was overcome when Brewster Brothers marked the completion of the structure on July 10th with a gala ball at which over 200 residents and visitors were present. Thereafter crowds increased somewhat, especially for the frequent dances sponsored by various local organizations. Some patrons were also willing to pay 35¢ to see the productions of such groups as the Sherman and Platt Stock Company and to view the novel moving pictures of the London Bioscope Company, which were reported to be "free from their iridescent sparkle which is so often noticed in animated pictures."

Despite numerous details to attend to at Banff in connection with the launching of the company's new endeavours, Jim became restless to get back on the trail. On July 17th he set out as guide with an important party headed by Preston Scott of Boston. The fishing and hunting trip would take them up the Spray River to Mount Assiniboine and then by way of the Kootenay and Beaverfoot Rivers back to the railroad at Leanchoil some six weeks later. A good guide for such a party was necessary, but one of the company's experienced and trustworthy men, such as George Harrison or Fred Tabuteau, could easily have handled it. It was becoming increasingly obvious that Jim's heart was not in the new aspects of Brewster Brothers' operations to the same extent as his brother Bill's. It was to become even more apparent over the course of the following winter.

Soon after the partnership was formed in 1904, Jim and Fred Hussey found that they immensely enjoyed each other's company and over a few drinks hatched all sorts of schemes. More often than not they carried through with them. During 1904 Brewster Brothers had taken Henry Molyneaux Paget Howard, nineteenth Earl of Suffolk and Berkshire, on a hunting trip. Jim had got on well with the Earl, a dynamic man who had the distinction of cornering the world wheat market for an hour. On the hunt's completion Jim was invited to visit his estate near Charlton Park, Malmsbury. In the autumn of 1905 during one of their drinking bouts, Jim and Hussey remembered the invitation and decided to take the Earl up on his offer.

Evidently the pair made quite an impression on the upper crust of British society during a rather tumultuous visit. On one occasion the Earl's other guests were somewhat taken aback when Jim appeared for the traditional fox hunt attired in his buckskin shirt and grizzly bear chaps. Nonplussed, he soon got the hang of enjoying the sport:

> The dogs started to bark and I made the first fence alright, and that horse was the finest horse I ever knew. I passed the Duke of Beaufort, who was the Master of the Hunt, and then I passed the whips, who look after the dogs. I passed the hounds without stepping on any of them, and we were getting on fine when the thing was called off and a fresh lot of flunkies appeared with fresh horses. They loaded me onto another horse, and after a time I found the saddle bags had flasks of whiskey in them and we had a fine afternoon.

When they returned to Banff from their trip abroad early in 1906, Jim and Hussey decided to pull out of Brewster Brothers. Certainly they had not been involved to any degree in the previous years' developments, leaving that aspect of the company's business in Bill's and, to a lesser extent, Phil Moore's hands. For their part, Bill and Moore must have felt that they were doing the lion's share of the work. Consequently an agreeable deal was a fairly easy matter to work out. For his interest in the company Hussey received a promissory note dated April 1, 1906 for $25,000 bearing interest at six percent per annum. Jim, not so anxious to burn all his bridges, accepted a

**Buggies and tally-ho on Corkscrew Drive**

chattel mortgage dated April 5, 1906 for the sum of $10,000 bearing six percent interest and maturing on January 1, 1907. The mortgage was against the store, including all stock situated in it, and the livery stable, including all the horses, buggies, wagons, saddles and harness which were on the premises.

With large sums of money owing to Hussey, Jim and the CPR, Brewster Brothers was in a tight financial position at the beginning of the 1906 season. The remaining partners realized that only hard work would clear these debts. The most pressing concern was the money still owing to the CPR for the livery plant, a debt they hoped could be worked off by the end of the year. When the season began there was every indication that increased business would make this possible.

Unfortunately Bill and Moore quickly ran into a series of legal entanglements that were both distressing and time consuming. Difficulties with some of the drivers employed for the summer season developed and to some degree reflected inexperience in handling the large number of employees the livery concession entailed. The company hired some local men as drivers but preferred to recruit men from the east since it felt they would be less likely to quit in the middle of the season. Advertisements were placed in several large eastern newspapers offering wages of thirty to forty dollars a month and a reduced rail fare to Banff on the CPR. Most of those hired were put to work driving the various sightseeing conveyances, the predominant rig being three-seater buggies manufactured by the McLaughlin Company. Generally the work was quite pleasant, involving driving tourists to the various points of interest, with the trips to Lake Minnewanka and along the five miles of road extending up the south side of the Spray River being among the most popular. Runaway teams created some hair-raising moments as did the passing of other vehicles on the narrow roads or on difficult grades, such as the tortuous Corkscrew Drive on Tunnel Mountain. The only other complaint of the drivers was that they had to answer the questions that tourists perpetually ask, the bane of generations of Brewster drivers. Typically a driver of a rig crossing the Bow River bridge would be asked, "Driver, what makes the river so green?" Usually the queries would receive courteous answers, but sometimes, as on one occasion, the company's men could not resist a smart reply: "Two or three tourists fall in every month."

While problems associated with tourist driving were few, drivers were sometimes given less desirable tasks to perform. The CPR livery contract called for Brewster Brothers to keep three wagons available solely for the use of the hotel. These were mainly employed in hauling coal for the heating of the hotel and hauling away ashes and garbage. Here lay the root of the trouble.

On June 14th James Houston, a recent employee at the upper (CPR) stables, was summoned to court for refusing, on June 8th, to perform the duty of teamster for which he had been hired. This was contrary to Chapter 3 of the Ordinances of the NWT, 1904, relating to masters and servants. Evidence given related how Houston, along with several other men, had been hired through an advertisement in an eastern paper and a subsequent interview with Charles Fenwick, overseer of Brewster Brothers' livery stables. Fenwick testified that on hiring the defendant he did not detail to him the precise nature of his duties, but merely told him he would have to drive tourists and do what he was told around the stables. Houston stated he and three others, also hired in the east, had spent most of their time driving the swill wagon to and from the Banff Springs Hotel and hauling and unloading coal. Feeling that this was not what he had been hired for, he stayed off the job part of one day until advised by Fenwick that he should go back to work and would get his fair share of tourist driving.

Bill Brewster, witness for the company, made it fairly obvious in his testimony that he had feared some kind of revolt in the ranks of his employees and had decided to come down hard on the agitators in order to make an example of them. Although Houston and the others had been off work less than a day, Bill called them into his office and told them to go back and get their time. When they returned he informed them that the question of their payment would have to be decided by the court. Magistrate Boswell, who heard the case, found that Bill had acted within the terms of the ordinance and found against the defendant Houston, fining him $15 and costs. The case showed that the law allowed the company to keep a tight grip on its employees and that management intended to exercise that right.

A second court case illustrates some of the difficulties entailed in running an outfitting business. On July 12th Bill and Phil Moore were charged with having in their possession twelve sheep heads, one goat head and five goat skins, contrary to the game laws. It was necessary for those in possession of such items to have a sworn affadavit from the hunter who had taken the game. Brewster Brothers had not secured these affadavits and Bill stated that, as the heads belonged to parties in the east, some time would be needed to get them. Paddy Nolan, representing the defendants, offered no defense but objected to the confiscation as being beyond the powers of a justice of the peace under the act. Judgement was reserved for ten days while the evidence was submitted to the Attorney-General of Alberta. When the justice handed down his decision he agreed that the point of law raised by Nolan was correct and dismissed the possession charge. Nonetheless he issued a court order confiscating the heads as the defendants had not proved their legal right to them. Undoubtedly the parties who had taken these trophies were none too pleased with Brewster Brothers when they were informed they would not receive them.

In spite of their legal entanglements, the partners benefitted from the increase in tourists visiting the park in 1906. In 1904 some 11,750 guests had registered at Banff's hotels with the number increasing to 17,600 in 1905 and then almost doubling to 30,100 in 1906. This meant larger profits for the livery service as well as for other ventures such as the store, opera house and blacksmith shop. As a result, Brewster Brothers was able to pay off most of its debt to the CPR by the end of the season and at the same time was able to acquire further interests. Primary among these was a small store and dwelling on Lot 13, Block 2 (126 Banff Avenue) purchased from John Walker. The first tenant was a Mr. Joy from Calgary operating a newspaper venture called *The Climber.* Bill, who did not see eye to eye with *Crag and Canyon* publisher Norman Luxton, quickly cancelled all the company's advertising in the older paper in favour of the new one. However, *The Climber* proved to be shortlived and thereafter the company did no local advertising for several years.

Once the livery plant debt was reduced, Brewster Brothers negotiated a new contract with the CPR retroactive to the expiry of the original contract of 1905. By its terms the company again had to pay $1500 per annum for the livery concession and rent of the CPR stables. In addition, it had to promise that it would not assign its interest to any party without the CPR's consent nor would it use the premises for any business other than the livery service. With this matter successfully concluded, the company's future looked secure and bright. But once again an unexpected change intervened to alter its make-up and future course.

As mentioned, when Phil Moore and Fred Hussey entered the Brewster Brothers partnership it was their intention to remain silent partners. Hussey in the main stuck to his intention, but not so Moore, who soon found that he enjoyed being involved in all aspects of the company's activities. In the spring of 1905, he, Hussey and Bill applied for leases on Lots 1-3, Block 21 (440-446 Banff Avenue) and agreed to build on them a dwelling valued at not less than $300. Contractor William Wade began putting in the foundation for the forty by forty-five foot one-storey structure in May and it was ready for occupancy by the middle of July. The three quickly dubbed their house the 'Brewster Bungalow' and agreed that it would be for bachelor purposes only. The bachelors' pact stipulated that if any of them married he would forfeit his interest and the last to remain single would become the sole owner.

Moore immediately moved in and determined to make Banff his permanent residence. Already he was becoming attracted to his partner's spunky young sister, Pearl. She was not easy to miss, sporting a personality and reputation fully as colourful as her brothers'. The only girl in a family of six boys, she early exhibited her determination to be their equal in all things. Before she had reached her teens she was already an accomplished outdoorswoman, able to shoot or fish with the best. Her prowess as a horsewoman was unmatched by any woman and few men in the vicinity. Even a stint at a New York finishing school had failed to take off the rough edges, but Moore was convinced he was the man who could do it. The courtship did not prove an easy one but persistence paid off and in August, 1906 the two were engaged. The wedding took place on January 15, 1907 at the bride's home and was followed by a reception and dance at the Banff Opera House, the likes of which the town had never seen.

Soon after the marriage, Moore decided to sever his business arrangement with his new brother-in-law. Possibly the two were not seeing eye to eye or perhaps he felt it was not wise to be in business with one's relatives. Whatever his reasons, on May 30, 1907 he turned over his interest in Brewster Brothers to Bill for approximately $21,000. Some $6000 of this was paid in cash while the remaining $15,000 was left on account at six percent interest, money which he quite likely never received. After his withdrawal from the business he and his new wife settled down in a beautiful log home he had built at 407 Banff Avenue. That summer he received an appointment as fire and game guardian for the park but this lasted only a short time. Most of the next few years he spent in military training, having joined a militia unit, the 15th Light Horse of Calgary, the previous year. Meanwhile, Bill prepared to carry on Brewster Brothers on his own, little realizing that before too long he would face a decision as momentous as Moore's.

**Pearl Brewster**

MOUNT ASSINIBOINE

**BREWSTER BROS.**

C. P. R. GUIDES

CAMP AND PACKING OUTFITS FOR
HUNTING, FISHING, ALPINE
AND EXPLORING
PARTIES

PACKING HORSE

Banff, Alta., December 6th 1906

STATEMENT OF THE AFFAIRS OF MESSRS BREWSTER BRO'S BANFF .AS

AT 31st JANUARY 1906

| ASSETTS | | LIABILITIES | |
|---|---|---|---|
| Sundries debtors as per schedule | 4,975.62 | P A Moore Capital A/c | 6,500.00 |
| | | W A Brewster " " | |
| | | J Brewster " " | 10,000.00 |
| Stock & fixtures in store as per inventory | 17,068.66 | F B Hussey " " | 25,000.00 |
| | | Bills payable as per schedule | 2,191.88 |
| Buildings, Lots, Ranch, Cattle Horses and sundry stocks as per inventory 30th Nov' 06 57,701.29 | ~~57x701x29~~ | Sundry creditors | 3,837.41 |
| | | Bank overdraft as pass book $436.83 | |
| | | Outstanding checks 171.61 " " | 608.44 |
| Purchased since Feb'1st-06 8,973.29 | ~~$48x923x55~~ | Difference being Excessof Assetts over Liabilities | 22,634.31 |
| | $48,727.76 | | $70,772.04 |
| | $70,772.04 | | |

Brewster Brothers' first financial statement

# IV: The Shattered Dream

On taking over as sole owner and operator of Brewster Brothers at the beginning of June, 1907, Bill realized that after three years of rapid development and unsettling change a period of consolidation and stability was necessary if he were going to pay off some of the company's mounting debts. He devoted most of his time over the next two years towards this end.

Although Brewster Brothers' first ever annual financial report, dated December 6, 1906, showed net assets of $70,772 and excess of assets over liabilities of $22,634, its cash position was poor. With the exception of some $5000 owing from sundry debtors, all assets were in the form of buildings, lots, inventories, equipment and livestock. On the liability side were the outstanding accounts of Fred Hussey and Jim Brewster, amounting to $35,000, and, after the end of May, an additional $15,000 owing to Phil Moore, all at six percent interest. Obviously what was needed was a clever bookkeeper who could handle the increasingly complex accounts that the company's expansion entailed and find ways to increase the cash flow. Bill was fortunate in finding a man who not only had an excellent aptitude for these matters but one who as time went on exhibited a superior skill in grasping the intricacies of business dealings and in recommending the correct financial decisions. This was Lou Crosby.

Louis Sydney Crosby was born on July 8, 1887 at Summerside, Prince Edward Island, the son of a local druggist. Initially educated in Charlottetown, he later went on to business college and gained his first training in accounting. Upon graduation he found employment as a junior clerk in a lobster processing firm, where his duties were mainly bookkeeping but on occasion also extended into financing of the business. At the age of twenty, taking stock of his possibilities for advancement, Crosby decided to head west to seek greener pastures. His travels took him to Calgary, where at first his prospects did not appear too bright. Living at the local YMCA, he managed to keep body and soul together by doing some part-time work for a grocery wholesale company.

Meanwhile, Bill was looking for a new bookkeeper. Arthur Saddington, who had originally filled the dual role of store manager and bookkeeper, had left to become Banff's postmaster in 1906. His replacement, Charlie McGruder, an acquaintance of Hussey's from New York, in the spring of 1907 was found to have a drinking problem which was making him lax in the performance of his duties. Since the local scene was devoid of candidates of the calibre that Bill wanted, he began to ask his business acquaintances if they could recommend a good man. During a conversation with the manager of the grocery wholesaler in Calgary, from whom he was purchasing goods for the store, Crosby's name came up. Bill asked that he be sent to Banff as quickly as possible. The next day, August 10, 1907, Crosby arrived on the train and after a short interview was hired on the spot. His career would span an incredible 57 years and would eventually see him rise to the presidency of the company.

With one problem solved, Bill turned to other pressing matters. A facet of the business that was proving a constant thorn in the side was winter pasturage for the company's horses, numbering some 164 head by 1907. In the early days of their outfitting activities, Bill and Jim had wintered their horses around Morley and at the mouth of the Kananaskis Valley. As the stock increased, they began to look for other good grazing lands; soon their gaze fell on an area their father had visited years earlier with William Twin, located on the Red Deer river north-west of its junction with the Panther River. William called the area "Ya Ha Tinda," meaning "Mountain Prairie," an open grass covered plain about seven by five miles in extent encircled by mountains. In August, 1904 the newly formed Brewster Brothers applied to the superintendent for a grazing lease on some of this land (Twp. 32, R. 12, W. 5) which had been included within Rocky Mountains Park in the boundary extension of 1902. The application was refused on the grounds that grazing was contrary to the intent of the Rocky Mountains Park Act. The next year, upon the Brewsters' reapplication for two townships of

**The Ya Ha Tinda Ranch**

grazing land in the area, Deputy Minister of the Interior W. W. Cory approved the lease of one township at an annual rent of $100. Undoubtedly the company's firmly cemented association with the CPR by this time had something to do with this change of heart.

Cory's approval did not solve all problems; the lease required renewal annually and would not allow the construction of buildings to house Brewster men on the site. In May, 1907 Bill reapplied for a longer term lease, stating that the company was prepared to construct buildings to a value in excess of $7000 and would pledge to protect game in the vicinity. After due consideration Minister of the Interior Frank Oliver wrote Bill in July informing him that a new lease was granted but that it would still have to be renewed annually and should not exceed ten years. However, Oliver did approve a lease on an additional 640 acres on which the necessary structures could be located. Actually a rough log building seems to have already been constructed prior to the granting of this right.

Bill continued to experience problems with the ranch, mainly in connection with completing a survey of the land and submitting a blueprint of it to the Department of the Interior. He did not have to bear this responsibility alone as he soon entered into an agreement with two rather interesting partners, James K. Howard and Schaffer Graeme.

The Honourable James Knyvett Estcourt Howard, Viscount Andover, was the younger brother of the Earl of Suffolk. Born in 1887, he had been well-educated in English schools and had then gone on to study electrical engineering. Apparently his heart was not in it and his brother began to cast about for something which would both occupy him and keep him away from home. As early as the summer of 1905 the Earl had written Jim on this score: "I have got a brother who is doing no good at his present job, viz. electrical engineering. Would you be inclined to pound the tar out of him — and if you think him worthy — eventually take him on in the firm. He can put in about £5000." Brewster Brothers was not in the market for any additional partners at the time, but Jim agreed to do what he could.

Howard soon appeared in Banff and bunked in at the Brewster Bungalow, quickly finding the lively atmosphere conducive to his tastes. In effect a remittance man, he also found that his funds from home could not support the wild parties he frequently threw at the Banff Springs Hotel and he was forced to go to work on the trail for Brewster Brothers. His suave English style quickly made him a favourite with the tourist parties he accompanied, and guests at the Banff Springs soon began referring to him as "the Viscount." But the Brewster guides and packers jokingly dubbed him "Lord Jim" and this name stuck.

When "Lord Jim" came back to Banff in the spring of 1908 after a winter spent in England, he brought along his friend Schaffer Graeme, the son of an English admiral. Together with Bill, the two hatched a scheme for establishing a ranching venture at Ya Ha Tinda and formed the Ya Ha Tinda Ranching Company, Limited with authorized capital of $37,500, consisting of 375 shares valued at $100 each. The distribution of the shares is not known but it is likely that each partner subscribed approximately a third. One of the company's main objectives was to raise cattle, and by the year's end forty-three head shared the grazing at the ranch with Brewster Brothers' horses.

Late in the fall of 1908 Howard and Graeme visited the ranch to look over its operation and set off for their return to Banff, three days distant, in cold, snowy weather. Inexperienced with such conditions, they missed a shack erected as a stopping place a day's journey from the ranch and spent the night in the frigid air. On reaching town both were discovered to have suffered frostbite in their feet and were treated at the Sanitarium Hospital before departing for England. Soon afterwards the populace of Banff was amazed to hear reports of "Lord Jim" lying at the point of death in New York's Waldorf-Astoria Hotel. Ever eager to produce an exciting story about some well-known personage, the press stated that Howard, "one of the wildest and most reckless spirits that ever accompanied a pack-horse party on a mountain adventure in the West," was in precarious condition as a result of a terrible experience while out hunting in the wilds of British Columbia. One of the reports supplied details of the experience:

> Accompanied by the Baron Schaffer, a German nobleman, he came to this country two months ago to hunt moose and bear.

"Lord Jim" Howard (right rear) and some of Brewster Brothers' guides. Left to right (rear) — Frank Wellman, Bill Potts, George Harrison, Bob Logan; (middle) — Fred Brewster, Bert Sibbald, Paddy Ryan (NWMP), station agent, George Brewster; (front) — Donald King, Pat Brewster, Jack Brewster

About a month ago they arrived at Banff, Alta., where their party was further augmented. They then went on to British Columbia. There were about twenty-five in the party and after travelling for two days, facing weather that registered below zero, most of the party decided to turn back, after vainly trying to induce Howard and Baron Schaffer to follow their example.

On the return trip to Banff a blizzard obliterated the trail and the men became lost. By turns they cried for assistance but no response came. Fatigued and weak they lay down on the skins of three heavy bears that had fallen before their guns. It took a searching party six days to reach them and they were found unconscious. . . .

When Banff was reached skilled surgeons were called in and they passed the opinion that the two men were dying. On Howard's statement that if he were going to die he wanted to pass away in London, he was placed on a train, taken to Montreal and from there to New York.

In an article that he wrote for the English journal *Canada*, Howard set the record straight, but he and Graeme felt the effects of the frostbite for the remainder of their lives.

Overall the Ya Ha Tinda ranching venture fit in well with Bill's consolidating and stablizing Brewster Brothers' interests. Another deal in which he became involved in 1908 seemed a departure from this end as it encompassed a major expansion of the company's operations. It was simply a case of an opportunity too good to refuse but it also had far reaching ramifications, for it was the company's first step toward monopolizing the tourist transport business in the mountains of Western Canada along the line of the CPR.

As mentioned, Tom Wilson had won the CPR livery and outfitting concessions at Lake Louise and Field in 1902. Finding that the two locations were too much for one man to handle, he had taken in a partner, Robert E. "Bob" Campbell. Campbell had come to Banff as a school teacher late in 1896 and thereafter spent his summer vacations working for Wilson on the trail. After the formation of Wilson and Campbell in 1902, the two operated out of stables at the Lake Louise Chalet and across the Kicking Horse River from Mount Stephen House until 1904, when Campbell bought Wilson out. They had initially outfitted major trail trips and supplied daily saddle horse hire, as the number of drives suitable for sightseeing vehicles was limited. In 1904 the situation began to change with the initiation of work on roads at Moraine Lake and the Yoho Valley and the utilization as a road of the old CPR grade between Field and Ottertail where the railway had been realigned. By 1908 sixteen miles of carriage roads at Laggan and thirty miles at Field compared with eighty miles at Banff. Meanwhile, Campbell was taking advantage of these developments to build up his livery plant, experiencing fair success offering sightseeing trips from the two locations.

In the winter of 1907-08 Campbell's contract with the CPR expired and on April 1, 1908 the railway offered Brewster Brothers a new contract which included Laggan and Field along with Banff. Campbell's desires about relinquishing his concession are unknown, but the suspicion exists the CPR gave him no choice. The railroad apparently felt it desirable for all its livery and outfitting concessions in the Canadian Rockies to be in the hands of one company. Certainly within a short time the CPR was being roundly criticized for its monopolistic tendencies by, among others, A. O. Wheeler, Director of the Alpine Club of Canada, who suspected all competitors were being driven from the field.

Acquisition of the Field and Laggan concessions meant further major changes for the company. The agreement included a very welcome reduction in the annual CPR concession fee to $1000 and an extension in its term to five years. But the railway did demand an additional thirty pack and saddle horses and at least seven driving teams and passenger vehicles with a total seating capacity of no less than fifty persons be kept at Lake Louise and that twenty-five pack and saddle horses and driving teams with passenger vehicles capable of carrying at least thirty persons be kept at Field and Emerald Lake combined. Brewster Brothers purchased some of the necessary rigs from Campbell, although he decided not to sell his horses, and Bill quickly had to reapportion the company's existing livestock to meet its commitments. Offsetting the additional investment required, a revised livery tariff specifically outlined the charges for each particular drive or trip. Typical of these were: $3 return for a single rig between Field and Emerald Lake; $3 return from Field to Ottertail for up to three persons;

**Pack train leaving Brewster headquarters at Field**

and $4 from the Banff Springs Hotel around the Loop and to the Cave and Basin for up to three persons.

The change in ownership of the livery operations meant that existing staff had to be dealt with. Since Lake Louise was a major outfitting point, particularly for longer trips to the north, it was fortunate that a considerable number of guides and packers on the payroll chose to stay. Added to them were some of Brewster Brothers' men who had previously guided out of Banff. Included were George Harrison, who was soon to be made the chief guide at Lake Louise, Nello "Tex" Vernon-Wood, an English immigrant who had worked on a ranch before joining Brewster Brothers in 1906, and Herbert Alonzo "Soapy" Smith, a native of Vermont whom Brewster Brothers had first hired as a harness maker in 1905.

For manager of the entire Lake Louise operations Bill chose the extremely capable James I. McLeod. Born at Manitowaning, Manitoulin Island, Ontario on March 26, 1879, McLeod had attended business college at Owen Sound. During a visit to the east in 1906 in search of an accountant, Bob Campbell had visited the college and hired him because he had the finest handwriting of any of the students. Initially McLeod's responsibilities at Lake Louise had been in the office, but as he was constantly exhibiting his skill in handling horses Campbell eventually decided to move him outside and make him general manager. At Field, where the staff was somewhat smaller, other Campbell men such as chief guide George Hankins and Jack O'Leary, whom Bill placed in charge, also stayed on.

With his additional responsibilities, Bill experienced a rather hectic 1908 season. All his measures to increase the company's profits were insufficient to make any real headway on its debts. During 1907 the various aspects of the company's business earned in excess of $15,000 in profits, with the store ($7400), the lower livery stable ($3800) and outfitting ($2400) being the most lucrative, CPR operations ($220) somewhat less so. But Bill's personal drawings and interest on the mortgage and notes ate up much of the profit and he chose to leave the rest in the surplus account against future uncertainties. In 1908 profits on the CPR operations increased dramatically to $3500, a result of extinguishing the debt against the CPR's livery plant, but other accounts decreased correspondingly. As a result, by the year's end the $35,000 owing against the mortgage and note of 1906 and the further $15,000 owing against Moore's loan of 1907 were still outstanding.

Corresponding to his financial predicament were some personal problems which Bill was experiencing during these years. As a handsome young bachelor with a business of his own he was fair game for the numerous young unattached ladies of Banff. Bill, who fancied himself a ladies' man anyway, responded enthusiastically to their attentions and gained quite a reputation. For example, on his birthdays he was known to have held parties for himself at the Brewster Bungalow to which only members of the fairer sex were invited. About 1907 he married a girl named Isabella Lee but, although they were not divorced, they did not remain together for long. His favourite companion proved to be his sister-in-law's sister Tead Froste who, as mentioned, was the wife of local station agent William Froste. In fact, it was common knowledge that two sons born to the Frostes in 1901 and 1902 had actually been sired by Bill.

Fortunately Tead Froste spent a good deal of time in her sister's company, so Bill could see her frequently without providing too much fodder for the local gossip mill. Nonetheless, the situation became increasingly uncomfortable for all concerned. Finally she gave Bill an ultimatum: he could stay with the business in Banff or he could leave with her, the two young boys and an older daughter, Sylvia (Sid) Froste. It was an excruciatingly difficult decision to make, but love eventually won the day. His dreams for the great future of Brewster Brothers shattered, he departed with Tead and the children for New York early in the spring of 1909. On hand to pick up the pieces was Jim Brewster.

After he and Hussey left Brewster Brothers in 1906, Jim remained in Banff. Twenty-four years old and feeling that he had accomplished a great deal for one so young, he decided to enjoy himself. Together with Hussey he spent long periods out exploring, hunting and fishing in the mountains. When not on the trail he idled away many hours with the Brewster guides and packers, drinking, playing cards and generally having a good time at the Birdcage. Among those frequenting its confines there was such a degree of cameraderie that they formed a team which became involved in local baseball, football and hockey competition. Their prowess was such that in 1905 their baseball nine, relying on the strong pitching of Hussey and Sam Reid, another former baseball star at Princeton, defeated Wetaskiwin for the Brewery Trophy, emblematic of baseball supremacy in Alberta. Despite no longer being a member of the company, Jim played on all the Birdcage teams, as did Phil Moore. With an abundance of free time on his hands Jim also became increasingly involved in other local activities, serving as the assistant fire chief beginning in September, 1906, supporting the work of the local Masonic order, and helping to organize the annual Banff Indian Days.

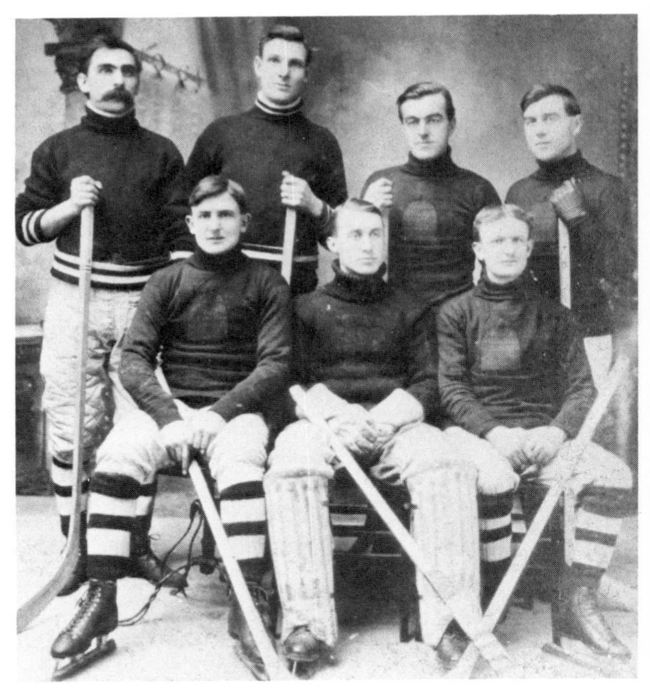

**The Birdcage hockey team. Left to right (rear) — Tom Dunsmore, Jim McLeod, Jim and Bill Brewster; (front) — Lou Crosby, Phil Moore, Percy Crosby**

But he was not completely idle. His uncle, William Brewster, had established The Brewster Manufacturing Company at Edmonton in the years immediately after the turn of the century. The firm manufactured farm machinery, mainly tractors, although William also invented one of the earliest combines ever produced in the country. By 1906 he was looking for capital to expand his business, and in May of that year he formed a new company, The Brewster Iron Works, Limited, with Jim and Hussey as partners. Each of the three took 100 shares of stock and they hoped to sell an additional 700 shares to other interested investors. The objectives of the company were extremely broad, including carrying on business as iron masters, steel makers, colliery proprietors, chemical producers, mechanical engineers and tramway operators, although it mainly continued to function as a producer of farm machinery and implements.

As time went on Jim became bored with his relatively uncomplicated lifestyle, so with Hussey he planned new schemes in which they could become involved. Particularly attractive were some real estate opportunities at the coast being touted by his father. John Brewster, after twenty years in the dairy business, had sold the Brewster Dairy to Frank Wellman early in 1907. Immediately afterwards, in May, 1907, he entered into a real estate brokerage partnership with two old acquaintances who had driven on the Winnipeg Street Railway with him, J. G. Howes of New Westminster and A. J. Carleton of Vancouver. The partnership, named John Brewster and Company, established its office at 1007 Granville Street in Vancouver. Land sales were booming at the time and his father soon advised Jim to invest in some lots. Taking the advice to heart, Jim had his father purchase some properties and then decided to move to the coast himself to look after these interests and perhaps acquire more. In the spring of 1907 he sold his house on Banff Avenue to the Presbyterian Church but did not actually move his family until September of that year.

Little is known of Jim's activities during his relatively short sojourn at the coast. He purchased a home at 1125 Yates Street in Victoria and probably spent much of his time involved in real estate speculation. It is known that his wife first purchased some lots at Point Grey and that he followed by purchasing an entire acreage. Meanwhile, some of his other lots increased in value so rapidly that within two years they were worth double what he had paid for them. Despite these successes the old lure of Banff was strong, and by May, 1908 he and his family had returned and taken up residence in a house purchased from Arthur Saddington.

While Jim was living in Victoria the second anniversary of the mortgage he held against the Brewster Brothers store and livery stable fell due. Its terms called for the principal and interest to be paid by January 1, 1907 but this date passed and only $600 in interest was rendered. Thus he had taken the precaution of filing a renewal statement to ensure its continued validity. Soon after arriving back in Banff he also acquired another very important instrument of interest in Brewster Brothers, Fred Hussey's note for $25,000.

It is difficult to determine why Hussey signed over "without recourse" his demand note to Jim in 1908. Probably it had something to do with a deal they made concerning some timber licences which Jim held on the Simpson River. The area around Simpson Pass and the Simpson River had been a favourite hunting territory for both Jim and Bill ever since William Twin had introduced them to it. Interestingly, during one of his hunting trips in 1904, Jim, his wife and Bob Logan had camped near Simpson Pass and while the men were out hunting Lade Brewster discovered an old blaze in a fallen tree. Subsequent examination showed that it recorded the trip of Sir George Simpson and John Rowand of the Hudson's Bay Company over the pass during Simpson's trip around the world in 1841. The blaze was carefully cut out and taken back to Banff where it became an item of great curiosity in the Brewster home.

Over the years Jim had become very familiar with the Simpson River country and in 1907 he decided that some of the excellent timber in it could be made a marketable commodity. He applied for and received a total of twelve licences allowing him to cut, fell and carry away timber on the lands described therein. These included lands on the west bank of the Simpson about four miles north of its junction with the Vermilion River as well as on the north bank of the east fork of the Simpson. Each licence required a payment of $115 per annum making for a total investment of $1380. In January, 1908 these licences were transferred to Fred Hussey for the sum of $1 and about the same time Fred signed over the aforementioned note to Jim leaving the impression that the two matters were somehow connected. Apparently Hussey never did anything in the way of developing his rights on these lands.

Regardless of how he acquired assignment of Hussey's note, it was Jim's key to the future. Combined with the mortgage he was in a postion to receive over $2000 in interest annually or, if he chose, call in the monies owing and gain control of Brewster Brothers at any time. He decided not to exercise the latter option in 1908 but certainly the threat of it hanging over Bill's head must have provided food for thought when he was considering his options. With Bill's decision to leave early in 1909 the affairs and the assets of the company went directly to Jim. While his interest in the activities of Brewster Brothers had vacillated considerably prior to his pulling out in 1906, such was no longer the case. Three years had passed, Jim had matured and now he had visions of his own for the company. He quickly began to take the steps to turn those dreams into reality.

Jim with three-seater carriage at the Banff Springs Hotel, ca. 1910

# V: A New Mould

Jim's new-found ambition and fertile imagination led him to envisage further developing the company's current interests and acquiring additional ones complementing its involvement in the tourist trade. He was certain the great expansion of tourism would soon present opportunities. His ability to recognize an opportunity had already been well-illustrated, but still undetermined were his abilities to grasp it and make it work when he was in charge. If anything, the years ahead would show that his mind sometimes went in too many directions at once. While he was farsighted and good at recognizing a business opportunity, his managerial abilities were not so good and he had to rely on the people around him to carry his projects through.

When Jim acquired Brewster Brothers' interests in the spring of 1909, the company's situation immediately improved; no longer standing against it were $35,000 in liabilities plus interest that had been owing to him. The company had been in fairly good condition when Bill departed as in the two years he had been the sole operator he had strengthened it considerably. Between 1906 and 1908, Brewster Brothers' net assets had increased from $70,800 to $97,800 and its surplus account had grown from $22,600 to $32,600.

Of even greater importance than the financial gains were increases in physical assets which accompanied them. These were substantial. By the end of 1908 the company possessed real estate with a book value in excess of $27,000, including the store, opera house, livery stable, bakery, blacksmith shop, ranch house and stable, warehouse and sundry other buildings and residences. It owned conveyances with a total value of $8800 including seven 'bus' coaches, two touring coaches, one tally-ho, fourteen three-seaters, two two-seaters, twelve surreys and buggies, one single rig and numerous wagons, sleighs and cutters; and it owned 205 horses valued at $15,700. Perhaps most importantly, Bill had left the company strengthened both by the rights it held vis-à-vis the CPR livery contracts and by the employees he had hired.

**Brewster Transfer livery and Brewster Trading store**

Despite the relative strength of the company he took over, Jim quickly decided to restructure it. In his estimation it had grown too large and diverse to remain a single entity. On April 30, 1909 he had his lawyer, Frederick S. Selwood of the Calgary firm of Short, Ross and Selwood, draw up memoranda of association to reincorporate Brewster Brothers' interests in two separate companies. The Brewster Trading Company, Limited took over the business carried on as general merchants and most of the real estate, and the Brewster Transfer Company, Limited took over responsibility for all business dealing with livery work, cartage and outfitting, including the CPR contracts. Brewster Trading's capitalization was $30,000, made up of 300 shares valued at $100 each, while Brewster Transfer's was $20,000 made up of 200 shares valued at $100 each.

**Brewster Transfer coach at the Banff Springs Hotel**

The manner of assigning the shares of the two companies was rather interesting. On June 10, 1909 Jim entered into agreements with Brewster Trading and Brewster Transfer whereby, in return for the total of 300 and 200 shares respectively, he transferred to them the assets of Brewster Brothers, excepting the leases on the properties held in trust for them in his own name. In the case of Brewster Trading he alloted 191 shares to himself, 108 to Fred Hussey and 1 to Fred Brewster, while in the case of Brewster Transfer, 127 shares went to himself, 72 to Fred Hussey and 1 to Fred Brewster. His brother Fred had just graduated that spring from Queen's University in Mining Engineering and Jim undoubtedly thought him a potentially valuable member of the two companies. As for Hussey, his shares were likely for the $25,000 note he had signed over to Jim and his previous financial backing of Brewster Brothers. Its shares assigned, Brewster Trading was duly registered with the Registrar of Joint Stock Companies. An unfortunate oversight, Selwood's neglecting to register Brewster Transfer properly, required several annoying appearances in the Supreme Court of Alberta to clear matters up.

After the creation of the two businesses, a meeting of their provisional board of directors and their shareholders to work out details of operation was called but since Hussey spent much of his time travelling or at his home in Allegheny, Pennsylvania it was difficult for him to attend. Finally, on November 15, 1909, Jim and Fred Brewster met alone to sanction the transfer of Jim's assets in Brewster Brothers to Brewster Trading and Brewster Transfer. To obviate possible similar delays in obtaining a quorum, Jim gave his wife Lade and his lawyer Selwood one share each in the two companies. At the shareholders' meeting which immediately followed all five shareholders elected themselves directors of the companies. Meetings of the boards of directors then elected slates of officers consisting of Fred Hussey as president, Jim as vice-president, treasurer and managing director, and Fred Selwood as secretary. These meetings also adopted the corporate seals of the two companies and appointed the Banff branch of the Imperial Bank of Canada as the companies' official bank. The bank's local manager, W. Foster, undoubtedly delighted to land the important accounts, perhaps would have had second thoughts had he foreseen the worry and sleepless nights they would cause him and his successors.

The seeds of their future insomnia were sown in the meetings of the directors and shareholders that followed the initial meetings. These meetings were really formalities to rubber stamp the decisions Jim made. He, of course, had controlling interest. Hussey, who never attended, always assigned his votes to Jim by proxy, and after the November meeting Fred Brewster no longer attended either. With Phil Moore and his brother Jack Brewster, Fred created a partnership eventually known as Brewster and Moore which initially worked at freighting on the construction of the Alberta Central Railway into the Nordegg coal fields. Later it became an outfitting and guiding concern at Jasper.

At subsequent meetings Jim moved by-laws allowing the companies to borrow from the bank or seek advances to the extent of $10,000 for each company and to mortgage, hypothecate or pledge their assets against these loans. As managing director or treasurer, he had the power to make such arrangements as he saw fit. While $10,000 was not an unreasonable amount for the companies to be borrowing, rarely a meeting would go by without the ceilings being pushed higher, eventually rising to $25,000 by 1913.

The primary reason for enacting these by-laws was that the companies were undercapitalized, their capital accounts consisting entirely of assets transferred from Brewster Brothers. No cash was put in by any of the shareholders. The companies could not function properly or undertake expansion without cash, but it seemed, in the heady days of 1909, they would have little problem repaying any loans as business progressed. Jim's optimistic attitude also pervaded the decisions regarding annual dividends. In December, 1910 a realistic dividend of ten percent on the capital stock of the companies was declared payable out of the profits and reserves of their business. However, subsequent dividends grew more rapidly than the rate at which the companies' limits of credit increased. By 1912 dividends had reached twenty-five percent for Brewster Trading and an amazing one hundred percent for Brewster Transfer. The monies might better have eliminated the increasing bank loans.

Jim did not foresee such policies would leave the companies vulnerable if hard times befell them. Managing them on his own, he lacked the experience to recognize such pitfalls. On taking over Brewster Brothers he had retained almost all

Lou Crosby speedskating

former staff, but the abilities of several key personnel, such as Crosby and McLeod, were still relatively unknown to him. Fairly quickly he took a liking to Crosby, probably impressed by his love of the outdoors and his prowess in speed skating and hockey. But Crosby's financial skills and good judgment Jim did not quickly or fully recognize. Although he became an assistant manager and chief accountant of Brewster Trading Crosby could not act on behalf of the companies until 1911 when a resolution was passed providing him with power-of-attorney to handle bank matters on their behalf. After this Jim increasingly relied on his skills and listened to his advice, and in 1913 he was given the one share in each company recently turned back by Fred Brewster. Jim

Jim McLeod (left) cutting ice at Lake Louise

McLeod, appointed as an assistant manager in 1909 responsible for the companies' "outside" or operating interests, in 1912 received power-of-attorney, but only when Crosby was absent.

Jim's optimism for the future of his two companies was consistent with the business atmosphere of the time. The growth in tourism and development the area was experiencing was occurring simultaneously with a pre-war boom in all of Western Canada. Investment in new companies and speculation, particularly in real estate, was rampant and ruined many people financially when the bubble burst. Jim was caught up in the spirit of the times and, initially, his optimism was well-founded. Brewster Transfer in particular performed well, turning a profit of $11,700 in its first year of operation and increasing it to $38,500 by the end of 1912.

The livery and outfitting service at Lake Louise, under the management of Jim McLeod, and the smaller, but still lucrative operations at Field proved the best money producers for Brewster Transfer. Jim, acutely aware the expansion into Lake Louise and Field had been a key development for the company, had strengthened his position in these two locations. At Field, he quickly replaced O'Leary, feeling he wasn't entirely honest in his dealings. As Jim, with typical humour, put it: "If you threw a dollar up in the air, it was mine if it stayed up and his if it fell down." In his place he put in charge Earl Gammon, a young man from Nova Scotia who, working for him at Banff as a carriage agent, had been impressive in his performance. In May, 1909 Brewster Transfer purchased Bob Campbell's horses formerly used at Lake Louise and Field, and in July, 1910 bought out the company's chief competitor at Field, Otto Brothers. Included in the $7000 purchase price were forty-seven head of horses, a few rigs, wagons and sleighs, a barn, a town lot and four timber limits.

With ample horses and excellent facilities at the two locations, business expanded rapidly, particularly in outfitting. Lake Louise and Field were outstripping Banff as points of departure for pack trips for mountaineering, sightseeing, hunting and fishing and scientific investigation. And Brewster Transfer continued to handle numerous prestigious pack train parties, people such as Felix Wedgwood, of English china and pottery fame, and Stuart Wing, a millionaire New York stockbroker. The purchase of Otto Brothers' interests also provided another valuable, if somewhat shortlived, shot in the arm for the company. Otto Brothers, appointed official outfitters to the Alpine Club of Canada, had received the exclusive privilege to outfit the club's annual mountaineering camps in the Rockies and Selkirks, a privilege which passed into Brewster Transfer's control. It did very well handling the 1910 camps in the Consolation and Yoho Valleys. But A. O. Wheeler, the club's director, was not fond of the Brewsters, his dislike stemming back to the time of the club's formation in 1906. Bill Brewster had attended the club's formative meeting at Winnipeg in March, 1906 and had promised, with several other prominent outfitters, to supply horses and saddlery free of charge for the club's first camp. When the time for the camp drew near, Bill had had a change of heart and withdrew from the agreement, leaving Wheeler in the lurch. The outspoken director, having never forgiven this desertion, quickly withdrew the official outfitter status after the

1910 camps. He also became a most outspoken critic of both the Brewster operations and the company's cosy relationship with the CPR, which to him smacked of monopoly.

The withdrawal of its status with the Alpine Club was not a serious blow to Brewster Transfer. Most of its best outfitting business came from sportsmen interested in fishing and hunting. In these fields it had excellent success, part of it attributable to the CPR's worldwide advertising campaign. The railway circulated such promotional pamphlets as *Hunting And Fishing Along The Line Of The CPR* which included information on the services Brewster Transfer could provide interested patrons. Jim, recognizing the value of such advertising, reinstituted advertisements in the local *Crag and Canyon* and approved the producing of a sixteen page brochure entitled *Hunting And Fishing In The Heart Of The Canadian Rocky Mountains* which was well designed and contained over thirty photographs, a map of the best hunting and fishing territory and a testimonial account by a successful New York hunter. It first appeared about 1912 and eventually went through several editions. Proving the form of advertising effective, it was the first in a long line of pamphlets, leaflets and brochures the company issued over the years.

With the growth in outfitting at Lake Louise and Field in the years after 1909 Jim increased his staff of guides, packers and cooks. Several new and interesting men thereby found their way into the Brewster corps of rugged individuals working the trail. A few were students employed for the summer, youths such as Sam Reid, a student at Princeton, who worked several seasons as a guide before graduating and becoming a successful New York attorney. But most were ex-cowboys who came to Lake Louise from prairie ranches and found the guiding life to their liking. A bunk house was erected near the Chalet for the use of all Brewster employees but many preferred to use a tepee where they would sit around the campfire in the evening swapping tales, singing and having a few drinks. If they were lucky they might even attract one or two of the comely young female guests at the chalet to their nightly revelry. The period between 1909 and the First World War was a golden age for the company's outfitting business at Lake Louise, and many employees treasured the memories of those days for years to come.

Some of the "Brewster Bunch" at Lake Louise, ca. 1913

## THE BREWSTER BUNCH

I ain't much of a Poet and seldom take a hunch,
    But I'm going to make an effort and tell you of the Bunch.
Just a bunch of dirty Packers but mostly white inside,
    Who used to work together, but now are scattered wide.
Bill Potts adopted Khaki and hit for the sound of guns,
    He did his bit for his country, and was captured by the Huns.
Wattie, his younger brother, has quit the single life,
    And tho' he is still a Packer, has got himself a wife.
"Soapy", one of the oldest, has had to quit the game,
    Rheumatiz has got him, but we remember just the same.
The "Farg Kid's" promoted, he's one of the bosses now,
    But he's just as white as ever, we all of us allow.
"Tiny" a six foot husky who seldom went sober to bed,
    Quit fighting "Johnny Walker" — He's fighting the Germans instead.
"Lord Jim's" another at the Front, he surely stood the test,
    And when the Bunch had broke him in, he showed up with the best.
Bob Logan he done quit us, the one of the oldest crew,
    Has settled down to ranching, he got married too.
Jack Giddie, "Poor Old Ugly", homely but full of wit,
    He's out on the Deserts of Egypt doing his little bit.
Fat Cain got hitched up double, so did Texas Wood,
    They quit and hired as wardens to teach us to be good.
Billy Lewis, he done left us, and beat it with his wife,
    Down to the Eastern States to lead a town-guy's life.
Walt Jordan, he's another, who knew the trails a few,
    He's sold his spurs and saddle and joined the soldiers too.
Com and Wesley Latam, youngsters at the game,
    Who also quit the packing to hold up Britain's name.
"The Hooknosed Kid" has settled down and owns a husky team,
    He's plumb subdued — his wildest sprees are nothing but a dream.
Bert lost a foot beneath a train when they hollored 'All Aboard',
    He's quit the life, has got a wife, and runs a dinky Ford.
"Big Bill" has wandered far away, he's listed with the "Strays",
    He's drifted back across the line to his cowpunchin days,
Jack Bevan too has quit the job and chose a warden's life,
    He's got a shack out on the "Red" and lives there with his wife.
Last but not least is our boss "Jim" — few better hands there are,
    He's done his share of the Packer's life and now speeds up a car.
Then "Windy", he's the writer of this here little "Pome",
    Who with this bunch has worked and played and with 'em made his home.
And now they're scattered far and wide as you can plainly see,
    But if this Bunch e'er meets again, there'll be some Jamboree.

**by Stan J. "Windy" Carr**

Loading ice blocks from the ice harvest onto boxcar

Apart from its livery and outfitting operations, Brewster Transfer soon became involved in other profitable ventures. One was the development of the timber limits near Field acquired in the Otto Brothers purchase which were run in conjunction with several other small logging operations the company undertook near Laggan and Castle Mountain. By 1911 the various "wood accounts" stood at over $11,000 with most of the sales being to the CPR for ties and pit props. As time went on, the company became involved in the retail end of the wood and coal business for domestic heating, opening a wood and coal yard on Banff Avenue in 1913.

The CPR provided opportunities in two other areas that also proved to be valuable for the company, particularly since they were activities carried out during the winter tourist doldrums. Because of the demands for accommodation by the increasing flow of tourists to the area, the CPR was almost constantly expanding its facilities at the Banff Springs and its other mountain hostelries. In 1910 the railway commissioned its chief architect, Walter Painter, to design essentially a "new" hotel at the Banff Springs, and during the winter of 1911-12 work commenced on his famous eleven storey centre tower. Up to 400 men worked on the structure over the next few winters, requiring the haulage of huge amounts of building materials. While Brewster Transfer's CPR concession related only to the summer livery and outfitting business, there was an agreement the CPR would award contracts to the company for off-season freighting and cartage provided its rates were competitive. Brewster Transfer was provided with some $14,000 in revenue for the year 1911 alone through these contracts.

A second need of the CPR the company filled over the winter months with the ice used in refrigeration in all the railway's western hotels. Ice cutting at Banff had begun as early as 1901 when the Arctic Ice Company of Winnipeg harvested the Bow River, but not until 1911 did Brewster Transfer become involved. The work, usually beginning in January when the ice had attained a thickness of about two feet, often utilized up to fifty men and twenty teams of horses. The ice blocks, weighing up to 700 pounds, had to be loaded onto sleighs for hauling to the railroad where they were transferred into boxcars. Eighteen to twenty cars could be filled on a good day and, as the contract usually called for the

Brewster Trading store with Lou Crosby, "Bub" Dunsmore and Tom Dunsmore at right

filling of up to 700 cars, the job lasted up to six weeks. The work, although performed in less than ideal conditions, provided winter employment for the Brewster men kept on the payroll over the winter. Although ice cutting was dangerous, the weather conditions that it was performed in caused the most hardship. George Harrison recalled one day when the men began working early in the morning. Around ten o'clock someone commented how cold he was feeling. On checking the thermometer it was found to register at $-60°$F. so they decided to quit for the day. Despite such experiences the ice harvesters were usually glad to have any winter work at all. And for Brewster Transfer, the harvest provided a respectable profit of between $2000 and $3000 annually.

Brewster Transfer's business flourished in its first few years, but Brewster Trading's growth was much more painstaking. Its profits increased from a meagre $2200 in its first year of business to only $10,850 by the end of 1912.

In 1908 Brewster Brothers had hired Tom Dunsmore, a young man from Oxford, Nova Scotia, to work at the store and the following year his brother Arthur (Bub) joined him. Lou Crosby had for a time been both store manager and bookkeeper but when his duties increased he had to relinquish the former responsibility. Tom Dunsmore, appointed manager about 1910, attempted to increase the business with frequent specials and sales. But competition in general merchandising was keen and Brewster Trading's chief competitor, Dave White and Company, gained the lion's share of the market. Also a large amount of money was tied up in accounts receivable. As the store offered credit to its customers — and most took advantage of it — the literally hundreds of small accounts were very difficult to collect. In 1912 over $7500 was outstanding for sundry accounts receivable under $100 and the total accounts receivable amounted to over $27,000.

Despite the fact that the store made only minimal profits, Jim upheld his reputation for treating his staff as generously as possible. For example, in the fall of 1909 he was giving the whole staff a holiday by turns. The firm treated the Dunsmore boys to a week's visit in the Yoho Valley and gave another employee, Eddie Wilson, a trip to the Seattle Fair. Jim's fair treatment extended to other facets of the Brewster operations as well. Walter James, an employee at the upper stable who didn't see eye-to-eye with the stable boss, was fired on three separate occasions. Each time he reported for his cheque Jim rehired him, the third time with instructions to stay on the job until he came up and fired him personally.

Difficulties also plagued Brewster Trading's Banff Opera House. When Brewster Brothers had originally constructed the opera house the company hoped it would be an immediate success. The success with plays, concerts and bioscope productions in its first years of operation proved shortlived, particularly after Dr. Brett opened the rival National Park Theatre located on the Sanitarium grounds in June, 1908. Brett's building had a seating capacity of 500 and consistently booked better productions than did the Banff Opera House. In 1910 Byron Harmon opened the town's first movie theatre which immediately attracted a good patronage. The only major attraction of the year at the opera house was the annual Packers' Ball in October. Sponsored by

**Brewster Transfer rigs at the Mount Royal Hotel, 1912**

the Brewsters since its inception in 1902, the ball was held in honour of those who worked the trails in the vicinity and always proved to be the highlight of the town's social season. However, it did little to improve the financial situation of the opera house, which consistently made only slightly over $100 per annum in profits.

Despite its relatively poor performance, Jim did not despair of the future for Brewster Trading. Quite the opposite. In 1912 his optimistic outlook led him to look for remedies to the company's problems and additions to its interests. The store was not large enough to carry the quantities of stock in a selection needed to make it competitive. To correct this situation the company announced in October, 1912 it would move the old store back to the lane and erect a new and up-to-date structure at the front of the lot. By the end of 1913 over $7000 had been expended on this project. The Banff Opera House's location on Lynx Street on the fringe of the downtown area was a disadvantage and in November, 1912 the company announced it would move it to a new location near the site of Jim's recent and major purchase, the Mount Royal Hotel.

Acquiring the Mount Royal was a major manifestation of Jim's involvement in the pre-war boom in Banff. In what the press termed "one of the biggest real estate deals ever made here," he, with Hussey's backing, agreed in May, 1912 to buy it from owners Dave and Annie McDougall of Morley for $75,000, a tremendous amount of money in 1912 which he could not raise all at once. Therefore he paid $20,000 down and the McDougalls carried the balance in a mortgage bearing seven percent interest to be paid off in three equal installments due in November 1912, 1913 and 1914. These dates were never met and carrying the mortgage many years resulted in the payment of heavy interest charges. Yet, despite the hotel's eventual cost, it was one of Jim's wisest and most lucrative acquisitions.

The major item in the purchase was the hotel itself. Originally opened in the spring of 1908 under the name of the Banff Hotel, the red brick structure, complete with a lead roof, boasted some sixty guest rooms as well as a spacious dining room and billiard room. As well, the deal included the Bow Livery and its rigs and equipment, a business first opened by McDougall and a partner Rattray in 1906 on the lot adjacent to those on which the hotel would eventually be built. When the hotel was completed the livery moved further down the block, allowing for a clear space of lawn between it and the hotel. Finally, in addition to the structures themselves the sale included the leases on Lots 18-19, Block 2 (136-138 Banff Avenue) on which the hotel stood, Lot 14, Block 2 (128 Banff Avenue) on which the Bow Livery was located and the three vacant lots in between on which future expansion could take place.

It was not long before Jim indicated he was ready to go ahead with such expansion. Upon

taking over the business he hired an experienced manager, George Colladay, formerly of the New Washington Hotel in Seattle. By the fall of 1912 Colladay unveiled plans for an extensive renovation and addition to the hotel, enlarging the dining room by cutting an archway through to the billiard room, installing an elevator and adding fifty bedrooms. Moving the opera house to a location across Caribou Street from the Mount Royal on the east half of Lot 1 and 2, Block 7 was part of the scheme. The opera house had recently had a gallery added to it and Jim hoped that, moved and redecorated, it could serve as a dance hall reserved for hotel guests three nights a week and open to the public three nights a week.

In the winter of 1912-1913, while work went ahead on the hotel, preparations were made to move the opera house. The structure would not fit on Lot 2, Block 7, fronting on Banff Avenue, as its staircase to the second floor would overhang the adjacent lot, owned by the Imperial Bank. A compromise was to have it front on Caribou Street, sitting mainly on the east half of Lot 1 (132 Caribou Street).

The move itself was never forgotten by anyone who witnessed it. Carried out by E. E. Knight and Company of Calgary during March of 1913, the job required about ten days. The crew began by raising the building and getting timbers underneath and then winching it on to a sort of carriage which had four sets of fourteen rollers under it. Tracks were laid and an ingenious arrangement of blocks and inch-thick cable leading to a horse-drawn capstan inched the building slowly forward, a tedious chore. It took from Tuesday through Friday to move it the two blocks down Wolf Street from Lynx Street to Banff Avenue. The building's seventy-five foot width necessitated removing the electric light poles lining the street. Yet when the building was safely on its new foundation the contractor proudly boasted that not a window had cracked nor had the slightest bit of damage been done.

Once the opera house was moved and redecorated, Jim decided its new situation warranted a new name. It was thereafter known as Brewster (or Brewster's) Hall. The first event hosted within its confines was a basket social presented by the Loyal Orange Order on April 24th. By early May three dances a week were being held, two of which were ordinary style and a third at which "ragging," the newest dance sensation, was allowed, "within reason."

While Jim's involvement in his business activities in the Rockies took up much of his time, he still found room for other personal ventures outside the area. Perhaps influenced by the success of the Brewster Iron Works, his favourite locale for these interests was Edmonton. One of the smaller and shorter lived of them was a taxidermy business known as Brewster and Wolfe. William de Wolfe, who had come to Banff shortly after the turn of the century, had worked on the trail for a number of area outfitters. However, by 1905 Norman Luxton began employing him as a taxidermist in the Sign of the Goat Curio Store, where his excellent work came to Jim's attention. De Wolfe made Jim a beautiful ptarmigan diorama, which graced the Brewster home for many years. In June, 1909 the two formed a partnership to carry on business in a store owned by Jim on 102nd Street in Edmonton. The partnership lasted only about a year before de Wolfe and Ashley Hine, another taxidermist who had worked for Luxton, convinced Jim to sell his interest at a handsome profit.

Jim's other interests in Edmonton and area were more grandiose. As mentioned, the pre-war years were an age of rampant speculation and he was by no means immune to the golden itch. In June, 1909 he purchased two quarter sections west of Edmonton, land formerly part of the

J. I. BREWSTER　　W. WOLFE

BREWSTER & WOLFE

TAXIDERMISTS

A speciality of Mounting Big Game Heads. All work done on the New Modelling Process: Lifelike, Lasting, Mothproof.

The finest work possible on Birds, Whole Animals and Fish. Furs Tanned and made as Rugs, Mats, etc.

Game Heads for sale. Coyote and Bear Rugs, etc. for sale

648 SECOND STREET
EDMONTON, ALTA　May 21st 1910

Stony Plain Indian Reserve, for $3284. The same year he purchased an additional quarter section in the next township north through which the right-of-way for the Edmonton and Slave Lake Railway passed. This land, which cost $17,500, he immediately subdivided into some 300 lots to form the subdivision of Dominion Park. Finally, in 1911 he and an acquaintance from New York, John G. McLochlin, purchased forty-eight lots in the new subdivision of Hempriggs in the northwest part of Edmonton for $13,000. As well, Jim owned two lots on Jasper Avenue, one lot on McDougall Avenue, four lots in the Norwood subdivision, two lots in the town of St. Albert and six lots in the town of Athabasca Landing.

On acquiring these extensive properties, Jim immediately set about attempting to sell them for a profit. The lots in Dominion Park moved particularly well, many of them being sold to Brewster employees such as Crosby, Dunsmore and McLeod at somewhat inflated prices. Jim initially looked after the sales himself but after the purchase in the Hempriggs subdivision it was impossible to devote to them the necessary time and attention. Therefore, in September, 1912, he entered into a partnership agreement with McLochlin in the real estate and brokerage firm of Brewster and McLochlin, joining over thirty similar agencies and over 300 individual agents involved in the Edmonton market at the time. McLochlin, managing the company out of an Edmonton office, took a brief fling at the Banff market as well. During the summer of 1913 Brewster and McLochlin advertised a Banff branch which, in addition to selling the Dominion Park and other Edmonton lots, solicited listings on Banff properties.

Another of Jim's schemes in Edmonton was a direct result of the real estate boom. With so many properties being developed the construction contracting business appeared to be a good investment. Together with Edward M. Read and Harold G. MacDonald, both civil engineers, Jim entered into partnership in Read-MacDonald-Brewster Limited, Engineers and Contractors in March, 1912. His investment of $10,000 gave him a one-third interest in the company, which his two partners co-managed out of an office in Edmonton's prestigious Tegler Building. The company immediately proved successful in acquiring major contracts, particularly in Edmonton itself, but it also secured the contract for renovating and enlarging the Mount Royal Hotel in October, 1912, Read personally supervising the work. Within a few years of its creation the business was paying annual dividends to Jim in excess of the amount of his original investment, and in 1916 it opened an equally successful branch in Minneapolis, Minnesota.

Because of his active participation in the development of Brewster Transfer, Brewster Trading, the Mount Royal Hotel and his other interests in the boom prior to the First World War, Jim, on paper, quickly became a wealthy man. At the end of 1913 his net worth amounted to approximately $375,000. But paper value in 1913 and real value a few years later were two very different matters, particularly in light of what was to transpire with regard to property values and his businesses during this period.

Brewster Transport's first "auto tally-ho" in front of Brewster's Hall, ca. 1919

# VI: The Gamble

His business interests proliferating locally and further afield, Jim continued to remain actively involved in the Banff community. By the eve of the First World War his numerous successes had brought him to a top rung on the local social ladder. Befitting one of his position, he had constructed a sturdy brick home, one of the town's showplaces, at 202 Bow Avenue on two lots acquired in his wife's name in 1908. This beautifully appointed eight room house he soon adorned with his numerous hunting trophies and mementos from the wealthy and famous whom his companies had served and he had befriended. As an adjunct to it, he had a floating boathouse constructed on the Bow River to house the Waterman speed boat he had purchased in Detroit in 1910.

Jim's social prominence was by no means affectation. Extremely fond of people, he wanted to be involved in everything going on around him, to the extent that virtually every local organization had his support and many had him on their executives. Several of these organizations were sports-oriented, since this is where one of his main areas of interest lay. In addition to his participation in hockey, curling and baseball activities, he took part in the formation of the Banff Rifle Club in 1909, and was elected president, the Banff Boating Club in 1910, of which he was appointed commodore, and the Banff Springs Golf Club in 1911. In 1912 he helped to create the Banff Winter Sports Club to promote winter activities and break the image of Banff as a one season town. In 1917 the club helped to organize the first Banff Winter Carnival, and Jim then headed a new organization, the Banff Winter Sports Association, formed to pursue this initial success. Other organizations on which he served to "boost" Banff were the Banff Indian Days Committee and the Banff Board of Trade, created to apprise the federal government of local wishes and needs. Recognition of Jim's efforts on behalf of the town was perhaps best summed up by the *Crag and Canyon* which in 1913 stated that he "has done more to put the town on the map . . . than all other residents combined."

Included in his efforts to "put the town on the map" was spreading the gospel of Banff during his frequent and wide travels. He usually made at least two major trips a year, one of which was always to eastern Canada to meet with both CPR and government officials and press for changes in contracts and regulations or promote development which he felt would aid the tourist trade and his companies' particular place in it. He was soon on familiar terms with both railroad and government officials and, in the case of the recently appointed Dominion Parks Commissioner, J. B. Harkin, made known the view and desires of Banff citizens on a variety of issues. As time went on his influence on parks policy as a spokesman for Banff became considerable. His political influence also began to grow in this period, as he took advantage of his trips to consult with those in the upper echelons of the Liberal Party. Jim's loyal support for Sir Wilfrid Laurier became particularly apparent when he took a rather unpopular stance favouring the former prime minister's position on conscription in 1917. Such loyalty would not go unrecognized during better days for the Liberals in the future.

In addition to visiting government and railway officials, Jim paid calls on tour agencies in eastern U.S. cities, arranging bookings and distributing information for the increasingly large number of group tours that were coming to the mountains. Raymond-Whitcomb, the first agency in the field, continued to be the best contact, but other agencies such as Gillespie, Kinport and Baird, and Thomas Cook and Son also became important. With the increasing frequency of this type of contact as the decade progressed, Jim also began to send Crosby and McLeod on junkets to drum up business with these and other agencies.

While in the east, Jim also made a point of attending as many of the various sportsmen's shows as possible. The annual Madison Square Garden show continued to be a favourite. The outfitting branch of the company was usually well represented with head guide George Harrison holding down the spot of chief publicity agent previously so capably occupied by Jim himself.

His visits to New York during the show also allowed him and Fred Hussey to hold forth at an annual party at the Waldorf-Astoria Hotel for their past and prospective customers. These parties quickly gained a reputation for their wine, women, and song, and both guests and hosts enjoyed them equally. Fred had opened an office on Wall Street and married a prominent socialite, Ethel Dean, and his enhanced social standing attracted many of the guests. But they also came to meet or re-acquaint themselves with that "diamond in the rough," Jim Brewster, whose name was quickly spreading.

That these guests were often from the wealthiest sector of the eastern upper class did not by any means guarantee that they were overly free with their money. At one of the parties a man approached Hussey and stated that Fred reminded him of someone, but couldn't remember just who. Fred played along but later had a good laugh with Jim when he recalled that the man had been a Brewster Transfer customer the previous year. Barn boss Bert McCallum had been short of carriage drivers, and a game Fred had immediately thrown on some livery garb, jumped in a rig and driven up to the Banff Springs Hotel to pick up the gentleman. Fred took him for a drive around the Loop, stopping to talk on the points of interest as Brewster drivers were supposed to, and delivered him back to the hotel after a very pleasant trip. The patron, expressing his pleasure, handed Fred a twenty-five cent tip!

While Jim was busily promoting Brewster Transfer and the Canadian Rockies, changes were taking place in the transportation world that would inalterably affect their future. By the turn of the century the "horseless carriage" was making its presence felt on the North American scene. Initially the automobile was the sole preserve of the wealthy, but as the second decade of the century began, Henry Ford's dedication was bringing it within the reach of the common man. The effects were apparent to Jim and gave him cause for thought. While living at Victoria he had owned an automobile for a short time and had become an immediate convert to its capabilities and possibilities.

Soon after the creation of Brewster Transfer, Jim identified a suitable opportunity for testing the viability of motorized transport in the tourist business. Transporting passengers by buggy from the CPR station at Laggan to the Lake Louise Chalet over a very steep and rough road had always been exceedingly hard on horses and passengers alike. As a result, in November, 1910 Crosby formally approached the park superintendent for permission to operate motor buses on this route. The superintendent relayed the request to the Superintendent of Forestry, under whose department parks at that time fell, recommending that, since "we have representatives of societies complaining of the cruelty to the animals driven on the road" and that "Brewster Transfer are the only ones driving on this road," it be allowed the privilege. In March, 1911 the Department of the Interior informed the superintendent he could issue a permit in favour of the company, good for one year, and that the licence fee should be the same as that paid for a horse-drawn vehicle. By the summer of 1911 the situation had changed and Brewster Transfer decided not to use a motor vehicle on this road, undoubtedly because the CPR proposed constructing a tramline between the station and the hotel which, when it became operational in 1912, would preclude Brewster Transfer's use of this route.

Jim's first car in Victoria, 1908

Despite the abortive attempt, establishing motorized transport retained a prominent place in Jim's mind, but, mainly due to two factors, one having to do with government regulations

Coaches and automobiles at Banff station, ca. 1917

and the other with economics, he did not resurrect it for some time.

As the second decade of the century began, government regulations were essentially anti-automobile. An Order-in-Council passed in September, 1905 prohibited the use of cars of any description in the park, a rather needless piece of legislation since no road linked Banff with the outside world. But by 1909 work on the Banff-Calgary coach road had made it possible for the odd Calgary motorist to make the perilous trip. The local magistrate came down hard on such offenders. Matters remained relatively quiet until 1910 when a deputation from the Calgary Automobile Club, composed of some of the city's most influential citizens, waited on the Minister of the Interior and convinced him to amend the regulations to allow the use of cars on such roads and under such rules as he authorized. In April, 1911 an Order-in-Council allowed motorists to drive into Rocky Mountains Park, but on reaching Banff they had to register and leave their keys at the office of the superintendent or at the police barracks. To the chagrin of local residents, a group from the Calgary Automobile Club arrived in town in late July and completely ignored the regulations, driving their "buzz wagons" all over town. From this point onward a trend began which gradually whittled down the automobile restrictions through successive Orders-in-Council passed in 1912 and 1913 at the instigation of, among others, Senator James Lougheed, himself a summer resident of Banff who preferred to drive. Despite this trend no allowance was made for livery cars in the regulations of 1913.

Although government regulations prevented Brewster Transfer from engaging in motorized transport in the early part of the decade, it is likely Jim favoured some restrictions. The *Crag and Canyon* probably reflected the local population's feelings quite well in its frequent attacks on Calgary motorists and their disregard for the regulations. Since the argument always hinged on the incompatibility of horses and motor cars, the Calgary press accused those who spoke out against cars of doing so to protect their livery interests, undoubtedly with some truth. *Crag and Canyon* proprietor Norman Luxton also owned the King Edward Livery Company, Brewster Transfer's major competitor in the livery business prior to the war. Other important people, such as Dr. Brett, also had livery interests and were keen on seeing the horse and carriage protected. Of course, Jim, with his company's extensive stock-in-trade of tally-hos, buggies and rigs as well as numerous teams of driving horses, had more at stake than anyone. If the motor car were going to replace the horse immediately he would lose a good deal of money on his stock and equipment and have to lay out substantial capital to buy motor vehicles. It was obviously in his interest to see a gradual transition to motorized transport, but Jim did not doubt it would come. Two things made this apparent. The first was the attitude of Dominion Parks Commissioner J. B. Harkin towards the automobile. He recognized that if parks demonstrated their ability to help pay their own way they would receive the appropriations to ensure their development. In 1913 he reported to his minister:

> It is a well established fact that motorists spend their holidays in their cars . . . . What motorist will be able to resist the call of the Canadian Rockies when he can go through them on first class roads? And what a revenue the country will obtain when thousands of automobiles are traversing the Parks.

Jim's discussions with Harkin soon made him aware of the commissioner's attitudes and gave him cause to consider their ramifications.

The second factor which brought home the

inevitability of motorized tourist transport was his brother Bill's experience at his new home of Glacier Park, Montana. Bill had left Banff in the spring of 1909, headed for New York City to join his brother George, a student at Princeton Preparatory School, and Lincoln Ellsworth, a man he had befriended during the latter's several visits to Banff. Ellsworth, later a famous Arctic explorer, had visited the Rockies in 1904 as a transitman on a survey through Yellowhead Pass. Then he had come to Banff to assist surveying coal locations for the then developing Bankhead Mines. He had returned several more times, the last in 1909 as resident engineer engaged in construction work for the CPR. Bill liked Ellsworth who was a rather footloose individual, much as Bill himself had earlier been, full of dreams and schemes. The three hoped to develop a partnership in a South American ranch and it appears they at least tried to carry it out. Bill moved his family to San Antonio, Texas, apparently thinking it was closer to South America than New York was, and then he and Ellsworth headed south.

Bill was gone more than a year, most of this time being spent with Ellsworth in Chile. After he returned he moved his family first to Reno and later to Lake Tahoe, Nevada. Apparently he had been expecting some money for his share of the capital account of Brewster Brothers but little, if any, ever arrived. Jim seems to have had only a vague idea where Bill was, stating to all enquirers that he was "somewhere in Mexico." Bill therefore was in strained circumstances financially when he was approached with an attractive proposition in 1912.

Louis W. Hill, the president of the Great Northern Railway, envisioned a system of hotels and chalets, much like those of the CPR through the Canadian Rockies, in the mountains of Montana after the creation of Glacier National Park in 1910. He was aware that to be similarly successful he had to offer the best in services. He wanted experienced people to run guiding and saddle horse hire in connection with the massive Glacier Park Lodge being constructed at East Glacier and other smaller lodges and camps throughout the park. Newspaperman Jack Farrell, an acquaintance of Bill's, suggested he had the prerequisites and Hill readily concurred. Bill arrived with his family at Belton, Montana in 1912 to organize the business, and Hill's influence soon secured for him the necessary licence from the U.S. Department of the Interior. Financing the business was not easy, and Bill eventually borrowed money in Montana and brought in a partner, his brother Jim.

Jim undoubtedly felt he owed Bill whatever help he could lend him. He insisted, however, he be a silent partner and that any agreement between the two should be strictly confidential, and neither the members of his own nor Bill's family were ever aware of it. The partnership, taking the old name of Brewster Brothers, in May, 1913 entered into an agreement with the Great Northern Railway, one similar in some respects to those the earlier Brewster Brothers had with the CPR. By its terms the railway company would direct clients to Brewster Brothers in return for their guaranteeing sufficient saddle and pack horses to meet the tourists' needs, providing adequate horse stage service on routes and schedules mutually agreed upon, and hauling supplies for the railway's hotels and camps at lowered rates. A significant difference was that Brewster Brothers did not pay an annual concession fee to the railway but rather to the government.

In the spring of 1913, Bill moved to East Glacier (Midvale) to prepare for the official opening of the Glacier Park Lodge that summer, with the help of his sons, Claude and Jack, and a few men he had hired. The company began operations with about sixty pack and saddle horses and twenty driving horses, all bearing Bill's recently registered Bar X 6 brand. Immediately a few buggies and tally-hos were also put into service, running on the road between Glacier Park station and Two Medicine Camp and between St. Mary's Camp and Lake McDermott Camp, both popular tourist drives. Bill quickly decided to operate automobiles on the same routes and brought in three Everts touring cars which proved unsuitable for the demands placed upon them. But the management of the Great Northern liked the idea so much that when renewing Brewster Brothers' contract in December, 1913 a clause was inserted that stated "the Railway Company shall have the right to maintain automobile service from, to and between any points in the park." These rights were soon given to Rowe Emery from Colorado, who had an interest in the White Motor Company. Emery set up the Glacier Park Transportation Company and began to operate White buses very successfully on the scenic routes in Glacier Park.

Rocky Mt. Goat

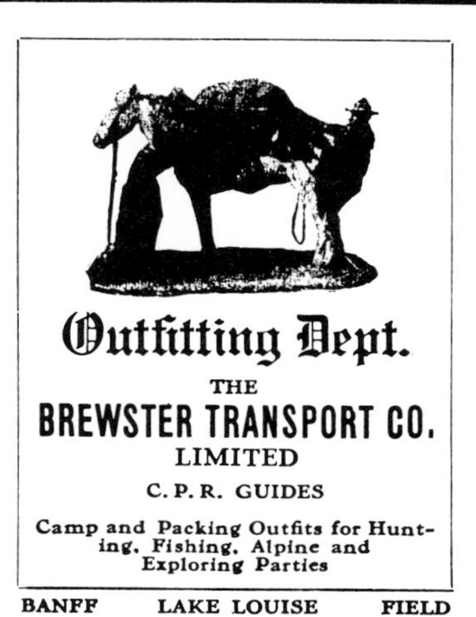

Rocky Mt. Sheep

Meanwhile, taking his cue from Harkin and the situation in Glacier Park, Montana, Jim had begun in 1914 to take steps to prepare for the inevitability of motorized tourist transport in the Canadian Rockies. First he changed his company's name and widened its scope of activities. On May 28, 1914 Selwood applied for a change in name from Brewster Transfer Company, Limited to Brewster Transport Company, Limited, a more accurate description of the company's function, since the word "transfer" had more of a connotation of cartage and hauling than of transporting people. Also the company began to acquire the buildings and lots related to its transportation activities. Prior to 1912, when Bow Livery had gone on Brewster Transfer's books, all real estate had been part of the holdings of Brewster Trading. By 1915 the blacksmith shop, the lower stable and numerous small workshops and buildings, totalling $16,875 in value, had become part of the assets of Brewster Transport. Also in its assets, beginning in 1914, were the Ya Ha Tinda Ranch, valued at $8000, as well as 329 head of horses.

A second step was taken in late 1914 during negotiations with the CPR for a renewal of the company's livery concession. As the experience in Montana had shown, it was not wise to take the railway's approval of motorized transportation rights for granted. During 1914 Hayter Reed had retired from his position of manager-in-chief of CPR hotels, F. L. Hutchinson replacing him. Jim and Hutchinson eventually became close friends, but at first Jim found the new manager-in-chief a hard bargainer. Coming into force on January 1, 1915 the new contract allowed Brewster Transport "the privilege of carrying on the automobile service, provided the Dominion Government permit the lessees the privilege of this service in the Rocky Mountains Park, except between Lake Louise Station and Chateau Lake Louise." In return the five year contract specified that the company pay the CPR $4000 per annum for this and their various other concessions, an increase of $2700 over the previous contract signed in 1912.

The CPR's backing secured, the government's restrictions regarding the operation of livery vehicles remained the only obstacle in Brewster Transport's path. The passing of an Order-in-Council on June 19, 1915 remedied this by promulgating new regulations respecting licencing, speed, hours of operation and other driving rules. Licence fees for vehicles used in motor livery were announced for the first time, amounting to $10 per annum for any motor vehicle to be used for livery purposes having a seating capacity of up to six persons and $15 for those having a seating capacity of over six. A motor vehicle used for draying or transfer was to be licensed at a fee of $10 per annum, and each chauffeur or driver of a motor vehicle used for livery or transfer purposes had to secure a Park Driver's Licence at $1 annually. Rates of speed were set at eight miles per hour in and about Banff townsite and fifteen miles per hour on public highways outside the vicinity of the townsite. Whereas previously no automobile had been permitted to drive after dark, now motor vehicles could "be driven from any hotel except those situated on the Upper Hotel Springs road, via Banff Avenue, Caribou and Lynx Streets, to and from the Canadian Pacific Railway Depot, at any time for the purpose of meeting and despatching guests on trains." Finally, as in the past, it was left to the discretion of the Minister of the Interior to decide on which streets and roads motor vehicles could be operated. Immediately after the new regulations came into force it was announced that all roads would be open, excepting the Sundance Canyon road from the Cave and Basin onward, Tunnel Mountain Drive and the Lake Minnewanka road between Bankhead and the lake.

Although Brewster Transport could have established motorized tourist transport in June, 1915, Jim did not immediately take the gamble. By 1915 the company owned a large stock of horse-drawn vehicles — three "hotel buses," twelve tally-hos, nineteen three-seaters, twenty surreys, eighteen single rigs and numerous miscellaneous rigs, baggage wagons and cartage wagons — as well as 146 head of driving horses. Some of these would have to be sold off, probably at a considerable loss, at the same time as expensive motor vehicles were being purchased. Therefore Jim wanted to make certain the automobiles he chose were right for the jobs they would have to do in the mountains without wearing out too quickly. The reputation of the Overland touring car, manufactured in a Toronto plant by Willys-Overland Limited, was well established and even though it was more expensive than the ubiquitous Ford, he decided to try one out. In late June, taking delivery of a Baby Overland, Jim became the first Banff resident to own an automobile. He spent the rest of that summer appraising its performance. Later in the year the *Crag and Canyon* reported that "the Ford must perforce hereafter take a back seat as far as its climbing abilities are concerned. Jim Brewster most conclusively proved last Friday that his motor car can beat the Ford."

With the Overland's ability proven, the company ordered four 7-passenger Model 86-Ts and one 5-passenger Model 85 at a total cost of about $5700. Work began in April of 1916 to turn the Bow Livery into a garage. With a cement floor, metal sheathed walls, a resident mechanic and a new name, the Mount Royal Garage, the building began to fulfill its new function on May 1, 1916 after the five Overlands were unloaded from a CPR freight car. At the same time the company was selling off some of the twenty-eight head of driving horses it would dispose of that year, forcefully exhibiting a new age was at hand.

Later the same summer the company decided to experiment with motorized hauling and cartage, purchasing a large truck from the White Motor Company of Cleveland, Ohio for about $3900. After acquiring a special permit allowing it to run across the bridge, Brewster Transport put it to work doing company hauling around town. The machine took some getting used to because of its great weight and load capacity. On one occasion when it was backed up to the door of the lower stable on Banff Avenue to unload a few tons of oats its back wheels slowly sank up to the axles in the soft earth around the building's foundations.

When Jim took the gamble and invested in motor vehicles in early 1916 several unknown factors remained that were to affect Brewster Transport's chances of success. One of these was the government's future attitudes towards restrictions on roads open to motor vehicles. Jim undoubtedly hoped the restrictions would come off slowly, allowing the company to operate motor vehicles on some roads while others were restricted to horse-drawn vehicles, giving him the opportunity to make the change to a completely motorized operation over a period of time. The restrictions imposed by the Minister of the Interior in June, 1915 would keep certain of the major drives closed to automobiles, in particular Tunnel Mountain Drive and the road to Lake Minnewanka, thereby seeming to support these hopes. Furthermore, after his annual visit to Ottawa and a conversation with Harkin, he returned to Banff in early March, 1916 and informed other interested parties that Harkin had told him that the same restrictions would apply for the coming season.

Jim had not reckoned with other Banff businessmen who had now climbed on the automobile bandwagon and wished to see all restrictions removed. Under the leadership of Norman Luxton, these businessmen drafted a petition in March, 1916 addressed to local Member of Parliament R. B. Bennett, Senator Lougheed, and Harkin, calling for the opening of all roads around Banff and Bankhead by May 1,

**Jim driving the Prince of Wales in one of Brewster Transport's Overlands, 1920**

1916. From their point-of-view this would "materially benefit the people of the aforementioned towns" and would also benefit tourists, particularly those on one day stopovers who "by using motors exclusively . . . would be enabled to see far more of the sights for which Banff is famous at a smaller cost and a considerable saving of time."

Shortly after this petition was drafted, Jim wrote Harkin explaining why he had not signed it:

> They seem to want to allow the motors to run at large beginning the first of May, and specially mentioned the Tunnel Mountain and Lake Minnewanka Roads. Both these roads, as you know, are impracticable to motors and horse-drawn carriages at the same time, and I think it would be more or less suicide to the business this coming season to allow them to use these roads for motors until they are widened to be made more secure in some ways.
>
> You can see by the petition there are few, if any of the people who handle the transportation of tourists during the season here on it, and those who have signed, in my mind have done so purely from a selfish point of view and have not the real interest of the Park at heart.

Despite this protest and one the CPR made on Jim's behalf, Harkin sided with the petitioners. He instructed the superintendent to widen the Minnewanka road and to open it and other roads as quickly as possible. On July 7, 1916 the superintendent issued a notice to automobile drivers that the Sundance Canyon, Upper Hot Springs and Lake Minnewanka roads were open to traffic. Fortunately, from Jim's point-of-view, the cost of constructing a diversion around the treacherous Corkscrew on Tunnel Mountain Drive was too great at the time and it remained restricted to horse traffic until 1919.

It is likely the unforeseen quick relaxation of the automobile restrictions forced Brewster Transport into faster investment in motorized equipment than Jim preferred. Necessity being the mother of invention, he struck on an idea that would increase the company's motorized carrying capacity inexpensively and partially solve the problem of excess horse-drawn vehicles. In May, 1916 John Locke, proprietor of the Homestead Hotel in Banff, brought in a char-a-banc (open excursion bus with transverse seats) constructed on a Ford chassis, capable of carrying ten or eleven passengers. Taking his cue from this creation, Jim decided to utilize the tops of some of the company's tally-hos for similar vehicles. Brewster Transport purchased one new and two used Kissel delivery trucks, costing some $3000, and had them stripped down in the blacksmith shop. The upper framework of the old tally-hos, including seats, were mounted on the Kissel chassis, a few adjustments to the gear ratios were made and in 1917 three "auto tally-hos" emerged from their cocoons. One of them was an 18-passenger model and the other two seated 14 passengers. Some of the resident Banff drivers, such as Rusty Gowans, James Forteath and Jim Raby who had driven the vehicles as tally-hos, were outfitted in new top hats and coats and became the company's first bus drivers.

The larger "auto tally-ho" had been built for the relatively long trip between Banff and Lake Minnewanka. A typical excursion in it would set out from the Banff Springs Hotel or downtown Banff and, after stopping at various points of interest along the way, would reach the shore of the lake about an hour later. Here, by prior arrangement, one of the tour boats operated by Captain Jack Standly would take the passengers on a lake cruise. The passengers would then return to Banff after stopping to view the bison and other animals in the Animal Paddock en route.

The two smaller vehicles were built with the hope that the government might grant the company permission to operate motor vehicles at Lake Louise as it had in 1911. The company now desired to run them between the chalet at Lake Louise and Moraine Lake. Crosby wrote Harkin in March, 1917 requesting the company be allowed to run on the Moraine Lake Road, stating that the tally-hos were breaking up the road and that Brewster Transport wouldn't be interfering with anyone since it was the only livery service there. Not wishing to appear to be granting a monopoly, Harkin decided to open the road from Laggan to Lake Louise and Moraine Lake to all parties. After he did so at the end of May, Crosby informed the CPR's local passenger agent that Brewster Transport intended utilizing the two 14-passenger "auto tally-hos" and two touring cars on the Moraine Lake Road and for meeting special parties at the station.

Another factor which affected Brewster Transport's motorized services was the livery tariff the company would be allowed to charge. When the government passed regulations which permitted motorized livery in 1915, it made no provision for a revised tariff. By the summer of 1916 action was necessary because a considerable number of operators had taken out livery licences and, as a telegram from the superintendent to Harkin pointed out, people were beginning to arrive for the season and he wanted to head off any trouble between patrons and drivers over charges. Harkin suggested the superindendent meet with the livery people and discuss tariffs and arrive at an agreement fair to tourists and owners alike. The meeting, held on June 25, 1916 with Jim Brewster, Norman Luxton and several others in attendance, proposed charges on a per person basis for the various trips with minimum charges applying to some. Charges suggested for the more popular runs included: $2.50 per person from the Banff Springs Hotel to Lake Minnewanka and return, including boat trip; $1.00 per person for the Loop Drive from either the Banff Springs Hotel or Banff village; and $1.00 per person from Banff to Bankhead and return. These and several other trips would not start with less than four passengers, thereby establishing a minimum charge, and in addition a fee for waiting time exceeding fifteen minutes would be charged on the basis of $2.50 per hour for a 5-passenger car and $3.00 per hour for a 7-passenger car. Fees of $5.00 per hour for 5-passenger cars and $6.00 per hour for 7-passenger cars were suggested for drives without specific destinations. Although Harkin wanted to change some of the minimum charges, the superintendent received his suggestions too late to make them that year and the livery operators received exactly what they suggested.

Tariff negotiations with the government did not prove so fruitful the following year. On March 21, 1917 a meeting of livery men was held at the superintendent's office with Brewster, Crosby and McLeod representing Brewster Transport, L. C. Orr representing the King Edward Livery and J. D. Hansen, B. Rodgers, John Locke, Frank Howell, C. E. Sibbald and Edward Ellis representing smaller concerns. Harkin's points on the previous year's tariff were reviewed and the meeting reluctantly agreed to accept lower minimum charges on some drives and lower fees for waiting time, with the understanding basic charges for the trips would remain the same.

Prior to the 1918 season it appeared the Department of the Interior would not establish a new tariff, and Crosby wrote to Harkin, pointing out that, because of war conditions, the cost of everything in the livery business had gone up twenty percent. A subsequent meeting of auto and horse livery men drafted a petition asking that an annual licence fee of $100 on the first car operated by any liveryman be levied, with a refund of a least three-quarters of this amount at the end of the year to those operating the entire twelve months. The intent was to offset a perceived increase in the number of outside jitney drivers coming in and taking away business from local livery men during the lucrative summer months. The petition also requested a minimum twenty-five percent increase in the auto livery tariff because of the general increase in the price of cars, gasoline, upkeep and wages and a minimum fifty percent increase in the horse livery tariff because of the increase in cost of carriages, saddlery, feed and wages. Harkin cited the policy of the Parks Branch that the park was maintained by and for all Canadians and any resident of Canada must not be discriminated against. He felt that since Brewster Transport and King Edward Livery were the only year-round operators the suggested policy would damage the smaller livery operators in Banff. Nor would he grant the requested large increases in livery tariffs, feeling they would be detrimental to tourist traffic. He eventually did allow a ten percent increase in all livery rates and agreed to further consider the question of horse livery rates after receiving a letter from Crosby pleading with him to do so.

While the livery tariff was important in the struggle to make Brewster Transport's services profitable, the number of passengers carried ultimately determined success or failure. It is significant that when Jim was deciding to go into automobiles in 1915 his company's transportation business was experiencing its most successful season. The full effects of the war had not yet begun to be felt in Canada, the United States had not yet entered the conflict, and Europe was closed to travel. Combined with the numerous excursions going to or coming from the Panama-Pacific Exposition at San Francisco, these factors pushed the visitor statistics to a record 90,000. Brewster Transport's own statistics were equally impressive. From June through October they handled 336 special parties, composed of 15,500 people, in addition to ordinary patrons. These statistics translated directly into increased revenues, income at the CPR stables jumping from $10,500 in 1914 to $35,000 in 1915, and at Lake Louise from $10,900 to $27,800. The company's net profit rose from $2600 in 1914 to $36,000 in 1915.

Jim and Crosby astutely realized the 1915 season was an aberration caused by the Exposition and knew such incomes could not be relied on in the future. Nonetheless the season promoted an optimism which, combined with the belief the war would soon end, made the company's future appear bright. Not long after the investment in automobiles had been made, it became apparent the war would not end soon, and visitor statistics plunged within three years to a low of 41,800, well less than half those in 1915. In 1916 Brewster Transport handled less than a third of the number of special parties it had in 1915. Income from the Mount Royal Garage, which included all motorized operations, stood at a meagre $2900. More ominous was the fact that because of its purchase of expensive equipment the company experienced its first operating loss. It amounted to only slightly more than $1000 and the company was still able to pay out $25,000 in dividends from its surplus account, but by 1916 the loss had grown to over $12,000 and no dividends were declared. It was not at all certain Jim's gamble was going to pay off.

Jim in his buckskin shirt and grizzly bear chaps, ca. 1915

# VII: Declining Fortunes

The difficulties Jim began to experience with Brewster Transport after 1915 exacerbated the problems of his personal and other business affairs. He was the victim of a situation created by the war, but unwise additional investment, poor planning and just plain bad luck aggravated it.

Jim's personal life took a hard blow with the death of his wife in 1915. Lade Brewster had been an active outdoorswoman, her obituary noting that "few women in the field could equal her wonderful shooting and hunting qualities." But about 1913 she had begun to suffer the effects of tuberculosis. Jim travelled with her to warmer climes to try to offset its effects but to little avail. Over the winter of 1914-15 Bill Brewster and his family returned to Banff so that her sister Tead could be with her. In February the sisters departed for Salt Lake City, and Jim spent several weeks with them in early March. Returning to Banff, he expressed his belief the change in climate had been beneficial to his wife's health. A few days later word arrived that she had passed away at age thirty-three on March 27th.

With the death of his wife, Jim alone had to raise his daughter Fern. Their already close relationship was even further strengthened and the two became almost inseparable. To assure her future security he set up a trust that included title to his Bow Avenue residence. In addition, he provided her with everything a young woman could desire. Early in 1916, at age fourteen, she became the owner of one of the few cars in Banff, Jim's gift on his return from a trip to New York. Fortunately he eventually recognized the harm in tying Fern too closely to himself and in September, 1916 enrolled her in the Bishop Strachan School in Toronto.

While he was dealing with the loss of his wife, Jim was trying to recover from reverses in his outside business interests and the affairs of Brewster Trading. His extensive real estate holdings in Edmonton and vicinity had been hard hit along with those of thousands of other real estate speculators when the market collapsed in the middle of 1913. While the Hempriggs lots had mostly been sold off by Brewster and McLochlin,

**Fern at the wheel of her Baby Overland in front of Jim's Bow Avenue residence**

Jim still held the rights to 270 lots, with a book value of over $70,000, in the proposed Dominion Park subdivision. By 1914 McLochlin had pulled out of the failing market and Jim reincorporated under the name of Brewster Realty and Coal Company, with George Gittius as manager. As the war progressed it became increasing obvious that real estate had become a liability. Taxes on the unsold lots still had to be paid. Jim withstood the tide longer than most but towards the end of the war began to let his properties go for taxes.

Other ventures met a similar fate. His uncle William's departure to California necessitated the sale of the Brewster Iron Works, and Read-MacDonald-Brewster Ltd. abandoned the Edmonton construction market for lack of contracts in 1917. While Jim could withstand his losses in these ventures, similar reverses in Brewster Trading and Brewster Transport were more threatening to his financial stability. Brewster Trading had never lived up to expectation in its first few years of operation, returning mediocre profits for the time and energy invested in it. Then in mid-February, 1914 disaster struck in the form of a fire at the King Edward Hotel, next door to the Brewster Trading Company store. The fire hydrants near the hotel were frozen, and the local volunteer fire brigade experienced difficulty in bringing the blaze under control. The stock from the store was emptied into the street but some of it was smoke and water damaged. Not only that, but, as the *Crag and Canyon* disgustedly reported, "Ghouls, wearing the guise of men, took advantage of the excitement to loot," bringing the reported loss to Brewster Trading close to $15,000.

The loss, undoubtedly exaggerated, was partially covered by insurance, but the fire nonetheless marked the beginning of a downturn in the company's fortunes. Brewster Trading's balance sheet for 1914 showed a total loss of $12,900 on its various operations. In an effort to find the reasons, the company's chartered accountants found fault with the methods of financial control. They pointed out that no reserve covered accounts receivable of over $15,000, a substantial portion of which various Brewster family members owed, and they appropriated $3000 from the surplus account to cover them. They mentioned that the amount of money tied up this way was considerably curtailing the working capital of the company. They drew attention to the lack of a reserve for depreciation if major repairs or rebuilding the store and other buildings became necessary, and appropriated $7800 from the surplus account for such a reserve. Finally, they noted that the gross profit on merchandise amounted to less than six percent compared with an average of about fourteen percent over the previous few years. On this point they agreed with Crosby who felt the fire losses and the low prices on goods sold during two sales after it were the cause of the loss in profits.

Their knuckles rapped, the directors instructed Crosby to tighten up the running of the business. Proper reserves were set up and efforts made to increase profits from various aspects of the operations. The Brewster Hall continued to be a poor performer despite efforts to rectify it. The company decided to lease the property out and in 1915 Jim Hutchins, a former Brewster driver with a musical bent, took over its management. He immediately redecorated the premises and put together a dance orchestra that would become a well-known local institution. While the monies collected by Brewster Trading on the lease proved to be greater than its previous profits from the hall, they were only marginally so. Profits from the running of the bakery were equally hard to increase. Thus it was the Brewster Trading store in which a major turnaround in profit would have to be made.

Interestingly, Dunsmore and Crosby increased the gross profit on merchandise immediately, bringing it back to fourteen percent for the year 1915, almost exactly the same percentage as during 1911 when the business had experienced its best year ever. But in 1911 this percentage had been on sales amounting to over $136,000 while in 1915 it was on sales amounting to just over $64,000. Instead of ending the year in a profit position, Brewster Trading experienced a further loss of over $7000 and for the first time no dividends were declared.

In their year-end report the accountants pointed out that a profit margin of twenty percent would have to be reached and expenses pared further before the business could expect to show any profit. But, with the worsening tourist situation occasioned by the war, sales plummeted rather than grew; the profit margin proved impossible to increase. By the end of 1916 the business was in a precarious position. The company had experienced its third straight loss, its accounts payable exceeded its accounts receivable, its surplus account had shrunk from $51,000 in 1914 to just over $7000, and it owed $20,000 to the Imperial Bank.

At a meeting on Feburary 27, 1917, the shareholders of Brewster Trading made a motion ratifying a recent application by Crosby to the Imperial Bank for a general credit of $20,000. They hoped it would tide the company over until better times, but apparently the request was refused. The shareholders met again on June 25, 1917 to consider selling the store. A resolution was passed permitting Brewster Trading to borrow up to $10,000 from Brewster Transport to keep the company afloat in the short term and a second motion authorized Crosby to enter into negotiations to sell the store business at a price and upon such terms of payment as he deemed satisfactory. He was also authorized to lease the store premises to the purchaser of the business or to such other persons on such conditions as he saw fit.

A purchaser willing to enter into an agreement in these inauspicious times was not easy to find. As a result, the business continued to founder for several months and soon its creditors were persistently hounding Crosby for past due accounts. To avoid declaring bankruptcy, Jim and Crosby entered into negotiations with the Alberta Division of the Canadian Credit Men's Trust Association, Limited. This organization, which included some of the province's leading businessmen on its board, acted as an assignee and trustee in cases where businesses were experiencing financial difficulties. The Credit Men's Trust agreed to act as trustee for the company's creditors on the understanding that Brewster Trading would appoint it official assignee for the proceeds of any sale it could negotiate under the terms of the Bulk Sales Act of Alberta. This effectively removed the business from the company's hands as Frank Freeze, the Credit Men's Trust manager in Calgary, was placed in charge.

Working together with Jim and Crosby, Freeze was able to negotiate a sale. The buyers were W. B. Morris, an employee in the store, and James Serra, an Italian immigrant who had spent some time in the Crowsnest Pass before coming to Banff in 1912. Serra and Morris, as the new partnership was known, agreed to make an initial payment of $3000 on taking over the business on November 1, 1917. As well, they signed a series of notes falling due at various times over the next three years by which they agreed to pay an additional $23,200. All of this money was to be held in trust by the Credit Men's Trust pending the settlement with Brewster Trading's creditors and the paying of its own fee for handling these transactions.

Despite the seemingly small sum of money for a once thriving business at one of Banff's choicest locations, it was the best that could be hoped for in the circumstances. On January 12, 1918, Jim, Crosby and Selwood held a board of directors meeting and sanctioned the sale. At the same time they agreed to sell the chattels and goods of the company remaining in the store to Brewster Transport for its promissory note of $2376. The Brewster Trading Company engaged in no further transactions until 1923. The initial $3000 payment went to the Credit Men's Trust and probably became its fee. The purchasers defaulted on all succeeding notes and in 1923 Brewster Trading reached agreement with the

LAST DAY---MONDAY NEXT
IT'S NOT TOO LATE TO SECURE
Some Good Bargains Left
GREAT
SLAUGHTER SALE
of the ENTIRE STOCK of
The BREWSTER TRADING Co., Ltd.
Purchased by SERRA & MORRIS
20 Per Cent. Off Entire Stock
(Excepting Groceries)
GROCERIES will be subjected to a discount of 10 per Cent.
on all stock excepting Feed, Flour, Sugar, Eggs & Butter
BARGAIN TABLES will groan under goods marked away below cost
WE SHALL OFFER DURING THE SALE
Three Loaves of Bread for 25c.

Credit Men's Trust not to press for its collection "in view of the fact that we [the Trust] have received certain concessions from the wholesale trade in favor of the Brewster Trading Co., Ltd., more than offsetting the amount of these notes."

Not long after Brewster Trading entered into its agreement with the Canadian Credit Men's Trust Association, Brewster Transport began to seek a different service from the same company, the result of a decline in fortunes that outstripped in speed and magnitude those of its sister company.

The onset of the war and the declining number of tourists occurred just as Brewster Transport made its heavy investments in motorized transport in 1916. They also took place during a continuing expansion of the company's interests when, undoubtedly, it should have been concentrating on consolidating those it already held. But despite the times, Jim could not resist what he thought a good opportunity when he saw it. In 1916 he saw a chance to buy his own newspaper.

The *Crag and Canyon*, owned by Norman Luxton, had been pretty much Banff's only news voice since he had taken it over in 1901. Though

Luxton was a rival in the livery and hotel businesses, he and Jim were close friends, spending a good deal of time together hunting, serving on the Banff Indian Days Committee and in numerous other local activities. Luxton, tacitly a supporter of the Liberal Party, was more than likely to call things the way he saw them in his newspaper. Sometimes Jim did not agree with his point-of-view and often desired to voice his own opinions. In 1916 the *Rocky Mountain Courier,* a relatively recent newspaper venture in Banff, was on the verge of collapse. The *Courier* had begun its existence in April, 1914 in an office owned by William Warren on the corner of Banff Avenue and Caribou Street. It was backed by such local Conservative stalwarts as Warren and William Mather and was rumoured to be financed by R. B. Bennett, the local Member of Parliament, and Bob Campbell, the local Member of the Provincial Legislature, both Conservatives as well. The paper had experienced a somewhat checkered early career in competition with the older, more popular *Crag,* going through several changes in editor and suffering from a fire in June, 1915. In April, 1916 Jim had Brewster Transport offer to purchase it, eliminating an organ of the hated Conservative Party and providing a new Liberal mouthpiece for himself.

While Luxton relished competition in other areas of business, he could not see Jim as a newspaperman, and acrimonious, sometimes scathing commentaries about their competitors began in the columns of both papers. Luxton led off in his initial reaction to hearing of the Brewster Transport purchase: "A hypnotist stopped off in Banff last week long enough to work his spell on the Brewster Co. who are now the proud and happy possessors of that junk heap known as the Rocky Mountain Courier. It will be interesting to watch J. I. and L. S. in their efforts to switch from C. to L. gear."

Crosby, given the job of managing the paper until an editor could be found, proved no match for the acerbic Luxton, who constantly poked and prodded in his columns. Often it was Jim himself who was the object of his derision as, for example, when he acted as host to the Governor-General, the Duke of Devonshire, on one of his frequent visits to Banff in 1917. Luxton reported as follows:

> Stopping off here on Sunday on his way to Vancouver, the Duke of Devonshire, Governor-General of Canada, was taken for a little run around to the various places of interest by James Brewster, Earl of Banff incog., and after an hour or so's airing he boarded the train and was handed over to Rajah Jas. McLeod at Glacier.
>
> The chief item of interest in connection with the visit was the fact that "Earl" Brewster blew along so fast that his guest lost his hat on the main street, but it was no trouble to find it again as the crowds were not so very dense at the time.

The *Courier* responded in kind to these barbs, and things remained on a relatively even keel until the conscription crisis began to split the ranks of the Liberal Party in 1917. At that time the two men's viewpoint diverged greatly, Jim remaining loyal to Laurier and Luxton supporting the unionist wing of the party. Then the feathers flew and the two got down to some genuine mudslinging, although the disagreement did not affect their friendship over the long run.

One of the few positive effects of Brewster Transport's entry into the newspaper field was a substantial increase in the amount of local advertising. Jim had always seen to it that some advertising appeared in the *Crag* but a plethora of new material now appeared in the *Courier.* Each edition would see a large advertisement enjoining tourists to "See America's Greatest Playground by Automobile, Tally-ho, Carriage or Pony using Brewster Livery Service, The Best In The Park." Also, after Brewster Transport became the official local agent for Willys-Knight and Overland cars in February, 1917, large space promoted their assets each week.

As time went on, the *Courier* carried numerous articles and editorials promoting the building of new roads in the mountains. In January, 1918 it unveiled a grand scheme promoting the idea of a circle tour and the construction of roads in such remote locations as Mount Assiniboine and Glacier, B.C. This, the newspaper maintained, was the only way to compete with American parks.

Although the *Courier* gave Jim free rein for his personal and political feelings and did its best to promote Brewster interests, it was not financially successful. Despite upgrading its presses and moving into larger quarters in the Brewster-owned building at 126 Banff Avenue, it never wrested loyal *Crag* readers or advertisers away from the older paper. As a result, it only turned a small profit on its first year of operation, this being almost entirely due to the auditor's re-evaluation of the plant. Thereafter it slipped into an ever-increasing loss position, becoming just one more burden on Brewster Transport. In 1918 it ceased to publish. In 1919 much of its plant was sold off — at a loss of $350 — although a paper did continue to appear periodically under the banner of *The Banff Advocate.*

A second opportunity which Jim could not resist came in the form of a chance to complete Brewster Transport's grip on the CPR concessions along the railway through the Rockies and Selkirks. Glacier House, located near the summit of Rogers Pass, had long been a mecca for mountaineers anxious to test their skills on the neighbouring rugged peaks. Consequently, the hotel had grown somewhat apace with the Banff Springs and Mount Stephen House. The outfitting and livery concession at Glacier was in the hands of Syd Baker, a well-educated Englishman who had received his outfitting experience in an earlier partnership with Banff guide Jim Simpson. By no means a large operator, he did fairly well providing saddle horses to tourists wishing to take rides to Glacier and Avalanche Crests, to viewpoints for the magnificent Illecillewaet and Asulkan Glaciers and to other local beauty spots. Similarly, he provided a carriage service over the rough and tortuous road to the nearby Nakimu Caves, where Charles Deutschman, their discoverer, had set up a successful business escorting tourists through them.

Until 1917 Baker showed no sign of being willing to relinquish the Glacier concession. Then after a period of rather strange behaviour, which some observors attributed to the altitude, he changed his mind. Brewster Transport purchased his interest and with it five 3-seater buggies, one surrey, two wagons and twenty head of horses. The CPR, taking into account the changed situation, provided a new agreement for Brewster Transport on June 1, 1917. This agreement, for Glacier alone, did not increase the total concession fee payable under the five year agreement of 1915, requiring the company only to provide transportation for CPR officials and do any hauling required free of charge. George Harrison was immediately sent from Lake Louise to take over the company's operations in its new locale, but there was little he could do to increase patronage. With the war Glacier House had entered on a period of decline that would end with its closure in 1925. On its 1917 operations the company lost $725 at Glacier, the only one of its concessions which failed to make at least a small profit that year. The following year it registered a further loss, a position in which it was joined by several other of Brewster Transport's interests.

Both of Jim's unwise decisions to invest in what proved to be losing propositions further impaired Brewster Transport's ability to deal with its deteriorating condition. With the situation in the affairs of Brewster Trading, prospects looked dim for the company's future. By early 1917 the board of directors and shareholders of Brewster

Transport were taking measures to prevent its slide towards oblivion. It quickly became apparent their actions might be too little and too late.

At a shareholders' meeting on February 27, 1917 at which all shares were represented, including the one share alloted to James McLeod after Lade Brewster's death, the shareholders ratified the actions of the general manager. These included applying to the Imperial Bank for a general credit of $30,000 and for special credits of $10,000 to carry out the CPR ice contract, $6000 to carry out a recently obtained wood contract for the CPR at Lake Louise, and $13,000 for the purchase of oats and hay for the coming season. Even though the company's surplus account stood at a respectable level of $84,000 by the end of the 1916 year, the losses experienced and its over $30,000 indebtedness to the Imperial Bank had left it in a poor cash position, necessitating the loan applications. The Imperial Bank, concerned about the amount already owing, advanced only about $10,000. The rest of the required funds had to be found elsewhere, namely in the selling off of 100 shares of Canadian Pacific Railway stock held by Brewster Transport at $160 per share.

The loss position of the company in 1916 and the continuing downturn in patronage made it evident economies would have to be made, particularly in the amount of dividends paid. In these circumstances Jim became concerned about his personal financial position, since he relied on dividends from his companies for his ready cash. To offset the situation, he agreed to accept an increased salary for his positions of vice-president and treasurer. At a board of directors meeting held on June 25, 1917 his salary was increased from $1500 to $5000 per annum. As well, he was allowed travelling expenses in the interests of the company up to $3500. A further resolution allowed the vice-president, general manager or treasurer to deliver a chattel mortgage on all the property and equipment of the company to the Imperial Bank to secure its loans. Its concerns growing daily, the bank insisted this be done immediately and a mortgage for $30,000 covering all stock, cars and equipment as well as an assignment of all the company's book accounts were made to cover its approximately $40,000 of indebtedness.

When the 1917 financial statement was complete, it was obvious the measures aimed at propping up the company had failed. The loss for the year was in excess of $12,000 and its liabilities had increased. After a further series of loans the Imperial Bank gave notice it intended to call in its notes. With insufficient cash to carry on business in the coming season, Jim approached his contacts in the CPR and asked what could be done to help him out. Now on close terms with F. L. Hutchinson, he undoubtedly made an appeal directly to him. Hutchinson, then spending his summers at the Chateau Lake Louise from where he directed the hotel department, frequently socialized with Jim. Mrs. Hutchinson was very fond of Fern Brewster, and when her husband told her Brewster Transport was in danger of going under she was heard to say, "We must save it for Fernie's sake." The CPR certainly had a vested interest in seeing the company maintain itself as well, and Hutchinson negotiated a new agreement covering Brewster Transport's concessions with the CPR. On March 1, 1918 it came into effect with terms the same as those of previous agreements with the exception of the clause stipulating the amount Brewster Transport was to pay for its various privileges. Whereas the fee had been placed at $4000 per annum in the 1915 agreement, it was now set at a nominal $1.00 per annum.

Hutchinson's largesse was not without its strings. To secure relief from the annual fee, Jim had to relinquish any direct control over the company's financial management and confine himself to its "outside" work. In addition, he had to agree to receiving no more than his $5000 annual salary from the company. To Basil Gardom, Superintendent of Construction for the CPR stationed at Lake Louise, Hutchinson gave general responsibility for overseeing the Brewster operation. But what was needed was a good man on the job with the power to make decisions for the company on a day-to-day basis. Apparently at the suggestion of the Imperial Bank, the CPR agreed to the appointment of Frank White, an accountant with the bank. At a board of directors meeting held on May 21st he was formally elected treasurer, replacing Jim in the position. With the appointment went entire control of funds, the power to check and keep accounts of all receipts and earnings, to control expenditures made and obligations incurred and to sign all cheques, bills, drafts, notes and negotiable instruments. White was to receive a salary of $150 per month and it was agreed that either he or the company could terminate his employment at any time. The same meeting resolved that Crosby would continue in his position of general manager at a salary of $1800 per annum but his powers were subject to and limited by those granted to White. Finally, and again with the approval of the CPR, the meeting authorized the company's officers to assign all monies payable to Brewster Transport by virtue of the concession agreement of March 1, 1918 to the Imperial Bank as further collateral security for its indebtedness.

Unquestionably the meeting of May 21st, which stripped him of control of his own company, did not sit well with Jim. Combined with the sale of Brewster Trading's store and the poor performance of the Mount Royal Hotel, which he was attempting to lease to the government as a convalescent home for returned soldiers, it made the future appear bleak. Jim had begun drinking heavily as his fortunes declined and in the summer of 1918 he became increasingly despondent. Adding to his frustration, the war appeared to be drawing to a close and he had not yet become involved in the defence of his country. In October, 1918 he made an earth-shattering decision. The *Crag and Canyon* announced that "James I. Brewster has joined the Siberian force and will take a place on the remount staff. It is needless to say that in this position Mr. Brewster will make good as all his life he has been mixed more or less with horses." In his despondency Jim had talked with Phil Moore about the future. Moore, who had served overseas and obtained the rank of Colonel, was then in charge of conscription for Alberta but was also looking towards his occupation at the war's end. He did not wish to return to Jasper, having already severed his ties with the Brewster and Moore Company. However, he was still interested in the tourist business, and Jim made him an offer. He would lease the business to him for a period of five years at an annual fee of $5000 plus one-half of the net profits of the operation in excess of $5000. Moore would guarantee to carry on a livery stable, motor livery and a transfer and cartage business during this

**Lieutenant-Colonel Phil Moore**

period. In addition, he would have the option to purchase the whole business for the sum of $66,-000, the degree of Brewster Transport's indebtedness to the Imperial Bank by this time.

Considering the circumstances, Jim obviously felt the agreement might give him the opportunity to retain control of the company. Of course, Hussey's considerable interest had to be taken into consideration, but he was serving overseas as a captain in the United States Army and had left his proxy in Jim's hands. At a directors' meeting held on November 21, 1918 at which only Jim, Crosby and McLeod were present, the agreement was unanimously approved. On a motion of Crosby it was resolved that the salary of $5000 heretofore paid Jim be terminated. The final link seemingly cut, he prepared to depart with the Canadian Expeditionary Force to Siberia to aid the Whites against the Reds in the bitter civil war underway in that far flung part of the world.

Brewster Transport touring car on Banff-Windermere Highway
below Radium Hot Springs Bungalow Camp

# VIII: The New Regime

No sooner had Jim made up his mind to forego attempting to keep Brewster Transport solvent and to join the Siberian Force than he changed it. Principally he did so because his creditors, particularly the Imperial Bank, were willing to give the company an extension of time on its debts. The individual who seems to have been responsible for the extension was H. P. Otty Savary, a partner in the legal firm of Savary, Fenerty and Chadwick in Calgary. While Short, Ross and Selwood had continued to be the company's solicitors and Selwood a shareholder, it had been recognized that the best legal and financial services were needed if Brewster Transport was to disentangle itself from its web of debts. At the same time Savary, a Nova Scotian who had set up practise in Calgary about 1908, was regarded as one of the brightest lights in the Alberta legal firmament. His considerable legal skills were balanced by an equal measure of financial acumen, exactly the mixture Brewster Transport's tenuous position called for. Consquently, the company had begun to consult Savary early in 1918.

The stay of execution which Savary had negotiated with the Imperial Bank and other creditors allowed the company to continue operating until May 1, 1919 when a decision concerning a further extension until the close of the 1919 season was to be made. This agreement secured, the next problem was the lease agreement with Phil Moore, due to take effect immediately. Savary suggested that Jim take up the matter with Moore to see if the agreement could be suspended until after the first of May, when the future of the company would be much clearer. The easy-going Moore listened to Jim's plea and agreed to forego his personal interests in favour of those of his brother-in-law.

The problem of finding sufficient capital to finance the company's current operations remained. The Imperial Bank could not be expected to make further loans, and, with the company's assets completely tied up as collateral for existing debts, nor could other banks. Yet if funds were not forthcoming, the financing of an ice contract recently secured from the CPR would be impossible and the company's hard won extension of credit would collapse like a house of cards. Fortunately in late December an agreement was reached with the Canadian Credit Men's Trust Association, through the good offices of Frank Freeze, providing a loan for the expenses of the ice harvest. Included in the agreement was a stipulation that Brewster Transport would assign the contract and the monies payable under it to the Credit Men's Trust, which in turn would distribute them to the creditors. The harvest proved a success and a profit in excess of $1000 was realized from it.

But the winter activities of the company were far less important than its summer ones, and in March, 1919 shareholders and directors meetings were held to look into the problem of financing these. The meetings did not arrive at any solutions but did appoint new officers for the company on the assumption that something would be worked out. Having decided the services of Frank White should be dispensed with, the new board had a ring of familiarity to it. Included were President Fred Hussey, Vice-President and Treasurer Jim Brewster, General Manager Lou Crosby and Secretary Fred Selwood. On a unanimously approved motion it was resolved that Jim would receive an annual salary of $5000 and Crosby $2100 and that they would have the power to make any financial arrangements they felt expedient to carry on the company. Jim, taking the directive to heart, consulted with Hussey and prevailed on him to advance $5000 towards getting the season's business underway.

The promised advance from Hussey arrived early in May in the form of a draft on his New York account and with it Crosby quickly opened an old company account at the Bank of Nova Scotia. At the same time Jim began negotiating with the company's creditors to gain further extensions. This he accomplished, entering into an agreement with the Canadian Credit Men's Trust Association, the Imperial Bank of Canada and "the several persons, firms and corporations who are creditors of the company." The bank and the creditors agreed not to press for repayment of their debts until November 1st, in return for which the full management and control of the company would be placed in the hands of the trustee, the Credit Men's Trust. The trustee was to pay all monies earned firstly to the current expenses of the business, secondly to Hussey in repayment of his $5000 advance, thirdly for wages and salaries owing previous to January 1st, fourthly to itself for performing its services, and fifthly to the creditors. The agreement was followed by further discussions with Moore who, once again, agreed not to exercise his lease for the time being. With these matters settled, Brewster Transport then prepared to open for its first post-war season, hoping for a quick return to pre-war tourist levels and the opportunity to work itself out of debt.

It was apparent that if the tourists did return they were either going to arrive in their own cars or expect to have cars available for livery service. In spite of its financial difficulties, the company decided to increase its stock of vehicles, concentrating on those which, like its existing "auto tally-hos," had large carrying capacities yet were not to expensive to obtain. Added to the fleet in 1919 were two 14-passenger "auto tally-hos," one built on a Kissel chassis and the other on an Alco chassis, a 10-passenger Cadillac "auto tally-ho," and a 7-passenger White "auto tally-ho," the first of numerous White vehicles the company would utilize.

Recruited to drive were several new men, mostly former soldiers who had either been invalided home during the war or had been recently demobilized. A few of these individuals were to establish themselves as valuable additions to the company's personnel and would achieve long careers in its service. Two of the best known were Ralph Harvey and Walter Ashdown.

Harvey was a native of Nova Scotia who had spent most of his youth in Massachusetts before moving with his family to Medicine Hat prior to the war. During overseas service in the conflict he was wounded, invalided home and then discharged in 1918. As a rehabilitation project he was given a course in motor mechanics in Calgary, completing it in the spring of 1919. Brewster Transport had contacted the technical institute where he was studying in its search for new employees and Ralph immediately secured a position as a driver. The most popular drive at the

**Ralph Harvey, his wife Bessie and daughter Maryalice at Lake Louise, ca. 1925**

time was to Lake Minnewanka, but, as there was very little in the way of formal training for Brewster drivers, he ran into a bit of difficulty on his first trip. Chauffeuring a group of tourists in one of the "auto tally-hos," he took a wrong turn and ended up in the animal paddock instead of on the Minnewanka road. To cover his mistake he simply told his patrons that it was an extra thrown in at no additional charge, but then had to endure the wrath of Captain Standly, who had been kept waiting with his boat at Minnewanka.

Towards the end of his first year with Brewster Transport, Ralph was transferred to Lake Louise to drive the single "auto tally-ho" stationed there between the Chateau and Moraine Lake. At the latter point the Misses Strick, Dodds and Danks had established a tea room and tent camp, making the drive an extremely popular one in spite of the rather treacherous road. The driving conditions proved even more hazardous one evening when he drove some of the hotel staff to the lake for a picnic. On the return trip his acetylene headlights burned out. Someone fetched a barn lantern and by its feeble light Ralph gingerly inched his way back down to Lake Louise.

The following year at Emerald Lake he experienced even more risky driving. Laid off for the winter, he secured a job as a driving instructor at an automotive school in Calgary. The following spring Jim McLeod asked him back and assigned him to haul building materials for the CPR from the railway to the Emerald Lake Chalet. This in itself was not too difficult — except, of course, that the trucks were rickety, makeshift affairs constructed from tally-ho bodies and, in compliance with British Columbia law, had to be driven on the left side of the frequently treacherous roads. Nevertheless he persevered, and at the beginning of his third season with the company was placed in charge of transportation operations at Lake Louise, a position he was to maintain until the late twenties.

One of Harvey's fellow drivers in the immediate post-war period was Walter Ashdown, whose previous experience had been much the same as his own. Born in Kent in 1890, Walter had come to Canada at age fourteen and farmed at Brantford, Ontario for five years before moving on to Calgary in the hope of becoming involved in ranching. Unsuccessful in his attempt, he pursued his interest in automobiles and enrolled in an auto mechanics course in Calgary in 1912. Upon completion of the course he obtained chauffeuring jobs with Dr. McKidd and Senator Lougheed, among others, until the war broke out. Serving as a despatch rider he saw action on the Somme and at Vimy Ridge and Cambrai before being wounded at Passchendaele. Invalided home, he had taken a short stab at the jitney business in Calgary but continued to be bothered by his wounds. His doctor ordered rest and recuperation at Banff and during his stay in hospital he met Jim Brewster, who offered him a job.

Walter's first season with Brewster Transport was 1920, when he was put to work as driver on one of the company's remaining horse-drawn tally-hos. After two summers he graduated to driving motor vehicles, the majority of his trips being to the popular new tourist spot of Johnston's Canyon. It was a whole day's return trip and in the usual muddy conditions often a difficult one. Frequently he had to dig his car out of a mudhole while his passengers waited impatiently. However, his cheerful disposition made him immensely popular with the tourists, and, combined with his superior driving abilities, landed him the job of the company's celebrity chauffeur in the thirties, a position he would retain for more than the next forty years, piloting the wealthy and the famous safely over a million miles of mountain roads.

With men of the calibre of Harvey and Ashdown joining its ranks and with new equipment available for them to drive, the company was ready to handle the post-war tourist's desires. Quickly the number of those coming to the mountains rebounded from a 1918 low of 41,819 to a respectable 69,830 in 1919, the best season since 1915. There was a marked increase in rail traffic and those coming tended to stay longer, to the extent that an accommodation shortage resulted. This augured well for the Mount Royal Hotel which accommodated some 6250 guests on the American Plan that year, almost ten percent of the total number of visitors to the park.

However, one good season could not lift Brewster Transport out of the hole it had dug itself into. At the beginning of November the company's major creditor, the Imperial Bank, reexamining its position, decided to call in its loans. The bank took action in the Supreme Court of Alberta against Jim as a guarantor of the company's liabilities up to $30,000, dated January 6, 1915 (with Hussey as co-guarantor) and up to $50,000 dated December 1, 1916. The outstanding liabilities to the bank stood at just over $42,000 and were secured by a general assignment of book accounts, a chattel mortgage for $41,000 covering all stock, cars and equipment and a mortgage on sundry properties in Banff. Thus Jim again found himself approximately where he had been a year earlier. He once more became despondent and sought solace in drink. Undoubtedly this was a topic of conversation on the streets of Banff and thinly veiled references to it appeared in the *Crag and Canyon*. For example, the August 30th edition reported on the results of one evening's spree:

> Jim is practising for next year's provincial trapshooting meet using a motor car for a gun and an outhouse for a target. Not being dead sure of his sight he used L. S. Crosby's car for the initial performance. But he needn't have worried, conditions were right and he scored a perfect bullseye.

Despite the seeming hopelessness of the situation, the company again almost miraculously staved off collapse. Undoubtedly it was Savary who worked out the details of a new agreement with the Credit Men's Trust dated November 14, 1919. By its terms Frank Freeze, acting for the

Trust, lent Brewster Transport an undetermined sum of money in return for a chattel mortgage amounting to $62,000 on the company's automobiles, horse-drawn vehicles, saddles and riding equipment, ice tools and horses. The Imperial Bank's court action was dropped, apparently in return for Brewster Transport's immediately reducing its loan account by about $15,000. Since the company's equipment, which had previously secured the Imperial Bank's loans, was used to secure the loan from the Credit Men's Trust, caveats were registered by the bank on the store and stable lots. While the details are sketchy, it seems that, along with the Credit Men's Trust, the Imperial Bank and the CPR were to have a voice in the affairs of the company.

Brewster Transport at least temporarily back on the rails, its management hoped that increasing tourist visitation to the Rockies during the coming decade would help to right its situation permanently. Initially these hopes proved unfounded as the 1920 season did not build on the previous one to the degree that had been expected. Statistics showed an increase to only 78,802 visitors in 1920 and the company experienced a slight loss on its operations. In 1921 the number of visitors slipped back to 71,540. While the transportation operations at Banff and overall operations at Lake Louise continued to be profitable, other facets of the business, such as the Banff and Field stables, fell into loss positions at the same time as the total expenditures of the company were growing. Combined with this unexpected setback was the loss of one of the company's most competent men, Jim McLeod. Although "outside" manager and a member of Brewster Transport's board, McLeod was only receiving a salary of $1725 per annum when he first threatened to quit in July, 1919. He reconsidered when offered a raise to $2100 but his discontent resurfaced the following year and he left the company at the end of August, 1920. His decision may have been influenced by a much better offer from another Banff businessman, and fellow Conservative supporter, William Warren.

Whatever McLeod's motivation to resign, a replacement for him was not going to be easy to find. Analyzing the situation, the Credit Men's Trust realized the time had come for a major shakeup of the company's management. In consultation with the CPR it was agreed a new general manager should be brought in to handle most of McLeod's tasks and some of Crosby's as well. Their choice for this position may have been a shock for long time observors of the company and those working for it. The new general manager was Bill Brewster.

Forced out of the motorized end of tourist transport in Glacier Park, Montana in 1913, Bill had begun to face a series of difficulties. One of his main problems was that he was a Canadian running a successful business in a foreign country. From 1913 onward he had concentrated on his horse business and, working under the name of the Park Saddle Horse Company, built it up to the point where he owned almost 400 head by the end of 1918. Meanwhile, in 1914 his brother George, who had been working for Brewster and Moore at Jasper, came down to join him in business. About the same time Bill and Tead's respective spouses jointly filed for divorce in Calgary on the grounds of desertion and the two were finally free to marry. But just when things seemed to be going along smoothly and the company proving a success, several competitors decided to move in. In 1916 Bill outfitted a party of 150 people led by pioneer American dude rancher Howard Eaton for a trip through Glacier Park. The party, which included famous American author Mary Roberts Rinehart, was so large that Eaton had to bring three carloads of horses from his ranch in Wyoming to combine with Bill's. The trip received wide publicity and soon afterwards the United States Interior Department began to be pressured to have Bill's concession cancelled on the basis that he was not an American. Attempting to stave off this move, Bill began the process of taking out citizenship papers and considered bringing down George Harrison, who had been born in Iowa, to front the business for him. Before anything could be accomplished, though, the government withdrew the concession. An influential Kalispel lawyer named Noffsinger then bought up Bill's note at the bank and when things got tight was able to foreclose on it.

Bill was able to salvage some of his horses from this debacle and he put them to work at a dude ranch he had recently established on some land he had acquired. His Two Medicine Ranch was located at Kilroy, some three miles east of East Glacier, and received its first guests in July, 1919. In conjunction with the dude ranching operations, George Brewster, recently returned from a stint overseas in the Canadian Artillery,

**Jim and Bill in front of Brewster Transport's office, late '20's**

established the nucleus of a cattle herd. But patronage was sparse at the dude ranch and it took time to build up a good herd of cattle. Therefore Bill was essentially broke when the offer came from Banff in late 1920.

It seems likely the CPR suggested Bill's name as a candidate for the general manager's position. He had several friends among the railway's officials dating back to his ownership of Brewster Brothers, one of the most influential being General Passenger Traffic Manager C. E. Ussher. By the terms of his contract he was given full control of the company's day-to-day operations, reporting to the Credit Men's Trust and undoubtedly the CPR as well. For this he was to receive an annual salary of $2775, while Jim, who retained his positions but was again stripped of most of his power, was reduced to $1250 per annum. Crosby also lost some of his previous powers but remained in control of the company's financial affairs at the reduced salary of $2100.

Bill's task when he took over the reins of the company was formidable; not only was there extensive indebtedness to a number of creditors to be worked off, but his appointment coincided with the appearance of strong competition in the motorized transportation field. Up until the end of the war Brewster Transport's main competitor in the livery field had been Norman Luxton's King Edward Livery and to a lesser degree Dr. Brett's Sanitarium Livery, also eventually taken over by Luxton. In addition there were the numerous jitney drivers plying their trade along Banff Avenue by 1918. In 1919 several returned veterans secured government permission to establish a veteran's jitney stand and it received a wide patronage. As the press stated, when no fewer than five Bankhead car owners joined the local jitney brigade in one week, it appeared as though "the line of jitney cars will soon stretch to the river." Brewster Transport obviously did not relish such competition but could easily withstand it, armed with its large fleet and its CPR concession. However, the new and ambitious competitor, Rocky Mountain Tours and Transport Company, which appeared in 1921 quickly

**Rocky Mountain Tours' fleet of McLaughlins and Whites, 1924**

began to challenge the company's preeminent position.

Rocky Mountain Tours, as it was commonly known, was the brainchild of William Warren, a man who on political grounds — and perhaps personal ones — disliked the Brewsters. Warren had been a guide for Tom Wilson after coming out from England in 1903, and by 1907, with the assistance of Mrs. Mary Schäffer, whom he guided for several years, acquired his own outfit. The recently widowed Mrs. Schäffer, a moderately wealthy Philadelphia Quaker, had taken a liking to the handsome Warren, and after several more years of outings together married him in 1915. Warren had a good head for business and at once began putting his wife's money to work. He opened the Cascade Garage at 208 Banff Avenue in July, 1919 and then combined with former Brewster employee Bert Sibbald and his Ford Garage to form the Banff Motor Company. In 1920 followed the purchase and renovation of the old Alberta Hotel. His biggest investment came in May, 1921 when he announced he was building Cascade Hall, a rival for the dancing patronage of Brewster Hall, and that in partnership with Jim McLeod he had purchased the King Edward Livery from Luxton and had renamed it.

Working out of garage facilities purchased from Harry Brett at 207 Banff Avenue, across from Warren's Cascade Garage, Rocky Mountain Tours started out with three small Fords, a Cadillac and a Kissel "auto tally-ho." Under McLeod's capable management and with Warren's financial backing the company grew quickly. Three new McLaughlin Special 7-passenger touring cars, "the niftiest cars to ever burn gas in Banff" according to the *Crag and Canyon*, were immediately added to the fleet. At the beginning of the 1922 season these were complemented by the addition of the first of several 11-passenger White buses, touted as "the finest motor car manufactured on the American continent."

Brewster Transport should have had the advantage over its rivals since it was the only company allowed to have a transportation desk at the Banff Springs Hotel and its vehicles could stand at the CPR station while Rocky Mountain Tours' had to wait across the street. Nonetheless, Rocky Mountain Tours, with ticket offices at the King Edward and Bretton Hall Hotels, the Alpine Club of Canada clubhouse and the Cascade Garage, began to cut into the company's business. The situation was exacerbated further when Jim McLeod went on the road, renewing old acquaintances and picking up business from tour agencies he had originally contacted while working for Brewster Transport.

Bill Brewster fought back as best he could, considering the financial stringencies he faced. At the beginning of the 1921 season Brewster Transport purchased four new Studebaker Big Six 6-passenger cars to bolster its fleet and in 1922 added three Hudson Super Six 6-passenger models. While these measures helped to increase the company's carrying capacity, bad luck adversely affected it.

Early on the morning of September 19, 1921 the Brewster livery stable on Banff Avenue caught fire and was gutted in a matter of minutes. Because it had not been used for livery purposes during the preceding few years, only a few horses were inside at the time. However, the livery had been serving as additional storage for vehicles operating out of the Mount Royal Garage and three were on the premises. Two of them were pulled out in time but a third, a Kissel valued at $1500, was destroyed.

Difficulties experienced with some of the staff added to the situation. Numerous good drivers were working for the company, but the seasonal employees weren't always so dependable. A case in point was "a native son of Sweden," hired in 1922, whose exploits were reported in the *Crag and Canyon:*

> Driving one of Brewster Company's cars [he] endeavoured to transform the big Studebaker into a motor boat one day last week, with indifferent success. He had driven a party to the Fish Hatchery, where they alighted to look at the building, and neglected to either set the brake or turn off the juice. The car, left to its own devices, rolled into to the artifical lake in front of the Hatchery and it was necessary to tow it across the water before it could be dragged up the bank.

Shortly thereafter the same driver upset and damaged a car near Sundance Canyon, while elsewhere "a joyriding party was endeavouring to test the tree climbing ability of one of the Brewster Company's Studebaker cars," damaging it to the tune of $300. Experiences of this kind led Bill to keep a notorious 'black book' grading the performance of each driver so he could weigh the merits of hiring him again the following season. They also induced him to hire the best help available to keep his machinery on the road, and he was fortunate to have Malcolm Amos, a virtual mechanical wizard, in charge of fleet maintenance.

On the positive side, Bill's appointment as general manager came at the bottoming out of the post-war tourist doldrums. From 1921 onwards new and better roads attracted an increasing flow of tourists, a result of Harkin's development policy; and increased and varied accommodation, largely supplied by the CPR, was also proving appealing.

Over the war years construction of the motor road west from Banff had continued at a slow pace, mainly using alien internees as labour. At the war's end renewed appropriations allowed the work to carry on more rapidly, and in June, 1921, the Banff-Lake Louise motor road was officially opened. With its foothold at the Chateau Lake Louise, Brewster Transport was able to take advantage of the increased business this development generated. Company facilities included a substantial bunkhouse and corrals, which dated back to early outfitting days, two large horse barns which doubled as automotive storage space for the winter, and a large open shed for the protection of cars during the summer. As well, there was a ticket office in the hotel, although, as manager Harvey put it, the real office was in his vest pocket and moved about with him as he oversaw operations.

The significance of the Lake Louise motor road was overshadowed by the long awaited completion of the Banff-Windermere Highway in June, 1923. This project, first formulated as early as 1911, was the result of tripartite cooperation between the federal government and the provincial governments of Alberta and British Columbia. Conferences between the three governments resolved that Alberta should build the section from Calgary to the eastern park boundary, British Columbia the section from the Windermere Valley to the park boundary at Vermilion Pass, and Ottawa the section through the park uniting the other two. The road was open from Calgary to Vermilion Pass by 1914 but the B.C. government lagged on its stretch, completing only twelve miles. Little was added during the next five years, owing to the war, and by 1919 the federal government entered a new agreement with the B.C. government. Ottawa agreed to complete the remaining fifty-three miles before January, 1924 in return for British Columbia's ceding approximately 600 square miles of land along either side of the route to form the new Kootenay National Park.

The work was completed ahead of schedule, the last link forged in what the Parks Branch, and soon Brewster advertising, called the "Grand Circle Tour" comprising some 6000 miles. Connections from Invermere, B.C. could be made via

Cranbrook to Spokane and Seattle, Washington, Vancouver and Victoria, B.C., Portland, Oregon and San Francisco and Los Angeles, California. The western section of the Grand Circle, known as the "California-Banff Bee Line," complemented an eastern section, known as the "Grand Canyon Route," which led from California to the Grand Canyon, then north via Salt Lake City, Yellowstone and Glacier National park, and crossed the Border at Coutts to Macleod and Calgary. A thirty-five mile diversion led to the beauties of the Canadian Rockies' southernmost playground, Waterton Lakes National Park. Entirely within Canada was a smaller 600 mile circle known as the "Canadian Rockies Circle Tour" or "Scenic Lariat," made possible by the Transprovincial Highway over Crowsnest Pass which connected Cranbrook and MacLeod. In 1924 work began on a third loop with the start of construction on the Lake Louise-Field road, the "Kicking Horse Trail," which would link up with a provincial road being built from Golden to Field. Completed in 1928, it allowed travel from Banff to Golden and thence by a road in the Columbia Valley to Radium and back to Banff via the Banff-Windermere Highway.

With these variations possible, the completion of these roads unlocked the tourist potential of the large population centers of the western United States. Brewster Transport joined with interested companies at other points on the circle to form The Circle Tours Association, an organization which met semi-annually to promote travel on the circle and which in 1924 elected Lou Crosby its president.

The tourist statistics reflected the effects of the road construction immediately, rising from 71,540 in 1921 to 79,492 a year later and, with the opening of the Banff-Windermere Highway, hitting 94,930 by 1923. To provide new tourist accommodation for this growing volume of traffic, the CPR began building bungalow camps, at first in out-of-the-way places but later along the routes of the new roads. The bungalow camps were the brainchild of Basil Gardom, who felt that many post-war CPR guests would prefer to

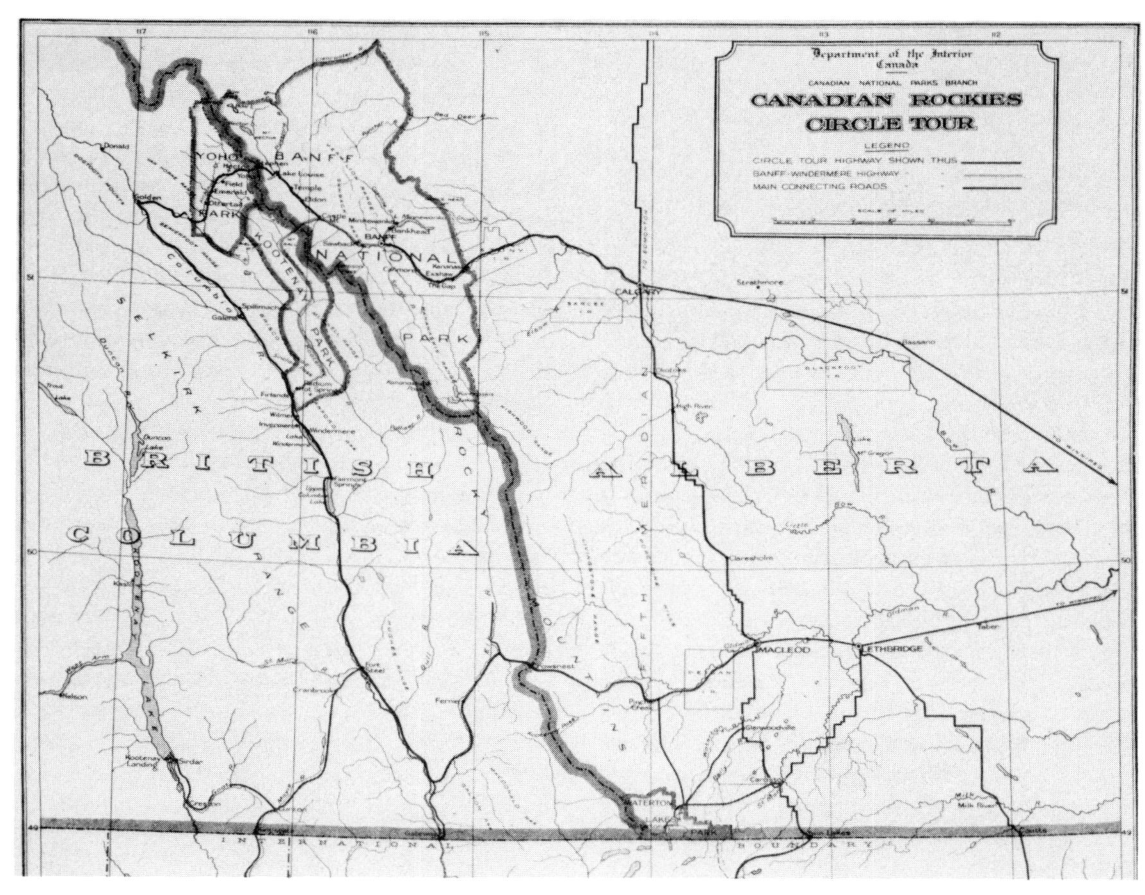

stay in smaller, quieter places where they might enjoy the beauties of the mountains more fully. In 1921 the first bungalow camp complete with a central lodge was built at Wapta Lake, near the summit of Kicking Horse Pass, and accessible by road to both Field and the Emerald Lake Chalet, thereby allowing Brewster Transport to establish a small transportation operation in conjunction with it. Gardom, recognizing the management of this first venture was all-important for its success, asked the polished and knowledgable Phil Moore and his lively wife Pearl to oversee it. Moore, who had been left on tenterhooks awaiting the outcome of Brewster Transport's efforts to survive, believed it unlikely he would be asked to exercise his lease agreement and accepted Gardom's offer. The Moores liked the experience of managing the camp and returned to run the CPR's new Yoho Bungalow Camp, at the foot of Takakkaw Falls, the following year. This was the first of many happy summers managing the camp which they interspersed by winter travel around North America, and eventually the world, during which Colonel Moore lectured and showed lantern slides advertising the Canadian Rockies for the railway. Meanwhile, Gardom's concept continued to expand with the opening of bungalow camps on main routes at Castle Mountain and Vermilion River Crossing in 1923.

Better roads and more widespread accommodation could not but help Brewster Transport. Bill's clever management, in the face of stiff opposition and a tight budget, combined with these factors to allow him to accomplish the task he had been hired for. At the end of 1922 Brewster Transport paid off its outstanding loans from the Imperial Bank and by early 1923 settled the account with the Canadian Credit Men's Trust. Bill had reason to be proud but also reason to be concerned. His mission had been accomplished but he had received little recognition for it, and thus he worried about his future security. To allay his fears he began to become involved in some business interests of his own.

The first of these was the Kananaskis Dude Ranch, established in June, 1923 near the mouth of the Kananaskis Valley on some land to which John Brewster had vague rights, dating from the late eighteen-eighties. Along with her sons Claude and Jack, Tead Brewster operated the ranch with some of the horses and equipment left over from their abortive dude ranch venture in Montana. There were many wrangles with the provincial government over the lease but they were worked out and eventually, mainly through support from the CPR, it became a going concern, offering typical dude ranch facilities and holding special rodeos and barbecues for organized groups not staying at the ranch. Later Tead's daughter Sid and her husband Syd Graves, whom she had met in Montana, joined them in its operation.

Bill's second interest proved more important than the dude ranch as a key to his immediate security. For several years Brewster Transport had been considering attempting to obtain the transportation concession at the Palliser Hotel in Calgary and in the summer of 1924 was about to make application to do so. Bill, recognizing a golden opportunity, prevailed on his friend Ussher to see it was granted to him instead of the company. On hearing of this, an incredulous Savary wrote Bill suggesting that there must be some mistake as surely he would not take out the contract in his own name while holding the position of general manager of the company. Bill responded that there was no mistake and that if the directors wished to discuss the concession he would be glad to do so at a directors' meeting. He suggested the same meeting could also discuss a new three year contract on new terms for himself and consider means whereby he could become a shareholder in the company. He pointed out that since taking over in January, 1921 he had regained for the company the confidence and goodwill of the CPR, reestablished its credit with the Imperial Bank and, by improvement of service and the addition of up-to-date equipment, had "entirely re-built and extended our business." An informal meeting which settled the question was held in mid-September. Bill received the security of tenure he had been seeking along with an increased salary and it was agreed he would keep the Palliser concession for the time being, although he was not given the opportunity to become a company shareholder.

Some of Royal Hawaiian Transport's Packard fleet, 1927

# IX: Broadening Horizons

The day-to-day management of Brewster Transport firmly in Bill's hands beginning in 1921, Jim was left to determine his role in the company. The restrictions on his powers meant he would have to concentrate mainly on financial matters, public relations, negotiations with the government and the railway, and planning for the company's future direction. If past experience were an indication, his exclusion from management would probably benefit the company, but his opportunity to contemplate the larger picture, Jim's forte, would be equally beneficial. It was often said of him he was a man of vision who knew where he wanted to go but didn't know how to get there. In Bill and Crosby he had the men to accomplish his objectives. The unlikely alliance, not entirely built on mutual trust, was to prove effective for more than a decade.

The most immediate result of Jim's new role was the opportunity to mend fences in his personal affairs. Since the time of his abortive plan to go to Siberia he had tended to let his interests and involvements drift, but in 1921 he took a positive step when he remarried. His new bride was Adele 'Dell' Sibbald, who had first come to Banff as a young summer visitor when her father Howard was Indian Agent at Morley. Later, when Howard Sibbald became the Chief Game Warden of Rocky Mountains Park, the family had moved to a home on Cave Avenue and soon afterwards, Dell, who had admired Jim from afar for several years, made his acquaintance. Her devotion, vivaciousness and charm were exactly what he needed. Soon after they married Jim rekindled his interest in other activities, once more taking a leading role in the organization of Banff Indian Days, the Banff Winter Sports Association and the Banff Advisory Council.

Another project receiving his active attention was the Trail Riders of the Canadian Rockies. The Trail Riders were essentially the creation of John Murray Gibbon, the assiduous General Publicity Agent of the CPR, a man whom, because of his personality and position, Jim would work closely with. Because interest in travel by horseback through the mountains had waned, Brewster Transport's and several other outfitting and saddle horse concerns' business had dropped off in the post-war period. Gibbon hoped to create an organization to revitalize horse travel and attract the wealthy and the distinguished to its membership. During its annual trail ride to a predetermined destination the patrons would be pampered with the best horses, guides, camps, cooking and entertainment available. Jim, enthusiastic both personally and from a business point-of-view, agreed to help Gibbon in any way possible. Gibbon in August, 1923 sent Jim a copy of the draft constitution for comment and in a covering letter asked for a favour. With a touch Jim would appreciate, Gibbon requested that "If you have anything to do with the Prince of Wales when he comes out, you might see that he rides at least fifty miles, so as to qualify for membership. It would help quite a bit if we could rope him in." Jim did have something to do with the Prince's visit but could not "rope him in" to riding fifty miles. He did continue to do everything he could to promote the Trail Riders, serving on its council in 1924 and lending his colourful presence to the proceedings on the annual ride. He became a popular figure on the rides and when the organization's song sheet was published in 1926 he was immortalized in a ditty entitled "Oh, Mr. Brewster!":

> Oh, Mr. Brewster! Whatever shall I do?
> I've gone and lost my pony and I'm feeling pretty blue;
> Fetch me out a new one as quickly as you can;
> Oh, Mr. Brewster! What a silly girl I am!

At the same time as he was revitalizing his personal life, Jim was finding his feet in the company's new circumstances. Ever interested in expanding Brewster Transport's interests, he took advantage of a long awaited release of government lots at Lake Louise in 1922. All the rights Brewster Transport enjoyed and the property it occupied at Lake Louise were a result of the CPR concession, but the government's decision to open about thirty lots near the lakeshore for commercial development allowed the company

**The Brewster gang during a trail ride. Left to right (rear)— Bill, Tead, Jack, Pat, Jack (son of Bill), Wilma; (front) — Phil Moore, Pearl Moore, Edmee Moore, Fern, Jim, Dell, June, Bessie Harvey**

to secure some property of its own. Jim acquired leases on two lots (Lots 4 and 7, Block 3) and in early 1923 had the latter cleared for the erection of a drug store. A business of this nature at such a location may have seemed a bit unusual, except that prohibition was still in effect in Alberta and drug stores were the only legal outlet for alcohol. Jim partook of enough spirits to know that the only liquor outlet in the area was going to be profitable considering the ease with which "prescriptions" could be obtained.

Jim was not the only opportunist at Lake Louise; several other businessmen picked up valuable pieces of property, among them Lou Crosby who, at his wife's insistence, applied for a lease. Gertrude Crosby, who had worked as a telegrapher and telephone operator at the Banff Springs Hotel and the Chateau Lake Louise before their marriage in 1911, was determined to get into business at Lake Louise if the opportunity presented itself. The Crosbys erected a handsome sixty by forty foot log building known as the Lake Louise Trading Company, one-third of it devoted to a small store and two-thirds to a cafe. Mrs. Crosby, with her strong will and good head for business, soon expanded the operation. Within a few years they had purchased the neighbouring Deer Lodge from George McKenzie and a chalet from the YWCA, launching themselves into the hotel business. Meanwhile prohibition was repealed in Alberta in late 1923 and Brewster Transport's interest in the drug store languished. Soon it was moved to make way for a service station to handle the needs of the increasing auto traffic. The service station, in operation by 1926, was run by the Crosbys as a matter of convenience because of its proximity to Deer Lodge.

Jim's involvement in the developments at Lake Louise occupied only a small portion of his attention. Two pressing matters concerned him more: capitalizing further expansion of Brewster Transport's business, and consolidating the interests of the Brewster Trading Company and the Brewster Hotel Company with those of the Brewster Transport Company. While Bill had done an excellent job of pulling the company out of debt by early 1923, the financial effects were transitory. Brewster Transport's credit rating had been reestablished, but to keep pace with the expected growth of tourism further capital borrowing would be necessary. Most pressing was the need to expand and diversify the motor vehicle plant to keep up with Rocky Mountain Tours. Brewster Transport's carrying capacity was greater but its rival's acquisition of White buses, the transportation standard in U.S. parks, gave it the edge in passenger comfort and operating efficiency.

Undoubtedly a prerequisite for obtaining additional capital funds was bringing all the Brewster interests under one umbrella. The store business had, of course, been sold to Serra and Morris as part of an agreement with the Credit Men's Trust in 1917, and by 1923 any attempt at collecting their notes had been abandoned. Other aspects of Brewster Trading had also fallen on dark days. Brewster Hall, which had rung with the music of Jim Hutchins' band for several years, fell silent in 1921. That year Hutchins leased Warren's new Cascade Hall and Brewster Hall was ignominously relegated to storage for Brewster Transport's livery rigs and automobiles. Brewster Trading's only other going concern was the bakeshop in the Birdcage, always a small revenue producer.

The Mount Royal Hotel (legally known as the Brewster Hotel Company) had some problems too. A continuing difficulty was finding a reliable manager who would stay with the job for any length of time. In 1916 J. M. Sherlock of Golden, B.C. had been named manager, but he was succeeded by Harry Broad of Calgary in 1917. By 1919, shortly after Jim failed in his attempt to lease the hotel to the government as a veterans' convalescent home, Earl Gammon replaced Broad. Gammon, in turn, was found to have more valuable skills and in 1921 went over to Brewster Transport as transportation manager. Broad returned for another stint, and so it went, one manager replacing another. Nor was the hotel performing any financial wonders, its annual profits amounting to just over $1000 for each of the 1921 and 1922 seasons. The heavy interest charges on the McDougall mortgage resulted in a very slow reduction of its principal and the outstanding balance remained at over $12,000 by the end of 1922. Financial strictures had also resulted in an ironic situation: in 1920 the Mount Royal, owned by "the motorized transportation barons of Banff," was the only hostelry in town still using a horse-drawn hotel bus.

Of course, the real importance of Brewster Trading and the Mount Royal lay in their extremely valuable real estate holdings. Brewster Trading had already transferred the store lot and improvements, valued at $15,000, to Brewster Transport. But it still held the Brewster Hall lots and improvements, valued at $13,500, the printshop lot and improvements, which had become the new home of Brewster Transport's offices, valued at $6500, the Birdcage lot and improvements, valued at $2250 and miscellaneous unimproved lots, valued at $5000. Similarly, Brewster Hotel had already transferred the Mount Royal Garage lot and improvements, valued at $6500, to Brewster Transport. Remaining in its hands were the five hotel lots, valued at $27,500, and improvements thereon, valued at $60,000. Between them the two companies owned some $115,000 worth of real estate.

The directors and shareholders of Brewster Transport realized the potential of this real estate as collateral for the company's capital borrowing. Therefore, a shareholders' meeting held on April 30, 1923 approved agreements with Brewster Trading and Brewster Hotel for the purchase of their assets. These assets included accounts receivable, furniture and fixtures, and cash on hand bringing the total transaction to $153,700. Because Brewster Transport was to assume these assets, its shareholders passed a special resolution that "the capital of the company be increased to $125,000 by the creation of 1050 new shares of the par value of $100 each," allowing payment for the assets of the two companies to be made by issuing fully paid up shares in Brewster Transport. The final arrangement called for a price of $35,000 in paid up shares for Brewster Trading's assets, $50,000 in paid up shares for Brewster Hotel's assets, cash payments of approximately $57,000 and the assumption of slightly over $15,000 of Brewster Hotel's liabilities. Despite the fact they carried on no business, Brewster Hotel and Brewster Trading had to remain in existence as they still had assets in the form of Brewster Transport stock and in cash.

As it turned out, the only unforeseen hitch in the whole consolidation process was in the transfer of title on several of the lot leases. In 1915 titles had been registered in Jim's name as trustee for the various companies. To have all the leases standing in the name of Brewster Transport Crosby informed the superintendent in June, 1923 that "to simplify their accounting system" the companies were amalgamating and wished to have the sixteen lots transferred. Although the

**Brewster Transport White buses and Hudson cars at Banff Springs Hotel, ca. 1925**

request appeared fairly straightforward, a sharp-eyed Parks Branch employee brought it to the attention of the Deputy-Minister of the Interior that in previous transfers of these properties the leaseholder had agreed to erect a building with a minimum value of $800 within one year. Even though compliance with these conditions had been overlooked, other parties might view further lenience in the matter as an act of discrimination. The department's insistence forced the company to reluctantly agree to execute a bond undertaking to reconvey these lots to the Crown should it fail to comply with the building restrictions within a year, an agreement which would cause some anxious moments in the period ahead.

The consolidation now completed, Jim turned towards putting it to work. At a shareholders' meeting on May 28th it was resolved that the directors were empowered to borrow sums of money up to $100,000 for the carrying on of the company's business and were authorized to pledge, as security for these loans, debentures of the company on such terms as they saw fit. Four weeks earlier, on May 1st, the company had entered into yet another agreement with Frank Freeze, acting in trust for the Credit Men's Trust, a $100,000 mortgage against all Brewster Transport's assets. With the Trust's backing the company issued nineteen debentures of $5000 each and five of $1000 each, all dated August 1, 1923 and bearing eight percent interest. These debentures were immediately pledged as collateral for a loan of $63,000 from the Imperial Bank. Shortly after, in a move probably tied to this financial manoeuvre, both Freeze and H. W. Supple, the manager of the Imperial Bank in Calgary, were appointed company directors. They joined Jim, Hussey and Savary, the latter having replaced Fred Selwood.

By the time the financing was arranged much of the new equipment the company had ordered had already arrived. Included among it were two 18-passenger, Model 15/45 White buses built at the White Company plant in Cleveland, Ohio and costing in the neighbourhood of $7500 each. These buses had convertible tops that could be put up in bad weather but otherwise were left down to allow an enhanced view of the surroundings. Often the drivers had to wrestle with the tops to get them taut enough to button along the sides and clamp at the front and sometimes they even had to ask the passengers to help. When necessary each passenger was issued a Kenworth blanket to use as a lap robe. Probably they would have been horrified to know that these doubled as their driver's bedding when he bunked in at the Lake Louise bunkhouse. Despite their drawbacks the Whites were a marked improvement on the old "auto tally-hos" and in 1924 an additional six of them were purchased. In 1925 four new 18-passenger and one 1913 model 30-passenger Whites were added along with several new touring cars, including three new 6-passenger Hudson Super Sixes and three new 6-passenger Packard Sixes.

The new equipment once more gave Brewster Transport the edge over its competitors. Rocky Mountain Tours had eleven vehicles, with a total capacity of approximately 120 passengers, while the next largest competitor, R. F. Colebrook, owned six vehicles with a capacity of about 40 passengers. Brewster Transport now owned thirty-five passenger vehicles with a total capacity of approximately 320 and it also had several trucks. Jim could therefore turn his attention to other pressing matters.

Beginning in 1924 the most vexing problem was the unfulfilled obligations the company had with respect to the promised improvements on its lots. A building on Bear Street was upgraded for use as a beer warehouse, and a vulcanizing shop and extension to the Mount Royal Garage were constructed on another lot. Five lots on which nothing had been done were subject to performance bonds totalling $8000. The company received a letter from the superintendent enquiring about this matter in December, 1924 and Jim hurriedly planned a trip east to discuss it with the Parks Branch. At a meeting with Harkin he received the help he had been seeking. The commissioner personally drafted a letter from Jim to the Department of the Interior pointing out the work which had been carried out on two lots, explaining that because of heavy investment in motor vehicles he had been unable to comply with the other building requirements and requesting authorization to renew the performance bonds for an additional year.

Needless to say, the request was accepted, but Harkin made it clear the Branch would grant no further extensions, applying pressure on the company to solve the problem immediately. Bill came up with a clever solution for the erection of residences not only on the lots in question but on several others as well. Bankhead Mines, an operation of the Natural Resources Department of the CPR, had been closed by a miners' strike in 1922 and, because of its friable coal, was not to be reopened. Dismantling the extensive townsite had begun by 1925 and the CPR began selling off the houses at $25 per room, the purchaser responsible for moving them. In November, Bill, after consultation with the Department of the Interior, had submitted for approval plans drawn

**Moving a Bankhead house**

up showing four designs for remodelling the four-room Bankhead bungalows. The Department accepted these designs on condition the houses moved to Banff were remodelled according to any one of them and that no two buildings of similar design were erected within any one block. Permission secured, the company purchased at least seven of the houses and spent the early months of 1926 hauling them into Banff, placing them on new foundations and remodelling them. By one of those strange quirks of history, the company had profited both by the beginning of Bankhead, when W. & J. Brewster had done contract packing for its original exploration, and by its demise.

Another construction project undertaken at the time was to prove equally as profitable for Brewster Transport. From the time the old livery stable on Banff Avenue had been destroyed by fire in 1921, a valuable piece of the company's property had been sitting idle awaiting redevelopment. Because of the tight money situation nothing was done, even though Harold MacDonald of Read-MacDonald-Brewster Ltd. had drawn up plans for a two-storey structure. However, when Jim was away on his trip east in 1925 local businessman Arthur Unwin approached Crosby with the idea of erecting a hardware store on the site. Unwin was not interested in a two-storey building, but Crosby suggested that a one-storey structure could be built to standards which would allow a second storey to be added later on. As the cost of the initial building would be about

Brewster Transport fleet in front of company buildings on Banff Avenue, ca. 1925

$14,000 and he felt that it could be rented for about $2000 per annum, Crosby suggested Unwin erect it and occupy it rent free for seven years.

No agreement acceptable to both parties was worked out, but soon one with two Calgary businessmen was consummated on basically the same principle. In 1925 Constantine "Gus" Baracos and John Demore, both Calgary restaurant proprietors, approached Brewster Transport about erecting a restaurant on the lot. An agreement was quickly worked out whereby they would construct a one-storey building, to be known as The Banff Cafe, costing approximately $10,000 and capable of having an additional two storeys added to it at a later date. The entire cost of construction would be borne by Baracos and Demore but they would have neither title nor interest in the ownership of the building. Since the partners could not afford the entire amount necessary for construction at that time they agreed to deposit an initial $5000 in Brewster Transport's bank account which the company would pay out as work proceeded. When this was fully depleted Baracos and Demore would deposit a further $2000 they intended to borrow. The remaining $3000 would be paid to the building contractor, Arthur Unwin and Company, in the form of $200 monthly installments charged as rent by Brewster Transport beginning in June, 1927. Rent payments would cease when the entire principal and accrued interest at ten percent per annum owing to Unwin was paid off, but the lessee would continue to be responsible for all upkeep and taxes. At the end of six years the agreement would lapse and the company would give the lessees the first right to a new lease on the building if it did not need the premises for its own purposes. By means of this agreement, Brewster Transport was able to have a building erected at no cost to itself and after six years would be in a position to collect rents for the remaining life of the structure. A significant accomplishment, it set the precedent for other company developments in the years ahead.

Despite such financial foot work, there was little ready cash or uncommitted capital available in 1925 when Jim found he needed it badly because of an unexpected request from Fred Hussey to sell his shares in the Brewster companies. Hussey had been living in San Mateo, California for the past several years and had visited Banff only infrequently, the last time being in 1922

when he and his wife Ethel drove up from California in a new Cadillac. Although he and Jim were still close friends they saw each other rarely and Fred had been inactive in the affairs of the companies for several years. In February, 1925 he cabled Jim and asked him to buy out his interests for $60,000, pointing out in a subsequent letter that it was not too much to ask "when you look back over the history of the business." Jim realized he was quite right.

When he received Fred's wire, Jim was trying to negotiate an amalgamation of Brewster Transport's interests with unidentified members of the Circle Tours Association at the coast (possibly Pacific Stagelines). It appears he was attempting to get in some new money and simultaneously gain a partial interest in the CPR hotel concessions at Vancouver and Victoria. His initial reaction to Hussey's request was positive, since it seemed there would be enough money to carry it off, but by late February the proposed amalgamation with the coast firms had been abandoned and Jim was off on a new tack, proposing to the CPR that it purchase fifty-one percent of Brewster Transport's tourist transport business.

Such a proposal may have seemed out of character, considering Jim's past efforts to keep control of the company, but it reveals itself as a shrewd move on his part. His preliminary discussions on the idea were with Gardom and Jim later wrote to him outlining Brewster Transport's current position and suggesting two possible courses of action. The company needed to clear its existing liabilities of $109,180, most of which was owed to the Imperial Bank. This, Jim stated, was necessary so that if a sale were made to the CPR the assets the railway received would be unencumbered. Using figures from the 1924 balance sheet he went on to point out that the company's assets used directly in connection with tourist transport (about half of the total assets) were $150,585 and fifty-one percent of these would cost the railway $76,797. Applying this entire sum to the reduction of the company's liabilities would still leave $32,383 outstanding. Therefore, Jim suggested the best way to facilitate the sale would be for Brewster Transport to change its name to Brewster Limited and then incorporate a new company under the name of Brewster Transport Company, thereby keeping transportation activities under a name with which the public was familiar. The present company would then sell its transportation assets to the new company, accepting fifty-one percent of the purchase price in cash and forty-nine percent in shares of the new company. The CPR would purchase fifty-one percent of the new company in cash, thus providing the money for the new company to purchase the transportation assets of the old. The old company could then pay off its liabilities with the exception of $32,383. Then came the choice of course of action. One possibility was to enter into the agreement immediately but not have it come into force until the completion of the 1925 season, when Jim was certain the company would be in a position to pay off the remaining liabilities. The other possibility was for the CPR to lend or otherwise provide the company with the money to clear the debt, with the company pledging its remaining assets as collateral for the loan.

The advantages of the proposed deal to Jim and the company were fairly obvious. Brewster Transport would clear off all existing liabilities while maintaining complete control over its non-transportation related assets such as the Mount Royal Hotel and other real estate. The company would lose control of the transportation related half of the assets — but who better to be in partnership with than the CPR? Gone would be concerns over concessions, financing of new equipment and even day-to-day management, although Jim did include a clause that would see him kept on at an annual salary of $5000 for at least five years. It boiled down to eliminating debts and headaches for simply being willing to accept only forty-nine percent of the profits on transportation.

Somewhat surprisingly, the CPR was interested in the proposals, perhaps feeling that contending with Brewster Transport's numerous ups and downs was becoming a bit tedious. Gardom, delegated to continue the negotiations, sent numerous missives to Crosby requesting details of the company's finances throughout March and April. As time went on Jim began to suspect that Bill was using his friendship with Ussher and Gardom to sabotage the discussion for his own ends. But by the end of April an agreement based on the first option seems to have been achieved with the final details to be worked out at the end of the season in October. As that date approached the CPR began to have second thoughts and ultimately withdrew. Their reasons are not known but the suspicion remains that Gardom, who never seemed personally convinced of the wisdom of the arrangement, used his influence to queer the deal. Another possibility is that Brewster Transport could not come up with the $32,383 to clear its debts.

Whatever the reasons for its failure, Jim was back at square one so far as meeting Hussey's request. He had hoped that an agreement with the CPR would change Fred's mind about pulling out, but that possibility had now been exhausted. The only course of action that it now seemed he could take was to cash in some of his shares in the company for the necessary funds. Fortunately, he had been able to whittle Fred down somewhat, the demand now being $50,000 in cash and the cancellation of some $5000 in debts on the company's books from old hotel accounts and various advances. At a shareholders' meeting on December 18, 1925 it was resolved that the capital stock of Brewster Transport be reduced from 1250 shares to 800 shares valued at $100 each by the paying off at par value of 450 shares owned by Jim. It was further resolved that payment of $50,000 be made to Jim in respect of this retirement, with $45,000 coming from the reduction of share capital and $5000 from the surplus account. In an agreement dated December 31, 1925 Jim then paid Fred the $50,000 for his 72 shares in Brewster Transport, 341 shares in Brewster Hotel and 108 shares in Brewster Trading. Jim, in a further agreement, gave his promissory note to Brewster Transport covering both Fred's indebtedness of $5000 and his own indebtedness, which over the years had grown to about $38,000. The fact that he was now the sole owner of shares in Brewster Trading and Brewster Hotel allowed him to wind these companies up, and this he quickly did in January, 1926. The end result of the entire transaction was that Brewster Transport's capital account was heavily diminished but, on the positive side, Jim now owned all the stock except for the one share each held by Crosby, Freeze, Savary and Supple.

It was entirely characteristic of both Jim and Hussey that after ending some twenty years of association in the various Brewster companies they should immediately become involved in a new scheme. Neither could resist the temptation of an interesting offer. An extremely interesting one came Jim's way in 1926 from an old friend, Arthur Benaglia, formerly manager of the CPR's Empress Hotel in Victoria, the Palliser Hotel in Calgary and, beginning in 1917, the Banff

Springs Hotel. During his years spent at Banff, Benaglia and Jim became very close, often going on fishing and hunting trips together. Jim was sorry to see him leave in 1922 when he accepted an attractive offer from a New Orleans hotel firm. But they did keep in touch and in 1926 Benaglia told Jim the Matson Steamship Line had approached him about becoming managing director of the Territorial Hotel Company in Hawaii, in which it was a major shareholder. The Territorial Hotel Company already operated two hotels in Honolulu, the Moana and the Seaside, and was building a third, the magnificient 750 room Royal Hawaiian. Benaglia further informed Jim that as yet no transportation facilities were organized in connection with the three hotels and, were he willing to set up a company and make some investment, he could undoubtedly gain the concession.

In the fall of 1926 Jim took ship for Hawaii to investigate. Apparently the Matson people were quite taken with him and by mid-November the basis for an agreement had been reached. Crosby then joined him to work out the details. As it was necessary to incorporate in Hawaii the first step was to set up the Royal Hawaiian Transport Company, Limited (Hawaiian Territory) with authorized capital of $75,000 divided into 750 shares of $100 each. After Hussey was convinced to become involved, the shares were alloted as follows: Fred Hussey, 150 shares; Jim Brewster, 50 shares; Lou Crosby, 10 shares; Arthur Benaglia, 1 share; Paul Winslow, 1 share; and Wayne Stewart, 1 share. The remaining 537 shares were to be subscribed by the Royal Hawaiian Transport Company, Limited (Alberta), a separate Canadian company with its headquarters in Banff. All the shares in the latter company were to be held by the Brewster Transport Company.

Brewster Transport, to acquire the shares of Royal Hawaiian Transport (Alberta), had to seek further loans. To accomplish this its first issue of debentures for $100,000 plus accumulated interest was cancelled and a new issue of $200,000 made, these secured by a mortgage on the increased assets of Brewster Transport, including its shares in Royal Hawaiian Transport. The new debentures were then used as collateral for increased loans from the Imperial Bank. However, the bank would only lend $29,500 instead of the $53,700 that was required if the company were going to subscribe the 537 shares of Royal Hawaiian Transport (Hawaiian Territory) stock alloted to Royal Hawaiian Transport (Alberta). Thus only 295 of the shares alloted were subscribed.

A legal and financial framework for the Hawaiian operation established, the next step was to gain the concession from the Territorial Hotel Company. It was secured in the form of a personal agreement with Jim dated December 31, 1926; its main provision granting him a concession on the transportation business at the hotels for a five year period, including the use of garage facilities, in return for $280 per month garage rental and ten percent of Royal Hawaiian's gross receipts derived from its business in Hawaii. Hired as general manager was Wayne Stewart, a bright and extremely personable graduate of a business school in Seattle. The company fleet, consisting mainly of new Packard 7-passenger touring cars, although there was at least one Cadillac and one bus, was purchased in the United States for about $46,000. Stewart then hired a few drivers and began to offer tours around the island. The most popular of these was called the Pali-City trip, an all day tour of the city of Honolulu and surrounding country for $5 per person. Included in the itinerary were a drive through the business section of the city, up Nuuanu Valley to the famous Pali and then to Bishop Museum, Moanalua Gardens, Fort Shafter, Red Hill, Aala Fish Market, Diamond Head and the Punchbowl.

In its first year Royal Hawaiian Transport lost $6000, a figure at least partially attributable to start-up costs. But by 1928, with a boom in Hawaiian tourism, Stewart reported a profit of $4000 for the year. The first six months of 1929 were even better with the company $17,000 in the black. Jim, extremely pleased with the turn of events, expressed his pleasure at a board of directors meeting in Honolulu in February, 1929. A year later he was back again and, although the economic situation had taken a turn for the worse, the company was still on its way to a $13,000 profit for the first three months of 1930. Jim expressed his appreciation more tangibly by moving a resolution granting each director a $500 bonus in return for his faithful service. By the time another year went by Jim would question the wisdom of his generosity.

# THRILLING RACE WITH DEATH ACROSS THE CANADIAN ROCKIES

Roaring across the Great Divide . . . past dizzy precipices . . . . baffling curves . . . . breath-taking hills . . . . nerve-wrecking roads . . . . on . . . . on . . . . 50-60-75 . . . . a mad race with death . . . . a race with two lives at stake . . . . . . .

Here is a thrill that comes once in a lifetime . . . But the Buckingham thrill is always with the smoker . . . . every time he lights a Buckingham. Here in this quality cigarette . . . . perfect in blend . . . . original in flavor . . . . smokers find an unrivalled pleasure. Buckingham Cigarettes are a blend of all that's finest in the leaf . . . . the coolest, smoothest and most refreshing cigarette made. Always the same . . . . in quality, size and weight . . . . kept ever fresh by the patented sealed package . . . . . .

"Buckingham Cigarettes are ace-high with me. I get a thrill out of every puff. They're a wonderful cigarette for relieving tension and steadying the old pulse."

Walter Ashdown

**Walter Ashdown, Military Medallist,** is the hero of a recent exploit that has thrilled the continent. With a pulmotor in his car Ashdown raced from Canmore, in the Canadian Rockies, across the Great Divide to Monarch Mine—a stretch of 81 miles—in one hour and twenty minutes in a desperate attempt to save two miners dying from asphyxiation. Over rough, treacherous roads, high above dizzy precipices, round death-dealing curves, up and down dangerous hills, he averaged a break neck speed of 60 miles per hour and performed a feat unequalled in the annals of the Rocky Mountains.

**20 for 25c**

NO COUPONS
ALL QUALITY

"THE THRILL THAT COMES WITH BUCKINGHAM"

Advertisement utilizing Walter Ashdown's "thrilling race with death"

# X: We Work For Brewsters

While Jim was watching with enthusiasm the progress of his new "baby," the Royal Hawaiian Transport Company, matters were moving apace on the home front during the latter half of the twenties. At no time previously in the Canadian Rockies had there been such an explosion in tourism. The recovery from the post-war doldrums which the opening of the Banff-Windermere Highway had occasioned in 1923 when visitations to Rocky Mountains Park reached 94,300, by 1925 had got into full stride and the figure had risen to 104,241. Obviously with the easy money attitude of the "roaring twenties" more people were travelling every year and the Canadian Rockies became an "in" destination for everyone from the middle class to glittering movie stars and millionaires. By 1929 the number of visitors peaked at an incredible 236,801, having more than doubled in four years. These were the halcyon days of Canadian Rockies tourism and Brewster Transport was quick to cash in on them. A catch phrase soon became popular in the tourist industry: "Tourists come to the Rockies for a change and a rest. The CPR takes the change and the Brewsters take the rest."

After the unsettling period of consolidation, attempted merger and unsuccessful sale in the first half of the decade, the company grew almost without restraint in the second half. One final significant development in its structure occurred in 1926. After the war the livestock part of the business had declined with the daily saddle horse rental more-or-less holding its own but the outfitting department going down rapidly. Brewster Transport's concession with the CPR precluded abandoning the service, but it was becoming a burden. Recognizing this, Jim suggested to his younger brother Pat that the outfitting business was a good one-man operation which perhaps he would like to take over. After an air crash in the Royal Flying Corps during the war, Pat had spent several years running Brewster Transport's interests at Glacier and had show a particular affinity for outfitting. From Jim's point-of-view he could get rid of a bothersome and unlucrative aspect of the business, help out his brother and satisfy the CPR customers who expected to have a Brewster take them out on the trail.

Pat accepted the proposition on the understanding that Brewster Transport's outfitting equipment would be turned over to him, the company would lend him some money to buy horses and he could share company bunkhouse and stable facilities. Naming his new venture Brewster's Mountain Pack Trains, he immediately hired such former Brewster Transport cowboys as Ray Legace, Ernie Stenton and Jack Bevan and complemented them with new men like Guy Thomas and Pat Worthington. Business began with the opening of the 1926 season and Pat's first party consisted of twenty-two people led by the Marquis degli Albizzi, an Italian nobleman who was searching out the Rockies with an eye to winter ski development. The trip visited the region around Mount Assiniboine and three years later resulted in the beginning of Albizzi's Assiniboine Ski Camp in conjunction with Erling Strom. Meanwhile, because of the demand for his services by such organizations as the Alpine Club of Canada and the Trail Riders of the Canadian Rockies, Pat's business grew by leaps and bounds. He established his main horse camp east of Johnston's Canyon on the Hillsdale meadows, which his father had used for pasturage in the early days, and had a secondary base at the Middle Springs after purchasing some property adjacent to the Alpine Club clubhouse. Pat constructed other smaller camps at Egypt Lake and Sunburst Lake in the late twenties and during the same period, along with Bill and Jim, scouted out and began development of the Devil's Head Ranch for winter horse pasturage, just outside the park boundary east of Lake Minnewanka. This was necessary because the Department of the Interior had cancelled Brewster Transport's lease on the Ya Ha Tinda in 1917 as a result of alleged game violations by its employees, requiring the company to board its stock at various foothills ranches for several years. Overall Pat's success in restoring the outfitting business to its former

**Brewster Transport's large open White buses and touring cars at Banff station, late '20's**

importance can be measured by the fact that he had 488 horses on the trail in his best year, 1928. Meanwhile, Brewster Transport continued to do well on its daily saddle horse rental.

Having disposed of the outfitting problem, Jim, with Bill's assistance, focused attention on one objective — the building up of Brewster Transport's fleet of motor vehicles. The company was making major purchases annually to accommodate the growing tide of tourists. Initally emphasis was placed on the Studebaker Big Sixes manufactured by the Studebaker Corporation of South Bend, Indiana. Studebaker's line of large six-cylinder cars included touring models which were relatively inexpensive ($2504 for a 6-passenger edition in 1925). In 1925 four 6-passenger and one 11-passenger Big Sixes were purchased and the following year six more 6-passenger and seven enlarged versions capable of accommodating 14 passengers were added. Two enclosed 17-passenger and one enclosed 12-passenger models bought in 1927 and 1928 joined with the open touring cars to round out the Studebaker component of the fleet.

The largest Studebakers were the equivalent of buses, and they were complemented by the purchase of some large Whites in 1928, four used 1925 Model 50A enclosed 24-passenger buses used principally for the transfer of passengers between the stations and hotels at both Banff and Lake Louise. The White Company was perhaps the most aggressive large vehicle manufacturer in the marketplace at the time with branch offices in Montreal, Toronto, Winnipeg, Calgary and Vancouver. Advertising centered around mileage records which the company claimed "shatter all comparisons"; they were capable of standing behind their claims with lists of customers that included 282 owning Whites with 500,000 miles or over, 1181 with 300,000 to 500,000 and so on.

The effect of such advertising combined with the company's success with its previous Whites led Brewster Transport to the 1929 purchase of its most expensive pieces of equipment to date, four Model 65 Whites, two of them enclosed, with 22-passenger capacities at $11,325 each, two of them open, with 18-passenger capacities at $8400 each. The total purchase price of almost $40,000 was beyond the company's capability to pay all at once, but the White Company agreed to carry a series of notes falling due over the next few years. One other major bus acquisition, also in 1929, brought the company its first Yellow vehicles, two enclosed 17-passenger Model WAs costing $8200 and $6950.

Though these later model Whites and the Yellows had several advantages over the company's earlier Whites, the drivers' problems with the convertible tops remained perplexing. A single bar on which to slide the top had been added to the open models but even this did not prove sufficient to remedy them. Two Brewster Transport employees, Fred Nudd and Fred Styles, went to work to try solve the problems. Nudd, a native of Great Yarmouth, England, had a solid background in upholstery work, having served his apprenticeship overseas and then working as a foreman at Great West Saddlery in Calgary producing saddles for the Canadian Army during the First World War. In 1921 he joined Brewster Transport and took care of all upholstery work on company vehicles. Styles, originally from Alcester, England, had moved to Victoria early in the century and had been involved with Sir Arthur Currie in the recruitment and training of the Motor Transport Corps of Victoria during the war. He too had arrived in Banff shortly after the armistice and had gone to work in the maintenance department of the company, soon achieving the position of supervisor of maintenance. Combining their particular skills, Nudd and Styles devised a system based on a mechanically driven roller that would spread a cover over a skeleton frame without unduly inconveniencing the passengers when it was put up and which could be neatly rolled away. By terms of an agreement dated February 4, 1928 the inventors turned over their rights to the top to Brewster Transport in return for the company's promise to pursue Canadian and U.S. patent rights, to develop working models and to pay royalties if the covers were ever manufactured. A Canadian patent was obtained in 1929 but the U.S. patent proved unattainable because of similar inventions in that country. Even though the covers were never manufactured, the company's involvement in this project demonstrated its willingness to support the development of new and better equipment for the tourist transport industry.

In the touring car field where Studebakers had dominated in the middle years of the decade, Packards became more popular. The company had acquired its first three Packard Twin Sixes in

**Brewster Transport Packards**

1923 and that September Jim had used one to show the Prince of Wales the sights of Banff. More were added by 1925 but it was in 1928, after Packards had proven their worth in Royal Hawaiian Transport's fleet, Jim began his love affair with the beautifully designed cars. In 1928 the company purchased four new Packard Six touring models at $3840 each, five used Packard Six touring cars, two used 1925 Packard Six sedans, and one used Packard limousine. The year 1929 saw the acquisition of thirteen Packards, most of them eight cylinder models, four of which were purchased from Royal Hawaiian Transport. Six more were added in 1930.

Because of these major additions, by 1930 Brewster Transport's entire fleet had grown to 79 vehicles with a total carrying capacity of 880 passengers, a growth which required a considerable increase in staff compared to 1925 when its total capacity was only about 320 passengers. Beginning in 1920, when the company moved its offices into the old *Rocky Mountain Courier* building, the office staff had its first appreciable growth in many years. Lou Crosby, in his position of financial manager, headed up the staff. Initially his assistant accountant was T. H. Balderston but Herbert "Bert" Manley, who had started with the company in 1919 as a clerk in the Mount Royal Hotel, soon succeeded him. For Manley this was

**Frank Hayes at the wheel of a White bus, ca. 1930**

the next step in a forty-two year career with Brewster Transport, most of which would be spent in the position of comptroller. In 1929 a third accountant, William Morrison, was hired. Assisting the men in a position she would retain for almost twenty years was the only full-time secretary, Ruth Lane.

Also in the company office building were Jim's and Bill's private offices and the transportation manager's officer. This job Earl Gammon filled until 1928 when he left the company to engage in road construction near Cochrane. Ralph Harvey, whose many years as manager at Lake Louise had proved him capable of this key position, replaced him. Directly under him was the despatcher, Frank Hayes. Born in Ireland in 1880, Hayes had learned the sightseeing business in England, conducting tours from London to the seaside, before coming to Canada, first to the Maritimes and then in 1925 to Banff. His first job was driving the Mount Royal Hotel bus but his conscientiousness and diligence earned him a promotion in 1929. At Lake Louise, George Brewster, who had worked for a period at Jasper after returning from Montana, took over the reins from Harvey for a short period before being relieved by Elmer Smith.

As significant as the growth in office and managerial staffs were corresponding increases in maintenance staff, drivers and other operating staff. Maintenance work on company vehicles, originally carried out at the Mount Royal Garage, was largely shifted to a garage the CPR built in 1926 adjacent to the Banff Springs Hotel. At the so-called "upper garage" several mechanics worked year round keeping the vehicles on the road any way possible in the summer and overhauling and reconditioning them in the winter. Company branches at Lake Louise and Field had their own mechanics on staff for the summer months and at all company garages temporary staff in the form of "greasers" and "gasers" helped keep the vehicles serviced. Other summer employees included the various "carriage agents," stationed at hotel and railway station ticket offices, guides and "pony boys," who handled the company's saddle horse rental services, and several Chinese cooks, who provided hearty fare for employees at the company's cookhouses near the Banff Springs Hotel and Chateau Lake Louise. But by far the largest and fastest growing group of company employees were the car, bus and truck drivers.

Very little had changed in the character of company drivers from the horse and buggy days. A small group of drivers was hired locally, but the majority came from outside. By 1930 most of the local drivers were young men in their mid-twenties who had been born or brought up in the area. Among them were Joe "Shorty" Bleskan and his brother Johnny from Canmore and Norman Knight, Rupe Edwards, Peter Whyte and Herb and Ted Paris from Banff. These young men were usually assigned to the driving of the 6-passenger touring cars or one of the company's baggage trucks, tasks in which they were joined by a few university students whom the company was beginning to hire. Most of these students initally came from eastern schools where they were studying to become lawyers, doctors and dentists, but as time went on some from western universities joined them as well.

Earl Gammon, while he was transportation manager, devised a simple test to determine

**Brewster drivers in the mid '20's. Joe Bleskan (rear), Bernie Hansen (second from left), John Bleskan (third from left), Walter Ashdown (third from right), Peter Whyte (second from right)**

which of these untried younger drivers he would hire. He would ask the aspirant to drive up a rather tricky, switchback section of Tunnel Mountain Drive that required plenty of double-clutching. If he managed to make it to the Bow Falls Lookout, Gammon would ask him to turn the car around. If the driver backed his car towards the mountain he was in but if he backed it towards the cliff he was out.

For its larger machinery, the company wanted men with more driving experience. Apart from a few older local drivers, such as James "Scotty" Forteath and Rusty Gowans, it found them outside of Banff. Some of those hired as bus drivers, like Frank Vaughan, were normally taxi drivers from prairie cities who felt they could make more money working summers in Banff than at their regular jobs. The wages were not better, the average monthly salary ranging between $80-$100, but receiving substantial tips from satisfied tourists proved attractive. Tips were particularly good if the driver were able to produce a bear or some other such exotic beast for the customer, a fact which led to numerous drives to the town nuisance ground.

Finding good, dependable men to fill these positions remained a challenge for Bill and the transportation manager. Men who had worked for the company previously and had received a satisfactory rating from Bill usually had the inside track. On other occasions he and Gammon would accept the recommendations of contacts they had made in the transportation business all over the country. Even these strategems did not always prove effective as the entries in Bill's 'black book' illustrate. In 1929, the peak pre-depression year, there were almost as many drivers as there were vehicles but very few of them got Bill's 100 percent rating beside their name. Much more common were percentages ranging from 50 to 85 or a simple N.G. (No Good). The ratings were often accompanied by additional comments such as "always in trouble," "dismissed for speeding," "agitator and not too energetic," "drinks," and most commonly "left early." The few drivers who got 100 percents were the ones the company wanted back each year and it fortunately often succeeded. Among the top drivers were Reg Knight, Elmer Charlton, Bernie Hansen, Sing Johnson, Frank Vaughan, Hank Dyck and Vic Saunders.

The premier driver of the company continued to be Walter Ashdown, who in 1930 was to take a drive remembered as the most daring and widely publicized exploit a Brewster driver was ever involved in — an 81-mile mission of mercy over treacherous mountain roads at breakneck speeds. Descriptions of the wild drive appeared in many newspapers, but it was most fully recounted in the *Crag and Canyon*.

A death-defying 70 mile an hour race that covered 81 miles of curve-strewn mountain roads — curves where the batting of an eyelid would have been followed by destruction — one hour and twenty minutes of continuous flirting with death in an attempt to cheat the "grim reaper" of his prey — two victims on whom he had laid fast-tightening talons — constitutes a mountain epic that will go down in the history of these parts as one of the most thrilling and heroic acts of modern times. At 8 a.m. on Saturday, June 7 two employees of the Monarch Mine, situated across the Great Divide and about 49 miles from here are discovered dying from asphyxiation. Vainly a local doctor and first aid men try to recussitate the stricken ones, but oxygen, the aid most needed is not on hand. A long distance call is put through to the Banff Springs Hotel Garage. "Get a pulmotor as quickly as possible," is the urgent plea. Frank Hayes, the Brewster Transport foreman, ponders but a moment then, "Phone the Canmore Mine to have one ready and we will send a car for it," he answers. Canmore is 16 miles from Banff and in the opposite direction to Field. From his office Frank runs to where a short wiry man sits behind the wheel of a Packard 8. Not for nothing has this driver been cited for bravery in the Great War, awarded the Military Medal Passchendaele, served as motor machine gunner and special despatch rider.

"Life or death," Frank says quickly, "The speed limit will be off in a minute. Rush to Canmore get a pulmotor and take it to the Monarch Mine in the Kicking Horse Valley. Two men are dying there."

The car shoots like a bullet from the garage at 45 miles an hour, it threads the Main Street of Banff while pedestrians stare open-mouthed. A clear road ahead — except for curves — up to 75 goes the speedometer then, over and down the Anthracite hill — hill dreaded by thousands — the grey meteor flashes. Canmore Station — 15 miles in 11 minutes — no pulmotor there — should have continued on to the mine office. Death gained one minute in the race.

**Walter Ashdown at the wheel of a Packard**

Along the twisting Canmore street — a flashing grey streak — the office — an official hanging up the phone after receiving a call from the Monarch Mine; the car has almost beaten the telephone.

Three valuable minutes lost in getting and loading the pulmotor into the car, then, the eight cylinders roared, the driver's right arm lies heavy on the horn button sounding the warning incessantly until the highway is reached and the westward run begins. Half a mile distant a car shows on the highway — twenty seconds and it is a passed incident. The winding, twisting Anthracite hill is once more reached — into second go the gears and to the bottom the gas lever.

Fifty miles an hour round sharp curves — second gear speed — first would have labored and lost time. Like a rocket the car shoots down the other side of the hill, then once more through a startled Banff, and out on the west highway where the greatest dangers of all commence — more numerous curves and few straight stretches.

Seventy-three, seventy-four, seventy-five shows the speedometer — a quarter of a mile away a road-repair man is at work — the horn shrieks — the man jumps — before his feet touch the ground the flying demon is past him and he has not seen it. Fifty miles an hour around sharp curves — 70 miles an hour down steep grades — death's grinning features peer around each curve — death's clutching hooked talons reach up from below the precipice's edges hungry for another victim — the car speeds on. An easy curve — a warning cloud of dust — 70, 60,50,40 miles an hour — too fast — a herd of pack horses blocks the way. Almost a stop while the phlegmatic cowboys, indignant that a machine should so insistently demand a hurried right-of-way, leisurely press their charges to one side — little they know of the desperate hurry.

Up, up goes the speedometer again — another dust cloud — a slow, heavy horse-drawn grader occupies the centre of the road. The brakes bite home — slower, slower the chafing driver puts his speed.

Slowly, so slowly, the cumbersome grader moves to one side — with two wheels perilously on the edge of a ditch the car shoots by, missing the horses by fractions of an inch and causing the grader men to swear loudly.

Up, up mounts the speed — curve, curve, curve — the Bow Valley bridge at Lake Louise station — the three mile hill to the height of land — three miles of second gear, fifty miles an hour flying around bends — the height of land — a sickening descent to the Great Divide — a flashing past Lake Wapta, then, the long drop down the famed Kicking Horse Pass — down the old railroad grade that one time filled passengers' hearts with fear — passengers riding on slow trains of those days. A steady 75 shows the speedometer — over the high trestle bridges that stand hundreds of feet above the tumbling torrent in the gorge — a railway crossing — all clear thank heaven —a sharpish curve — a skid — a recovery — might have meant a widow and fatherless babe in Banff tonight — three men on the roadside — slow down that they may jump aboard — a sudden turn followed by a dash up a narrow trail — a trail winding around jutting rocks and big trees — fifty miles an hour where there is barely sufficient room to steer the car through — can't slow down — men are dying around that next bend. Buildings a little way ahead — shrieking brakes — a stopped car — men seizing the pulmotor and rushing away with it. The time — "TEN MINUTES TO TWELVE," shouts someone and the call had been received in Banff at TWENTY-EIGHT MINUTES PAST TEN. Eighty-one miles of death-sown road travelled in ONE HOUR AND TWENTY-EIGHT MINUTES [actually 82 minutes] by a driver whose nerves have snapped with the reaction and who is being assisted from the car.

A short rest — an expressed wish to see the stricken men — then Walter Ashdown, military medal man of the Great War and now Brewster Transport Company chauffeur at the Banff Springs Hotel, looks down on the faces of the two victims. Softly — trembling — he asks their names: "Max Weber and Sivert Peterson," he is told.

Suddenly realization dawns — realization that he, Walter Ashdown, who for more than thee years had faced death with but one ambition — the ambition to destroy as many of his country's enemies as he possibly could — has today, in a period of little more than one hour, risked his life scores of times in an attempt to save the lives of two of his former foes — two sons of the German Fatherland.

Walter's reputation as a result of this fearless drive stood him in good stead with the company which elevated him to the status of "celebrity" chauffeur. The next year the first of many "big names," the King of Siam, saw the sights from Walter's gleaming Packard.

Most of the company's drivers were laid off at the end of the season, except for a few who were kept on to haul gravel and building materials for CPR construction projects. In the twenties there was quite a bit of such work since Brewster Transport was involved in rebuilding projects on both the Chateau Lake Louise and the Banff Springs Hotel after the disastrous fires of 1924 and 1926 respectively. But even among the summer staff there was an *esprit de corps,* a pride in working for the company. The younger drivers especially remembered the years as the most enjoyable of their lives with their cameraderie and their interesting people and places. The memories of those working at Lake Louise seemed to remain particularly vivid — memories of parties with the hotel staff in the Brewster staff quarters; of boat rides to the end of the lake in the warm summer evenings to relax with a few bottles of beer cooled in the glacier; of trips into Banff to attend the dances at the Banff Springs Hotel and then staying overnight at the Mount Royal Hotel where Brewster staff could get a room for a dollar.

The attitude that working for Brewster Transport was a little bit special pervaded other aspects of the company's operations; a story related by one of their cowboys, Chuck Millar, best sums it up. Given the job of taking some of the company's horses to the Devil's Head Ranch in 1929, Millar asked the stable boss, Jim McNeil, if he had secured the necessary permit from the RCMP to drive the horses across the Bow River bridge. McNeil had laughed and told him to forget about it. Millar was apprehensive but then remembered that the previous summer two of the company's men, Percy Bennett and Wes Latham, had got the police after them for some infraction of the regulations with pack horses. When threatened with charges Bennett had exclaimed, "You can't do that — we work for Brewsters." Millar resolved that if he had any problems with the police he would try Bennett's "password" and confidently set off over the bridge with the horses.

With its enthusiastic staff and its extensive fleet of cars and buses, Brewster Transport was in a good position to take advantage of the tourist boom. The management, not content to wait for the business to come, made every possible effort to seek it out. Several new publicity ploys were tried, including publishing more elaborate annual brochures advertising the company and its services and distributing free passes to travel agents and other indviduals who might send business its way. The major effort in this vein, though, was in organizations of tour operators formed for the purpose of joint advertising and mutual cooperation.

The first such organization the company became associated with was the Royal Blue Line. Little is known of its make-up, except that it seems to have been a loose association of tourist transport operators in Quebec and Western Canada with which Brewster Transport became affiliated around the mid-twenties. For a few years some of the company's buses had the Royal Blue Line insignia painted on their sides, but the company seemed to take little interest in the organization and ceased using its name. That is until Rocky Mountain Tours picked up on it and began using it about 1929.

Rocky Mountain Tours' usurpation led to a drawn-out court battle that proved a difficult test for Brewster Transport's new solicitor, Campbell McLaurin. In 1927 the ever-valuable Savary had passed away suddenly and the young McLaurin, who had first articled with Savary, Fenerty and Chadwick in 1919, and later became a full partner, was asked to replace him. McLaurin accepted and began a long career as both the company's and Jim's personal legal counsel. His first action in the Royal Blue Line affair was to apply for an injunction in the Supreme Court of Alberta prohibiting Rocky Mountain Tours' use of the name on the basis that Brewster Transport had established a reputation for it in the Province of Alberta. The injunction was granted but later overturned in the Appellate Division after Paddy Nolan, acting for Rocky Mountain Tours, argued successfully that Brewster Transport had no exclusive right to the name. Eventually the case went before the Supreme Court of Canada where

White bus bearing Royal Blue Line insignia

the judgment, delivered in December, 1930, went in favour of Rocky Mountain Tours, but with two justices dissenting.

The company's participation in a second such organization, Gray Line, proved much more satisfactory. The International Gray Line Sightseeing Association, formed in Baltimore, Maryland in 1910, had spread around the United States picking up member companies which paid annual dues for joint promotion and advertising and participated in annual conventions to discuss mutual problems and plans. By the late twenties the organization had begun to spread outside the United States to Canada, Mexico, England, France, Germany, and Hawaii, where Jim probably came in contact with it when Royal Hawaiian Transport became an affiliate immediately after the company was set up. In 1928 Brewster Transport followed suit, paying out some $1500 in membership dues.

Membership in Gray Line produced immediate changes in the company's appearance. In 1925, for the first time, all its vehicles had been painted the same colour, cream, by its painter, a Mr. Bessette formerly of the City Sign Works in Calgary. But all Gray Line vehicles were required to bear the organization's colours, blue and gray (actually a creamy yellow on the vehicles), and the Brewster machinery was so painted in 1928. Uniforms came from a common supplier in the United States and included not only a cap, which the drivers previously had to wear, but also matching light gray Norfolk style jackets and pants. A company regulation which forbade them to be seen in the beer parlour wearing a uniform was, so far as the drivers were concerned, one drawback.

The value of the Gray Line affiliation seems to have been a debatable matter amongst Brewster Transport's management. Certainly Jim was personally in favour of it, particularly after he was unexpectedly elected president of the organization *in absentia* during the 1930 convention at San Francisco. At the very least it was useful if only because one company tended to pass along customers to the others and it was widely enough known to give customers a feeling of security in their dealings with the company. Also, it played a part in engaging Brewster Transport in a new phenomenon that began to appear towards the end of the decade, the all-expenses paid tour.

Previously, when making their annual visits to tour agencies in the United States, Jim,

**White buses on Rawhide Trail tour at Golden Lodge, late '20's**

Crosby and Bill had restricted their activities to the promotion of group tours through the Rockies and to the distribution of literature on Brewster Transport's services. With all-expenses paid tours the company offered its services to a tour operator who would sell them in a prepaid package to the customer. For each package he sold that utilized the company's services the agent would receive a commission. For the customer, the service let him know exactly how much his trip was going to cost and what these costs covered instead of knowing just what the travel costs were going to be. The more expensive "A" tours would include at least one night stays at the Banff Springs Hotel, the Chateau Lake Louise and one of the CPR's bungalow camps, Brewster Transport providing the transportation between accommodations and some sightseeing as part of the package. In the less expensive "B" tours accommodation was in the Mount Royal Hotel and Deer Lodge. All the tour agencies in the States with which the company had previously dealt eventually offered these tours but the American Express Company, formerly a minor agency, captured the largest share of the market.

Another development in the tour field was the company's first involvement in a venture which crossed the International Boundary. In December, 1929 Bill Brewster, after returning from CPR headquarters in Montreal, announced that the CPR and the Great Northern Railway had agreed on a proposal to run excursion trains from Chicago to the Rockies and return utilizing both companies' lines and facilities. The plans called for passengers to travel from Chicago to Glacier Park, Montana on the Great Northern and then be transferred to the railway's Prince of Wales Hotel at Waterton Lakes in the vehicles of the Glacier Park Transportation Company. At Waterton, Brewster Transport vehicles would pick up the passengers and take them around the Lariat to Banff where they would board the CPR for the trip back home.

Participation in these Rawhide Trail Tours, as they became known, demanded Brewster Transport's establishing a branch at Waterton Lakes, a development carried out in 1930 with the hiring of a commission agent at the location. Additionally, the company had to undertake heavy deadhead expenses, something hitherto avoided. The drivers of the two 18-passenger Model 65 Whites normally used on this run would deadhead from Banff to Waterton Lakes through Calgary on Thursday and stay overnight. At 9 a.m. the next morning they would pick up their passengers and drive that day to Cranbrook, where the entire group would stay at the famous old Baker Hotel. The next day they would make it to Radium for lunch and then on to Golden to stay the second night in the Golden Lodge, a location where Brewster Transport had begun maintaining another branch office in 1928. The third day the trip would be completed over the tortuous Golden to Banff road. Later the Rawhide Trail Tours were extended to four days, with the third night's stop at Lake Louise, and private cars were made available to patrons not wishing to travel by bus. Because of these operations, the company's deadhead expenses rose dramatically, reaching $3200 in 1931. The same year its profits from Waterton Lakes revenues stood at $8400, making the expenses incurred well worthwhile.

Two other significant developments that called for expansion of company facilities also occurred towards the end of the decade and both centred in Calgary. Bill Brewster's acquisition of the Palliser Hotel transport concession in 1924 he had used as a bargaining tool in securing his new contract. By the contract's terms he would continue to operate the concession for the time being, and he had sent his son Jack to Calgary to look after it. Most of the vehicles used in the operation were Yellow taxicabs purchased in Chicago, and with them it had initially done quite well. However, as time went on Jack Brewster began to have problems and in 1929 Bill agreed to let Brewster Transport exercise its option to take over the concession. Jim sent his brother George to Calgary to straighten out the situation and he soon had it turned around, making a profit of $5300 in 1929. Soon after, another company employee, Felix Monden, was sent to continue George's good work.

The second Calgary development established a regular bus service between the city and Banff. In 1928 Brewster Transport applied for and received provincial government permission to operate "stage lines" over provincial roads between Banff, Calgary and Edmonton. A few runs were made to Edmonton utilizing White buses but the route, unprofitable with this equipment, was soon dropped. The Calgary run, using the company's enclosed Yellow coaches, immediately proved worthwhile. The service necessitated a pick-up point in Banff, the Mount Royal Hotel, as well as one in Calgary. Negotiations with Eatons' department store resulted in an agreement to rent space from them and the service went into operation with a bus leaving Banff in the morning and returning from Calgary in the evening. The first year proved rather uninspiring as it resulted in a loss of $2400, but by 1929 the idea had caught on and a profit of $4500 was realized.

Brewster Transport's numerous new involvements, its ongoing improvements to services and the boom in tourism appreciably changed its financial picture. Net assets increased from $290,000 in 1923 to $496,700 in 1929, while net operating revenues (before general expenses and taxes) went from $93,400 to $199,700 in the same period. Yet operating and development costs increased just as rapidly, resulting in no very substantial increases in overall profits. The net profit of $15,900 in 1923 had only reached $22,100 in 1929 and the surplus account had only grown from $93,700 to $191,900 with no dividends being paid. Over the same period the company had increased its total indebtedness to the Imperial Bank by some $77,000, most of it in loans for the purchase of new equipment. Added to this was $32,700 in accounts payable to the White Company, also for equipment. The profit picture was on the verge of improving markedly if seasons such as 1929 continued to occur, but they didn't. The company's debts, just as they had during the hard times of the First World War, would bring Brewster Transport close to collapse in the coming depression.

Single rail White bus at Takakkaw Falls, early '30's

# XI: Darkness and Sunshine

If the last five years of the twenties were the halcyon days of Canadian Rockies tourism, the following five years were just the opposite. The business depression which began to grip the world in late 1929 strongly affected tourism, in essence a "luxury" industry. Initially the number of visitors stayed at a fairly high level. For example, in 1931 there were 183,946 entries into Banff National Park, only some 53,000 fewer than in the peak year of 1928. But for the tourist transport business the statistics were highly misleading. Beginning in 1930 road travel to the park noticeably increased and what was termed "long distance travel" decreased, the latter being what Brewster Transport mainly depended on for its patronage. Many of the travellers to the parks throughout the depression were those who could reach them in their own cars. They would usually camp during a short stay, spend little money in total and almost none at all on sightseeing transportation. As the depression deepened, even the auto visitor began to stay at home and the 1932 statistics plunged almost 45,000 people in one year to 139,669.

Brewster Transport felt the effects of the depression quickly and severely. Between 1929 and 1930 motor vehicle operating revenues decreased almost thirty percent, while net operating revenue from all company interests shrank thirty-six percent from $199,700 to $127,700. Equally ominous was the fact that a profit of $22,100 in 1929 evaporated to a $41,600 deficit in 1930. This became just the first of several serious losses resulting in the company's surplus account slipping from $180,000 in 1930 to $106,000 in 1932 and then to just $81,700 in 1933.

Management could do little except to tighten its belt and try to ride out the storm. New equipment purchases worth $26,000 in 1930 brought the total fleet value to $410,800, after which all plans for acquiring new equipment were postponed. Some of the existing equipment was "mothballed" and stored in the basement of Brewster Hall until business picked up again. Likewise, there were staff cuts with the most drastic being made in the number of seasonal drivers and employees. Those lucky enough to be kept on had to accept less for their services. Total wages paid transportation staff decreased from $42,500 in 1929 to $32,500 in 1930, and by 1933 had been pared to an incredibly low $12,-200.

As if the wages being paid were not meagre enough, sometimes there was even some doubt as to whether employees would be paid at all. Cash flow slowed to a trickle and other uncertainties intervened to make the likelihood of collecting a pay cheque seem dim. On one such occasion "Mr. Jim," as he was now being referred to by his staff, ordered one of his drivers to take him to the Palliser Hotel in Calgary a few days before payday. There he went on one of his famous benders, after ordering the driver to stay with him for the interim. The driver phoned and reported the situation to Crosby who ordered him to get Jim back to Banff any way he could to sign the cheques. Uncertain how to accomplish this task, the driver seized an opportunity when Jim passed out during a drive around the city. He quickly sped back to Banff and delivered his cargo to the company office before he came around. Jim was furious, but the driver wisely maintained that Jim had ordered him to return. The cheques got out on time, but Crosby gained one more gray hair in a growing collection.

Despite the measures the company took to pare down expenses, it could not even begin to make up for its lost earnings during these years. This situation placed it in extreme jeopardy considering its 1930 liabilities of $260,000 in loans, accounts payable and bills payable. Jim was forced to turn to the CPR for assistance, as he had done so often in the past.

Fortunately Brewster Transport was then enjoying a very good relationship with the railway. The affable Edward Beatty, President of the CPR since 1918, was on excellent terms with Jim, a relationship that would grow into close friendship. Jim also got along well with H. F. Mathews, General Manager of Western Hotels, and directed his first request for help to him in 1931.

**Jim McLeod and his family in the early '30's. Left to right (rear) — Jean, Doris, Rae; (front) Jim sr., Jim jr., Allan, Evelyn**

The CPR agreed to a plan that would see the commission Brewster Transport paid for its concession cut in half.

After the war, the 1918 agreement, whereby the CPR charged a nominal $1.00 for the concession, had begun to change. By 1921 the CPR charged a $1200 per annum rental for the premises the company occupied and in 1923 this sum rose to $3000. Then in 1925 it implemented a whole new system based on commissions, Brewster Transport paying ten percent of the net operating revenues derived from its motor vehicle and livestock departments. By 1929 this meant a payment of approximately $14,800 in addition to the rents. Because of some disagreement about what sorts of business commissions should and should not be paid on, the company's representatives met with Mathews in June, 1930 to discuss the issue. Mathews agreed that the CPR would not collect commission on business on which Brewster Transport was already paying commission to tourist agencies or other hotels or on any work done directly for the CPR under the terms of their contract. Nor would it collect commission on parties to which Brewster Transport gave cut rates to encourage their attendance at Banff Indian Days or other such promotional events. In fact, the company would be required to pay commission only on casual or so-called "unorganized" business.

The agreement of 1930 and the CPR's subsequent willingness to cut the commission rate in half to five percent in 1931 failed to get Brewster Transport out of its financial vise. By early November, 1931, even before the commission reduction had become official, Jim was again approaching Mathews, this time with a direct request for funds to pay off some of the company's more pressing debts. Mathews demurred, feeling that other ways of reducing overhead and inefficiencies might help the company pull through this dark period. He suggested Brewster Transport approach Rocky Mountain Tours and see if some sort of agreement might accomplish these ends.

Despite the fact they were both business and political rivals, Jim Brewster and Jim McLeod had kept their friendship intact. It was not in either man's nature to hold any grudges over past events. In April, 1931 McLeod began construction of a new home on the corner of Lynx and Caribou Streets, immediately behind Lou Crosby's home, itself just across Caribou from Jim Brewster's. The three men therefore lived within a stone's throw of each other and it was not uncommon for either of the two Jims to visit the other to discuss politics or some other interesting issue of the day. Consequently it should not have been difficult for Brewster Transport to enter into amalgamation discussions with Rocky Mountain Tours, although it appears that neither man was very keen on the idea.

Brewster Transport initially suggested the two companies maintain their individual identities but jointly set up a third company which would conduct all livery operations, the profits to be divided at season's end on the basis of present seating capacity of equipment or average gross earnings over the past three years. An agreement of this nature would curtail overhead, reduce advertising, eliminate one set of carriage agents, avoid duplication of local daily trips and postpone capital expenditures for new equipment. A memorandum outlining this suggestion was sent to Rocky Mountain Tours on November 7, 1931 and within two days there was a reply from their solicitors, Bennett, Hannah and Sandford. It was fairly negative, stating that a split on the basis of seating capacity would be unfair because Brewster Transport had more equipment but Rocky Mountain's was for the most part newer and likely to be utilized more. A split on the basis of gross earnings was felt to be equally unfair, and, it suggested, a basis of net earnings would be more equitable.

This response set off a series of negotiations mainly carried out by letter and telephone between the companies' respective lawyers, P. L. Sandford and Campbell McLaurin. McLaurin's immediate rejoinder to Rocky Mountain's contention about its equipment was that Brewster Transport's Packard touring cars were superior to anything on the road in the park and that, regardless, it was not the age of the equipment that mattered so much as the unused miles on it. Adding that a division of profits on the basis of net earnings was not objectionable, he appealed for McLeod and Warren to meet with Jim and Crosby to negotiate face to face. However, the principals of Rocky Mountain Tours were not prepared to do that and, although communications continued, it was apparent that they were not really interested in the idea. Early in January, 1932 Jim forwarded the file on the negotiations to Mathews so that he could see for himself that every effort had been made to come to an agreement. Mathews intimated he would intervene personally in the negotiations but when this too came to naught he admitted the plan seemed infeasible. That this was exactly what Jim had desired was made clear in a letter he received from McLaurin on January 9, 1932 in which the lawyer stated that the correspondence "should be quite satisfactory from your point of view as it culminated in the Rocky Mountain Tours' declining to even discuss the details of the proposed amalgamation."

Rocky Mountain Tours' refusal left the door open for Brewster Transport to make another direct appeal to the CPR for funds. The railway had little option but to acquiesce, realizing it would either have to support a new concessionaire or get into the livery business itself if Brewster Transport failed. McLaurin approached the CPR's chief solicitor in Calgary and convinced him that the company needed $150,000 immediately to pay off debts to vehicle manufacturers, tire makers, gas and oil suppliers and sundry other creditors. The CPR agreed if Brewster Transport would provide some security for the loan, a rather ticklish request in that all the company's assets were tied up as collateral for a $200,000 bond issue which in turn was pledged as security for $195,000 in loans from the Imperial Bank. Fortunately the bank agreed to release twelve automobiles from the bond security, and the CPR then accepted chattel mortgages on these vehicles as security for its loan.

As it turned out, McLaurin's skillful handling of the company's creditors resulted in the need for substantially less money than had been requested. Several creditors were convinced to accept only 50 or 75 cents on the dollar and when they had all been paid off he was still left with $25,000. McLaurin mentioned this to the CPR's chief solicitor who advised him to "take a damn good fee out of it" before returning the balance. Jim agreed and the remainder was used to reduce the amount owing the railway.

Although the CPR loan relieved the immediate pressure, it was still going to be an uphill struggle for survival if the depression deepened. Accordingly, the company had already begun streamlining its activities. It cancelled its plans to expand its operations into Jasper National Park, an idea which had first been brought up in 1930. That year Elmer Charlton, one of the company's newer drivers and George Brewster's future brother-in-law, led a group of four drivers equipped with Packards to Jasper to open a branch there in opposition to the CNR, which like the CPR was beginning to support livery services for its Jasper Park Lodge. However, the railway refused to allow them access to the station platform or the Jasper Park Lodge, thereby keeping their effectiveness to a minimum. In its first season of operation the branch grossed only $6100 in transportation revenues and turned a profit of $840. The worsening financial situation made the investment required to make the branch a going concern impossible, so it was discontinued in 1931.

Other interests outside the immediate vicinity of Banff suffered a similar fate, particularly those in Calgary. On November 1, 1931 the company agreed to sell to Felix Monden the Palliser Hotel taxi concession and the four Packard sedans with which it was being run. Monden was to pay $150 per month over a thirty-six month period, at the completion of which title to the cars would be turned over to him. But as time went on he fell seriously in arrears, obliging the company to carry him on its books. Eventually, the company had to repossess the four cars, although Monden did manage to survive and operated what became known as the Brewster Taxi Service for many years.

Another of Brewster Transport's Calgary interests which it released was the Banff-Calgary bus. Since returning to Banff from Jasper, George Brewster had been working for the company and the bus line had been one of his responsibilities. By 1932, faced with tight financial stringencies, Jim was having difficulty keeping him on the payroll. Finally his sister Pearl convinced Jim to turn over the running rights for the line to George on the understanding that Colonel Moore, who had just received a substantial inheritance, would provide a vehicle for him to operate it with. Moore purchased a small Ford bus which was more efficient and economical to run on the route than the big Whites that Brewster Transport had been using. The Brewster Bus Service, as it became known, began with Elmer Charlton driving the bus. It left Banff at 8 a.m. and, depending on the weather, the road conditions and the number of stops on the Indian reserve, usually arrived at the Herald Building in Calgary three hours later, returning to Banff at 8 p.m. The fare was $2.50 one way or $4.00 return. Again Jim not only got rid of an unprofitable aspect of the business but helped out a family member in the bargain.

The company also participated in a third, very shortlived venture in Calgary when it became involved with City Council in an experiment to test buses for city transit. Calgary was having great difficulty with its streetcar system, especially on some of the outlying runs; and the city commissioners felt that Brewster Transport's contention that gasoline buses would prove more economical was worth investigating. On February 20, 1931 the company contracted with the city to operate buses on the Elbow Park run for a minimum of two and a maximum of four weeks beginning on March 1st. Buses were to run every five minutes at peak periods and every ten minutes at off peak periods using the city transit department's fare schedule of three tickets for twenty-five cents. The experiment lasted three weeks during which time Brewster Transport used several of its 25-passenger White buses and supplied its own drivers but managed to clear a profit of only $183. Nevertheless, the company agreed to repeat the experiment when approached by the Mount Royal Community Club in April about running a half hour express from the district to the downtown core. Bill pointed out in his letter agreeing to partake in this experiment that it could only be temporary since the equipment would soon be needed for sightseeing purposes, a restriction which undoubtedly influenced the Special Transportation Committee's decision not to grant the Community Club's request. The decision did not end the company's involvement in such trials as it participated in a similar one on Edmonton's system beginning on April 28, 1931. This time the test lasted for five weeks and proved much more satisfactory from the company's point-of-view since it netted a profit of almost $3000. As in the Calgary case, though, Edmonton's transit department could see no way of implementing a bus system during such hard times and neither experiment was followed up.

More serious to the company than its elimination of the Calgary interests as the economic situation worsened was the contemplated sale of its subsidiary, Royal Hawaiian Transport. The depression had not hit the Hawaiian company as quickly as it had Brewster Transport, but eventually it hit even harder. In 1930 Royal Hawaiian finished the year with a profit in excess of $4000 and had, as mentioned, given a bonus of $500 to each director. During 1929 and 1930 the company's fleet had grown with the purchase of ten

Jim and Wayne Stewart with Royal Hawaiian Transport Packard, ca. 1930

vehicles, mostly Packard touring cars, to a total of twenty-two cars and two buses. One of the Packards, a beautiful twelve cylinder deluxe model, Jim bought for his personal use and after it was shipped to Banff he could be seen behind the wheel of the powerful machine in his wide-brimmed hat on a daily drive to the Banff Springs Hotel or ferrying some dignitary around to see the sights. Other interaction between Banff and Hawaii had been encouraged in these good years as well. In the summer of 1928 four of Royal Hawaiian's best drivers, Ed Kekahio, Henry Yates, Ed Wallace and J. W. Searle, drove at Banff and the winter of 1929-30 Brewster Transport reciprocated by sending Bert McCallum, manager of the Mount Royal Hotel, and Peter Whyte, a former carriage agent and driver, to Hawaii. Whyte, a recent art school graduate, took advantage of the opportunity to sketch some of the Hawaiian people, and had the chance to compare the way the two companies were run while working for Royal Hawaiian that winter. In the Hawaiian company the drivers received a small salary augmented by a fifteen percent commission on the business they carried.

When the depression began to be felt in the islands, Royal Hawaiian's rosy financial picture rapidly deteriorated. In 1930 its gross revenue from all operations, which in addition to tourist transport included sales of gas and oil, baggage hauling, Hawaiian luaus and a small "Drive-Ur-Self" car rental, stood at $164,000. Gross revenue had fallen to $106,000 by 1931, and by 1932 to $72,500. Over the same period the $4000 profit of 1930 had become a $12,400 loss in 1932 and the surplus account had slipped into a $6000 deficit position. Wayne Stewart had implemented numerous economies, "mothballing" nine cars and one bus in June, 1932, paring down his staff to an absolute minimum and cutting the salaries of those who were kept on. But these actions failed to stem the tide and in August, 1932 he admitted in a letter to Jim that "the Royal Hawaiian Transport Co. is broke and we owe plenty of bills." What had finally done him in, Stewart contended, was the $5000 the company had loaned to Jim in April, 1932 to help pay off some of Brewster Transport's more pressing debts and $8000 which had been paid out for Fred Hussey's stock.

The latter amount was part of a $15,500 settlement with Ethel Hussey after Fred's sudden passing at San Mateo in January, 1930. Fifty years old then, Hussey had been plagued by a drinking problem for many years and it had finally taken its toll. Jim's closest friend and a man who had often kept Brewster Transport afloat was gone and an era in Jim's life and the company's history ended.

Hussey's death may have given Jim cause to reflect on his own drinking habits, but he appears not to have changed them much. Observors working at Lake Louise during this period recalled his idiosyncracies, mixing up big pans of hot rum, bringing a bottle to share with staff, or taking cash out of the company's till in the Chateau to spend in the bar. On one occasion during a drinking bout with Lyle Currie at the Chateau, Jim ordered a private railway car to be delivered to Lake Louise. The next day he and Currie boarded with a good supply of liquor to begin what would be a five week odyssey taking them as far as the Waldorf-Astoria Hotel in New York City. Crosby, whom Jim had neglected to inform of his plans, was only able to keep track of his whereabouts by the rather large cancelled cheques he periodically received.

Loans of $2250 from the Bank of Hawaii and $2000 from Benaglia had temporarily solved Royal Hawaiian's problems. Stewart then assured Jim that the company could pull through and "be on top of the heap when the deal is over." Jim, not so sure, worried about both the bleak financial situation Brewster Transport faced at home and the reports he was receiving that Stewart and Benaglia were not getting along well. Benaglia, who had a very difficult personality, resented Stewart's taking any action on behalf of the company without first clearing it with him. Unable to afford a trip to Hawaii, Jim had to sit in Banff reading letters from the two men stating their respective cases, and then tried to keep the peace in his replies. To Benaglia he pointed out that Stewart was always acting with the best interests of the company at heart; to Stewart that Benaglia was not only a shareholder, director and creditor of Royal Hawaiian Transport but also the key to securing renewal of the company's contract with the Territorial Hotel Company.

Eventually the worry heaped on all of his other problems became too much and in October, 1933 Jim allowed Benaglia to discuss with Earl Thacker and Company a possible sale of the company. Earl Thacker, ostensibly a general insurance agent in Hawaii, also had many other interests and ambitions, one of which was to become involved in tourist livery on the islands. Through Benaglia, Jim let it be known he would let Royal Hawaiian go for $50,000, but Thacker and Company, quoting the company's audited financial statement of March 31, 1933, pointed out that its assets worked out to only $15,000 after current liabilities were deducted. Stewart, hearing of the plan to sell, appealed to Jim to reconsider since he had managed to finish paying off the Hussey stock and was making inroads into the Benaglia loan despite its being the worst year of the depression. Certain that business was just about to turn the corner — and rather than see the company sold so cheaply to Thacker — he suggested he be given the opportunity to raise the money to buy it himself. He did interest G. A. Schumann of the Schumann Motor Company in the project but he too would not pay the $50,000 asking price.

In December, 1933 Stewart suggested that Jim come to Hawaii to negotiate the sale personally, but Jim again replied that he could not afford to do so. He mentioned in the same letter that he had read Royal Hawaiian's most recent reports and that, all things considered, he did not think the picture looked too bad. Furthermore, Phil Moore and his family were about to arrive in Hawaii and Jim had decided to ask him to look the situation over and give his opinion about its prospects. Obviously he was beginning to change his mind about the decision to sell, something which became even more apparent in a letter to Stewart on December 23, 1933 in which he stated "I am not crazy about selling or giving the organization away to anyone, providing it can carry its own load, as we have to do here in our own plant." Intuition and foresight had apparently led him to the conclusion that things were about to change for the better.

Although all Brewster Transport's operations suffered to some degree during the depression, the Mount Royal Hotel performed amazingly well. This was somewhat surprising since its performance had been disappointing during the good years of the twenties. For example, in 1925, an excellent year for Brewster Transport, the hotel had generated gross revenue of only $13,000 and a profit slightly in excess of $4000. Such poor returns during boom times had eventually led to a decision in late 1926 to lease the hotel to the Lethbridge Brewery Company for a two year period beginning January 1, 1927. Since the annual rental was in the $8000 neighbourhood, the company benefitted over the previous situation. Nevertheless, it was anxious to regain control of the business when the agreement with Lethbridge Brewery expired at the end of 1928.

Fortunately the problem of finding a good long-term manager had finally been solved in Bert McCallum, a former manager of the company's livery stable between 1912 and 1917 and more recently the manager of a hotel in Revelstoke. A meticulous dresser who spent much of his own money on clothes, he was not one to waste a cent on anything he felt was unnecessary for the hotel. It was said of him that when he was hiring a new maid the first question he would ask in the interview was whether or not she could paint. Three times a day he would put aside his bowler hat, don a porter's cap and proceed to the Banff station where he would take his place on the platform along with station agents from other hotels and bark out the benefits of his hostelry. Although Jim often asked him to desist from the practice, since it tended to be somewhat embarrassing to have the hotel manager performing this function, McCallum would promise to try but invariably be back at it within a day or two. McCallum's penury in pursuit of profits for the hotel is well illustrated in a popular story told about him. During the thirties Dr. Frank Buchman, leader of the religious movement known as the Oxford Group (later Moral Rearmament), often chose Banff as the location for his annual convention of followers. Since the Banff Springs' rates were too high, he usually rented the entire premises of the Bretton Hall Hotel (formerly the Sanitarium Hotel) to house those in attendance. The Bretton Hall's disastrous fire in 1933 forced Buchman to look elsewhere for accommodation. There being no other hotel apart from the Banff Springs capable of singly handling the delegates, he entered into joint negotiations with McCallum and Lorne Orr, manager of the King Edward Hotel. Bargaining became tough at the point where the cost per room was under discussion, Buchman insisting that $2 per day was all he would pay while McCallum and Orr held out for the usual $4 per day. As the debate became heated, Buchman called for a halt to allow for a few moments quiet reflection during which he would call on God to

Mount Royal lobby with Bert McCallum, Lou Crosby and Bill Brewster at right, 1934

help resolve the impasse. A few minutes passed and Buchman finally broke the silence: "God has spoken to me and told me that $2 is the fair price." Unabashed, McCallum retorted, "Well, he spoke to me too and told me $4." Buchman was so taken aback that a compromise was quickly reached.

As McCallum was a manager capable of wringing every dollar out of a business, in 1929 he was allowed to undertake a major renovation of the Mount Royal, redecorating and remodelling the upper floor including the installing of hot and cold running water in twenty-four rooms and complete bathrooms in some others. The work had the desired effect as in 1929 the hotel cleared a profit of almost $19,000 with sixty percent of revenue coming from room rental and the other forty percent evenly divided between dining room and beer parlour revenue. In 1930 hotel profits slipped to about $11,000, with beer parlour revenue showing the smallest decrease, and then continued to slide until bottoming out in 1933 at $4000, the same profit as in 1925.

Overall the depression years proved difficult for all Brewster employees, but perhaps most difficult for Bill Brewster. As general manager throughout the excellent years of the twenties, he had received some praise for the company's performance; but when things began to turn sour, criticism far outweighed praise. Since he was the highest paid staff member, receiving an annual salary of $5000 compared with Jim's and Crosby's $3000, he also felt pressure to take a cut in salary. This he did in 1931, receiving just over $4000 for that year's labours, but as the situation worsened so did the feeling that he should be prepared to make even greater economies. His influence with the CPR had also disappeared with the death of C. E. Ussher and the retirement of Basil Gardom. These factors, combined with his continuing inablility to become a shareholder in Brewster Transport, weighed heavily in his decision to resign in 1933.

Having for the second time cut himself free of the company, Bill once more turned his attention to his own business interests. Within a few years he lined up both the lease on the new Texaco service station being constructed on the northwest corner of Banff Avenue and Caribou Street and the Ford Motor Company dealership in the area between Morley and the B.C. boundary. But, as had been the case over twenty years earlier in Montana, he had to rely on assistance from his family to get started. The dealership required his supplying $2500 working capital, a sum loaned in November by Phil Moore which Jim guaranteed. As part of the agreement Bill had to submit all cheques drawn on the loan to Jim or his designate, Bert Manley, to ensure that the money was being spent only for the purpose for which it was loaned. With this security in hand, Bill began what was to be a very successful business career in February, 1936, opening Brewster's Garage as a joint Texaco service and Ford dealership and repair.

Bill's departure from the company in 1933 put a great deal more responsibility on the shoulders of other employees, particularly Lou Crosby's. He too had been called upon to work a little harder and accept a little less during the depression, often bringing home the books at night and foregoing part of his salary in the slow winter months until business picked up again in the summer. In addition he had remained Jim's closest confidant and advisor, a position which required particular skill during a period when every decision regarding money had to be carefully weighed. Jim was inclined to go ahead with his schemes regardless of the situation while Crosby was cautious and examined all the pros and cons carefully. Often his temperate voice won out and he frequently prevented the company from getting into further difficulties. Beginning in 1933 his power and influence in Brewster Transport, which had been restricted to a degree during Bill's tenure as general manager, was unbridled and he became both respected and feared by employees and those dealing with the company.

Jim appreciated Crosby's loyalty and good judgement and in a measure repaid him for it by supporting his activities at Lake Louise. There were those both inside and outside the CPR who criticized him for operating a hotel in competition with the Chateau Lake Louise while being employed by Brewster Transport. Jim always stood up for him and defended his right to have a private business, particularly during Crosby's expansion of his premises in the spring of 1931 when Deer Lodge gained a new octagonal tower of Rundle stone and red brick which tied the two separate buildings together, giving it a fifty room capacity.

**Bill and Tead at the Kananaskis Ranch**

For Jim himself the depression years were the most frustrating and worrisome he had ever experienced. Apart from his companies' troubles, his personal financial affairs were in rough shape, leading to further drains on Brewster Transport's coffers in the form of $5000 bonuses he annually requested over and above his salary. Some of this money he needed because of his generosity in helping destitute families in Banff, assistance he refused to have acknowledged or repaid. Adding to his frustrations was the presence of a Conservative government in power at Ottawa led by his arch-enemy, R. B. Bennett. Bennett and Jim had had several run-ins over the years, a particularly memorable one occurring in the Palliser Hotel that ended with Jim calling the politician a "pot-bellied old buggar."

With Bennett as Prime Minister, Brewster Transport did not expect many favours at Ottawa, even though Bill Brewster had made a convenient switch to the Conservative party. Consequently much of Jim's time during these years was spent in political activity, beginning with his convincing Campbell McLaurin to run as the Liberal candidate in Calgary West in opposition to Bennett in the election of July, 1930. Despite the fact that McLaurin was beaten badly (365 votes to Bennett's 954 in Banff) Jim did not relent. His organizational work in the constituency continued and when Liberal leader Mackenzie King visited in August, 1933 Jim drove him from Calgary to Banff and Lake Louise while the press speculated that King would have "a heart-to-heart talk with the genial James I. before his departure, and the talk will not be altogether on the state of the tourist traffic through the park." Later on, in January, 1935, when an election was imminent and Jim was due to sail for Hawaii he was quoted as stating: "If Bennett calls an election before I get to Honolulu I'll jump off and start swimming back. If it is called before my visit is completed I'll get Amelia Earhart to fly me back. I've got to be in that fight no matter how I get here." When the election was finally held later that year he had the satisfaction of seeing King elected and having his own political influence reach its apex.

Skiing was another interest that Jim developed which helped to take his mind off the depression. Always keen on athletics of any kind, he could see that skiing would not only be enjoyable but would possibly hold the key to Banff's successfully breaking out of its mould of a one season town. Some of Banff's younger men, such as Cliff White and Cyril Paris, had already formed the Banff Ski Club in the mid-twenties and had begun clearing the slopes of Mount Norquay for ski runs and a lodge. Late in the twenties Jim himself learned to ski and in 1929 served as vice-president of the Banff Ski Club. In 1930 as chairman of the Banff Advisory Council, he called on the government to upgrade the access to Mount Norquay, and used all his influence to secure government and CPR support toward making skiing attractive to the visitor. In 1931 both he and Crosby were on the council of the newly formed Ski Runners of the Canadian Rockies, a CPR-sponsored attempt to do for skiing what the Trail Riders of the Canadian Rockies had

Jim and Mackenzie King

done for trail riding. Jim was also on the nominal executive of the Ski Club of the Canadian Rockies, Ltd., an organization likewise formed in 1931 to promote the development of the Skoki area north of Lake Louise. However, it was his own ski development on Sunshine Creek at the head of the Healy Creek drainage southwest of Banff that became his passion.

The Sunshine area had been a popular camping spot for trail parties ever since Walter Wilcox had passed through on his way to Mount Assiniboine in 1899. A. O. Wheeler, attempting to establish his Wheeler's Walking Tours to Mount Assiniboine, had used the meadows as the site for one of tent camps in the early twenties, and in 1928 the Trail Riders of the Canadian Rockies had built a cabin slightly to the north of the so-called Wheeler Flats. Some of the younger Banff skiers had used this cabin during the late twenties and early thirties but it was not until 1933, after being told of the possibilities of the area for ski development by his brother Pat, that Jim's interest was pricked. In late March, Jim, Dell, and Pat, accompanied by Ralph Harvey, Herb Paris,

Ed Hansen and Austin Standish, skied from Hillsdale through Shadow Lake to Egypt Lake and then over to the Trail Riders' cabin at Sunshine. Familiar with the area from summer visits, Jim had his doubts about its suitability for skiing dispelled. On returning to Banff, he and Pat reached an agreement to run a ski camp if the Trail Riders' cabin could be leased for the purpose. However, Pat soon withdrew because Jim placed Crosby in control of the financial end and thereafter Sunshine was run as a part of the Mount Royal Hotel.

Permission to use the "Sunshine Rest Cabin" for the spring of 1934 was secured from the CPR which, as sponsor of the Trail Riders, owned the structure. The eighteen by twenty-two foot cabin could sleep twelve people, ten guests and two staff to cook and guide for them. The first paying customers were a party from Vancouver who visted in February, 1934 and they were followed by several local patrons. One of these, Kay Jennings, daughter of the park superintendent, became Sunshine's first recorded casualty in late February when she fell and broke her ankle on the practice slope.

Jim, becoming more enthused about the area and its implications for the tourist business, mentioned in a letter that all the skiing "augurs well for developing more or less a winter resort in Banff and vicinity." Consequently he entered into a contract with the CPR in June, 1934 to lease the cabin for the following winter for $50. Staff were hired to run the cabin for the spring skiing of 1935 and information was circulated to various ski clubs quoting rates of $30 a week per person for food, lodging and guides. In February, 1935 a group from the Washington Ski Club took advantage of the offer and was guided by Ted Paris and Norman Knight during its stay. That year the CPR also put out its first ski brochure entitled "Ski the Canadian Rockies" advertising Skoki, Sunshine, Mount Assiniboine and Mount Norquay, a move which helped immeasureably.

By 1935 the country and the company were slowly beginning to emerge from the depression. Crosby, looking forward to a new period of expansion, and convinced that the Sunshine development could not carry its own weight, advised Jim to dispose of it. But Jim, with the bit in his teeth, for once strongly disagreed with Crosby's advice, feeling that Sunshine would eventually pay its own way. So sure was he that he renewed his lease with the CPR in the fall of 1935 and in 1936 negotiated for the purchase of their licence of occupation on the cabin and the quarter acre plot it stood on. In September, 1936, even before the purchase from the CPR was sealed, he had a gang of men at work near Simpson Pass getting out logs for the erection of a twenty-four by forty foot two-storey addition to the cabin. On October 20, 1936 the transfer of all the CPR's interests to Jim was completed. The total price — $300!

Pat, Dell and Jim at the Sunshine Trail Riders' cabin, 1933

Sunshine Suzy, ca. 1940

# XII: A Battle Joined

The enthusiasm Jim exhibited for Sunshine began to pervade other aspects of Brewster Transport as the depression loosened its grip. Recovery was neither rapid nor spectacular but it led to hope that the company was on the verge of an era of development akin to the twenties. Particularly heartening was the government's renewed attention to roads, both within and leading to the parks, resulting in the company's initiating several new projects.

Building and improving roads as relief projects had been the only benefit of the depression as far as tourism was concerned. In 1929 the Dominion and British Columbia governments jointly agreed to construct the Big Bend Highway, completing the western section of a cross Canada motor road. Avoiding the rugged Selkirks by following the northern arc of the Columbia River, the highway would link existing roads at Golden and Revelstoke and provide a "direct" route from the prairies through the parks to the Pacific coast. Both federal and provincial contributions to the project were cut at the depression's onset, jeopardizing the entire development until the Unemployment and Farm Relief Act of 1931 provided funding for some 200 men on relief to work on construction during the 1931-32 fiscal year. Another project utilizing unemployment relief funds, initiated in the fall of 1931, promised to be equally beneficial to tourism. This was the Banff-Jasper Highway that would provide a trip through some of the most majestic scenery on earth and access between the two largest mountain national parks. Work on both the Big Bend and Banff-Jasper projects went slowly, a result of the stipulation that they were to employ as much manpower and as little labour-saving machinery as possible. By 1934, when the Relief Act ended, sizeable portions of both highways still remained to be built, but both the federal and provincial governments were committed to their completion and work continued as the decade progressed.

Jim solidly favoured both the Big Bend and Banff-Jasper projects and the paving of the Calgary-Banff Highway, which was also progressing. He used all his personal and political influence in Ottawa to further them and also spoke in their favour as chairman of the Banff Advisory Council. In fact, the council meeting of November 6, 1936 endorsed his suggestion of "Canadian Icefields Highway" as the official name of the Banff-Jasper route. Earlier that fall both his historic connection with the route, harkening back to his part in the first Banff to Yellowhead Pass trip in 1904, and his company's future interest in the road were recognized when he was invited to accompany T. A. Crerar, Minister of Mines and Resources, on a tour of inspection of the highway route.

Although neither the Banff-Jasper nor the Big Bend Highway was officially opened until 1940, travel over their already completed sections before that time provided an additional attraction for tourists. Visitor statistics began to rebound from a depression low of 132,264 people in 1933 to a respectable 178,940 people in 1936.

Brewster Transport's financial picture tended to parallel these statistics. Its worst year was 1933, and then it began a slow but steady return to pre-depression levels. The company experienced a relatively small 1934 loss of $2700 and by 1935 it was back in the black with a profit of $5100. Unfortunately for the surplus account, that year Jim, advised by his accountants, eliminated the mounting personal account he had standing on the books from many years of charges and withdrawals. A dividend of $26,600 was declared in his favour, to wipe out his personal account, and a further $31,900 was charged against the surplus account as an adjustment for his travelling expenses from the inception of the company to date. These large withdrawals left the surplus account at a dangerously low $17,000, although the improving tourist situation quickly replenished it. Operating profits of $39,000 in 1936, $41,000 in 1937 and $21,000 in 1938 boosted the account beyond the $110,000 mark, and the company was making inroads into its heavy liabilities, Imperial Bank loans standing at $40,000 and CPR loans at $33,700 in 1939 compared with $180,000 and $97,200 respectively in 1934.

Brewster Transport 1937 Ford bus

The improvement in the financial picture came mainly from increased profits in the transportation department, even though it purchased little new equipment. During the six years between 1934 and 1939 it spent only about $100,000, the major addition coming in 1937 when it bought its first two Ford buses, 22-passenger models with bodies specially built in Winnipeg, through Bill Brewster's Ford agency. Other additions included three 5-passenger LaSalle sedans, one 6-passenger Packard sedan and two Ford baggage trucks in 1937 as well as three 5-passenger Packard sedans, one 5-passenger Ford sedan and two additional Ford baggage trucks in 1939. These barely accounted for replacement of old equipment: in 1939 fifty-two of the company's one hundred and three vehicles, with a replacement value in excess of $200,000, were more than ten years old. It is a fine testimonial to the mechanical staff's abilities that it was able to keep some of these machines on the road. All the staff, happy to have a job after the rough times earlier in the decade, pulled together to achieve these results.

The situation of company employees had improved steadily as the depression receded. Salaries returned to a reasonable level, about $70 per month for car drivers and $90 per month for bus drivers, by the end of the decade. In 1939 wages paid in the transportation department alone amounted to $30,400, a long way from the $12,200 of 1933. Additionally, employees were able to take part in a company group life insurance plan, the value of which was illustrated when the widow of a deceased employee who had been paying into it only four years, a total contribution of only $48, received a cheque for $2000. Management also benefitted from the improved situation, Jim's salary reaching $10,000 and Crosby's $6000 per annum by 1939.

As in the past, Lake Louise was the favoured company branch for staff to be posted to. Tom Kirkham, a young man from Lethbridge who had his first contact with Brewster Transport working at Waterton Lakes, secured employment with the company as a station despatcher at Louise in 1937 and recalled it fondly. His first day on the job he made all the tours around Lake Louise, the extent of his training, and then, issued a uniform and given instructions on how to sell people on using Brewster transportation services, he went to work. Part of the time, along with ticket agents Rupe Edwards and Ted Paris, he would stand at the front door of the Chateau and sell sightseeing trips to guests. Far more interesting was meeting the trains at the station where, like a circus barker, he would yell out "Brewster Transport for the Chateau Lake Louise" in competition with Rocky Mountain Tours' agent selling transportation to the Triangle Inn. When he had sold thirty 50 cent tickets or had collected as many pre-paid coupons from those on all-expenses paid tours, he turned them over to the driver who would then depart for the Chateau on his instructions. Train traffic was heavy, beginning with No. 1, the local from Vancouver to Calgary, in the morning, Nos. 3 and 4, The Maple Leaf or The Limited, at noon and then later in the day Nos. 7 and 8, The Imperial, and Nos. 13 and 14, the Soo Line train from Vancouver to Chicago.

Sometimes he would have orders for a private car which would be shined up and waiting at the station with a chauffeur. Usually these were for regular visitors who requested a particular driver they had become acquainted with and would wish to retain for the duration of their stay. Celebrities were almost an everyday occurrence and in 1937 included such notables as the Crown Prince of Japan, Ginger Rogers, Nordhoff and Hall, authors of *Mutiny on the Bounty,* and Douglas Fairbanks honeymooning with his bride, Lady Ashley. With this class of people using exclusive services, it was not unusual for a driver to receive a tip of one or two hundred dollars at the end of a visit.

One celebrity whose visit was not looked forward to, particularly by CPR employees, was Sir Edward Beatty, who annually made a tour of inspection of the western region. Those at the Chateau would work fourteen to sixteen hours a day to make sure that the hotel was spotless. The Beatty party's suite would be freshly painted and the print shop would work up special fluted-edged menus trimmed with gold leaf. Jim would drive Sir Edward wherever he wished to go during his stay and one such drive almost cost Kirkham his job. Coming down the hill from the Chateau in a company car, he met the Packard carrying Beatty driven by Jim "in the middle of the road as if he owned it" at a hairpin turn. To avoid hitting him Kirkham almost had to go over the edge of a precipice; the last thing he saw fading in the mirror as he continued down was Jim shaking his fist in the air. Luckily Jim's enquiries about the identity of the company driver who had almost run him and Sir Edward off the road were met with a shrug of the shoulders by other company employees.

In early August of that year a slide caused by a build up of meltwater escaping from a basin on Cathedral Mountain blocked the rail line. The CPR immediately called on Brewster Transport to form a land bridge around the slide, one of the severest tests the company had ever faced according to Kirkham, who was despatcher during the crisis. Fortunately there was a supply of buses at Field as some passengers normally got off the eastbound train there and visited Emerald Lake before being driven on to the Chateau. Kirkham got in touch with Lyle Currie at Field via a land line and together they organized the transfer of some five trainloads of passengers who were already backed up there. Using the vehicles he had, Currie despatched some passengers straight through to Banff where special trains were made up to take them on eastward. Once such a group reached Banff, the driver of the car or bus would return to Field and pick up the next load. Meanwhile, some trucks were hired to supplement the company's own baggage trucks and hauled the baggage to Lake Louise where the lobby of the Chateau, cleared of furniture, accommodated it until it could be shipped on. After three days the line was cleared and at the end of that time not one piece of baggage had been lost. Passengers expressed their pleasure at the manner in which the CPR had handled the situation and the railway handed the praise on to Brewster management and a very tired lot of company employees.

When Kirkham returned to work for Brewster Transport at Lake Louise in 1938, drivers could take their patrons as far as Peyto Lake on the Banff-Jasper Highway. Characteristically, Jim developed other new schemes to make the road a paying proposition. The first of these was the acquisition of a site for the construction of a combination hotel, restaurant and service station for those who would soon be travelling the new route. It was his brother Jack Brewster of Jasper who first brought the proposed site to his attention and suggested some sort of joint venture. The location was the choicest along the entire length of the highway, the foot of the stupendous Athabasca Glacier which reached down from the hydrographic apex of North America, the Columbia Icefield. The government granted permission for the construction of what would become known as the Columbia Icefield Chalet in 1938, although it was not until 1943 that the company submitted a survey plan showing the location and the government granted a formal licence of occupation (changed to a lease in 1966) for the ten acre site at an annual cost of $160. A plan, loosely based on a Swiss style chalet containing a three-storey central section and a two-storey wing, was settled on and Jack supervised the construction. Work began in the summer of 1938 and over $8600 was spent on the project that year; in 1939 an additional $28,000 was poured in.

At the same time Jim was seeking other ways to utilize the area. In 1938 Brewster's Mountain Pack Trains initiated horse tours from the uncompleted Lake Louise end of the highway to the Icefield. Jim accompanied some Hollywood VIPs on a trip in September, 1938, but the idea proved unfeasible because of logistical problems. By 1940 such trips were no longer necessary with the final completion of the highway, and he focused attention on getting the Icefield Chalet open for business. After the spending of another $6900 it was ready to greet its first customers that summer under Jack's management. Immediately it proved its worth, the 150-seat dining room initally being the most popular attraction. It grossed $18,000 compared with $5000 from room rental, $1700 from the garage and $1000 from the curio shop in the first season. This translated into a respectable $5700 profit.

Although the Columbia Icefield Chalet accounted for much of Brewster Transport's expenditures on real estate development at this time, several other important projects were on line. The growing enthusiasm for skiing dictated further development of the lodge at Sunshine and improved access to its location. Jim's personal efforts on behalf of the sport had helped secure the Dominion Ski Championships for Banff in 1937. Returning from the 1936 Winter Olympics in Germany, he was elected western vice-president of the Canadian Amateur Ski Association that April, whereupon he cooperated with other interested individuals to secure the championships. By fall they announced the success of their bid. Held during the first week of March at Mount Norquay, the event proved so successful that all transportation companies in Banff were taxed to the limit ferrying spectators back and forth. Jim realized it was the breakthrough in winter tourism he had sought so long. Immediately following the championship, in the second week of April, Sunshine held its first organized ski races. By the next spring these had become a popular annual event known as the Great Divide Championship Ski Tournament. The only factors which limited the numbers of spectators were the doubt there could be sufficient snow to hold races at Sunshine when there was none left at Banff and the difficulty of getting there.

Jim realized he must come to grips with the access problem if Sunshine were ever to fulfill its potential. Accordingly, in August, 1937, he requested government permission to improve the Healy Creek fire trail as far as Sunshine at his own expense. Approval was granted on the understanding that the park administration would direct the upgrading. Subsequently Jim did little or nothing, except use his influence to try to secure government involvement in the construction. Whatever transpired, the park had a crew at work on the trail beyond the Healy Creek warden cabin by December, 1937 and improvements continued the following summer with a small tractor, a plough and a grader. By December, 1938 it was possible to get a light truck in summer and a tracked vehicle in winter to "the ford" (today's Bourgeau Parking Lot), where the trail crossed Healy Creek some three miles from the lodge.

For access beyond "the ford" Fred Styles created a "snowplane" from airplane fuselage material. The machine, capable of carrying four people, was mounted on four skis and was powered by a five-and-a-half foot rear-mounted propellor, but it lacked the power to negotiate the steep grades. For the time being patrons had to ski the last three miles to the lodge. Two other

Modified Model "A" Ford at Sunshine Lodge, ca. 1941

Styles creations provided transportation from the Mount Royal Hotel to a halfway cabin built at "the ford." In the Brewster garage he fitted two Model "A" Ford Truck chassis with new engines and modified them with tank-like tracks on the rear and skis on the front. Capable of carrying only six to eight passengers, they were soon replaced by a specially built 1937 Ford bus which could be modified in a similar manner and could handle up to sixteen passengers. Described initially as a "snowmobile bus," this vehicle with its first driver, Lloyd Hunter, became very much a part of the Sunshine scene. One patron described it as "a species crossed between a sidehill gouger and a grizzly bear," but as time went on it became known affectionately as "Sunshine Suzy," probably the best-remembered piece of equipment the company operated. For a time its limit too was "the ford," but in the meantime, in spite of some government officials' opposition to the upgrading of a fire trail to a road for the sole benefit of Brewster Transport, construction continued on the Sunshine road at an expenditure of over $3000 of public funds. By the fall of 1940 it had reached timberline, just over a mile from the lodge, and in 1941 it was carried through to the lodge itself, allowing patrons to be delivered right to the door for a $1 fare.

At Sunshine the work on the lodge initiated in 1936, including the construction of a two-storey log addition with a large stone fireplace, continued in 1937 and 1938 at a cost nearing $10,000. Construction on a separate staff quarters was also underway. Accommodation and the price charged for it increased accordingly. In the spring of 1939 the house count reached sixty-five during the annual ski meet, taxing the facilities to the limit. The price on the American Plan was $5.50 per day or $35.00 per week for two or more to a room or $7.50 a day for single occupancy. A permanent staff ran the lodge and at least one ski instructor was on hand at all times. Fay Nowlin and his wife Madge were the first hosts and in 1938 Ina Mae Hummond, one of the company's premier "carriage agents" during the summer, succeeded them. The first full-time ski instructor was Ches Edwards, a local lad; after his departure in 1939 to become ski instructor for the Toronto Ski Club the first two in a long line of European instructors, Vic Kutschera and then Bruno Engler, replaced him. An innovation of 1938 was a radio communicating with the Mount Royal

Sunshine Lodge in summer use, ca. 1945

Hotel for messages about the number of guests to expect and their time of arrival.

Despite its improvements and better access, Sunshine did not immediately become a lucrative proposition. Gross revenue for 1940 amounted to only $9500 and, after deducting $2400 in inventories, $2900 in wages, $1700 in operating expenses and $500 in advertising, net revenue stood at $2000 before depreciation. An agreement with the government signed in April, 1939 to secure renewal of the licence of occupation required the company to pay a five percent concession fee on the net revenue after deducting interest charges paid on money borrowed for capital expenditure.

The small winter season returns from his investment led Jim to promote Sunshine as a summer resort for riding, hiking, fishing and climbing by the late thirties, bringing him into open conflict with the park administration which disliked non-government access on what was essentially a fire road in the summer season. Jim did not hesitate to use what influence he had in Ottawa and in 1941 an agreement allowed his vehicles one trip in and one trip out per day at designated times. Meanwhile, in an associated development, in October, 1938 the company purchased the Shadow Lake Rest House, built by the CPR in 1934, for $200. Jim felt it could be worked into the company's summer program at Sunshine quite well.

While Sunshine and the Columbia Icefield Chalet were new and exciting developments in the post-depression period, some attention was also going to Brewster Transport's older properties in Banff. The Brewster Hall had languished unoccupied for several years. Since the company had no plans of its own for its resurrection, management responded favourably when the Diamond brothers, owners of Braemar Lodge in Calgary, inquired about renovating and re-opening it as a cabaret in the summer of 1937. Sam Diamond agreed to pay a $25 monthly rental and to improve heating, flooring and doors. With music supplied by the Braemar Lodge Orchestra, "Norquay Lodge," as it was renamed, proved fairly successful, except that renovations cost the Diamonds much more than they had anticipated. The company cut the rental in half and the Mount Royal Hotel agreed to lease back the premises for the winter months and offer them to local clubs and organizations for meetings, socials and dances. Further renovations on the upper floor provided a six-lane bowling alley for the coming season. Haplessly, the bowling alley was short-lived; in July, 1938 an early morning fire caused by a careless smoker gutted the upper floor. After Brewster Transport collected on its insurance policies and paid the Diamonds $1800 for lost improvements, the top storey was removed and the building again lapsed into somnolence, serving mainly as a dormitory for company drivers.

Its parent across Caribou Street, the Mount Royal Hotel, was on the verge of its first major expansion in several years. The hotel's problems in the second half of the decade, after having performed so admirably during the depression, reduced profits from near $4700 in 1935 to $670 by 1936, largely because of the increased costs of repairs to the building and more realistic depreciation rates on furniture, fixtures and equipment. Through 1938 revenue remained almost constant, but operating costs increased appreciably, leading to a $1275 loss for the year. On the positive side, in 1938 management eliminated the final $4500 owing on the original McDougall mortgage for the purchase of the hotel twenty-six years previously. Free of encumbrances, the company now felt secure to approach the Imperial

Mount Royal Hotel 1940 addition and Garage

Remains of Brewster Hall, 1938

Bank to borrow money for a much needed expansion.

Construction on the addition to occupy the space between the hotel and the Mount Royal Garage commenced in February, 1940. Plans included thirty-one new rooms, retail space opening onto Banff Avenue on the main floor and renovations to several rooms in the old part of the hotel. The work was performed by Lars Willumsen at a total cost of $69,300, and the addition was ready for occupancy by June, 1940. Adorning its façade, in a tribute to Brewster Transport's origins, was Charlie Beil's plaque illustrating two men packing a horse. Manager McCallum quickly put the new space to good use and got back on the right track with a profit of $2200 for the year.

Brewster Transport's subsidiary, Royal Hawaiian Transport, also had a substantial impact on the company in these years, proving that Jim's faith in its future during the depths of the depression was not misplaced. In 1934, as the islands began to emerge from the depression, Jim resolved for the next couple of years to reduce its capital debts, a commitment that included acquiring no new vehicles in favour of renting cars when the company's fleet of eighteen could not handle the load at peak periods. With the return of numbers of tourists to Hawaii, the policy produced immediate results with net operating revenue of $35,400 and a profit of $5200 in 1934 compared with net operating revenue of $19,200 and a loss of $5200 in 1933. A profit of $11,100 in

**Royal Hawaiian Transport buses at the Royal Hawaiian Hotel, mid '30's**

1935 got Royal Hawaiian out of the red, and in December of the same year a reevaluation of the capital stock helped to erase the company's debts. The major debt on the books was $21,800 still outstanding on the 530 shares of Royal Hawaiian Transport (Hawaii) stock originally owed for by Royal Hawaiian Transport (Alberta). However, this stock Brewster Transport had owed for directly since 1934 when the Alberta company was dissolved. The best way for Brewster Transport to eliminate this debt and a further $11,000 it owed on purchases of vehicles from Royal Hawaiian was to devalue the authorized capital. This step was taken in December, 1935 when the stock was decreased in value from one thousand shares at $100 each to the same number valued at $25 each.

Jim's objective now reached, the company invested in some additional equipment, four new Dodge sedans in 1935 and ten vehicles, mostly used Cadillacs, Packards and Oldsmobiles, in 1936. For the first time in its history the company declared a dividend, sixty percent of the surplus account amounting to $9200. The following year it acquired two service stations, at Waikiki and Nuuanu, and still managed a $6100 profit and a fifteen percent dividend on profit.

Given the improving situation in the affairs of Royal Hawaiian, it was somewhat a surprise in 1938 when Jim decided to sell out. His reasons for doing so are not known but likely had something to do with the lapse of his contract with the Territorial Hotel Company and the negotiations for renewal. Another possibility is that the worsening international situation led him to conclude Brewster Transport should shed its vulnerable foreign ties. Whatever the motivation, a sale to Earl Thacker netted Brewster Transport a profit of $12,600 over and above its share of the book value of the company. Three years later the deal looked like a stroke of genius when, after Pearl Harbor, tourism in Hawaii was completely shut down, a blow the company could never have withstood.

The beginning of the forties found Brewster Transport in a fairly strong position vis-à-vis its properties and its total financial situation. However, the transportation department, although it was performing well, would soon face the problem of aging equipment. Two other dark clouds loomed on the horizon, the effect of the war on tourism, and new competition in the transportation field. Although the war had not produced any serious effects by 1940, Jim and Crosby, recalling what the First World War had done to the company, feared the coming years. More immediate was the threat the changing transportation picture in the mountain parks presented.

Competition in livery business, be it horse-drawn or motorized, had always been a fact of life for the company, and it philosophically accepted competitors such as Rocky Mountain Tours and other small resident operators. But when the question of non-resident operators had first become controversial in the early twenties, Jim and the company management consistently fought against them, albeit rather unsuccessfully. The issue took on a renewed relevance with the imminent completion of the Big Bend and Banff-Jasper Highways and the Edmonton-Jasper road, which would undoubtedly attract more outside competition. Particularly worrisome were the actions of a fast-growing stage line, Greyhound Lines, operated by the secretive transportation genius George B. Fay.

Fay, originally from Chicago, began as a bus salesman for General Motors in Western Canada, but in time the possibilities of operating inter-community bus service in the area intrigued him. With Speed and George Olsen from Victoria, who had transportation interests at the coast, and John Learmonth, who ran a small bus company out of Nelson, B.C., he began a company called Canadian Greyhound Coaches in 1929. Initially it ran buses from Calgary to Waterton Lakes and then on to Nelson, but by 1934 it had twenty buses running on routes north to Edmonton, west to Trail, B.C. and east to Swift Current, Saskatchewan. Brewster Transport had, of course, earlier held the rights to several stage line routes in Alberta but, with the exception of the Banff-Calgary run, had let them lapse. Fay desired the Banff run more than any other and had set his cap on acquiring it at all costs. Jim felt it was secure in his brother George's hands, but Greyhound had been able to acquire running rights between Edmonton and the Jasper Park gate. Jim's concern was that with improvements of the Edmonton-Jasper road and the completion of the Banff-Jasper Highway Greyhound might gain entry to Banff through the back door.

Since other resident operators in Banff and Jasper had similar fears, they sought a way to protect themselves. Beginning in the fall of 1938 Jim and Crosby discussed with them and with the government officials ways to achieve such protection. Quickly it became apparent from government response that if they acted as individuals they would accomplish little, but an organization embracing all resident livery operators might bargain forcibly. There were inherent dangers for Brewster Transport in the idea since, as company lawyer McLaurin warned, it could seriously weaken the company's preeminent position unless the company could have a voice in the organization's affairs corresponding to its status as the major operator in the parks. Nonetheless, Jim decided to proceed and met with other Banff concerns. At the same time the three largest interests at Jasper, Jasper Park Lodge, Mountain Motors and the Athabasca Hotel, met and decided to proceed in concert with the Banff interests. The formation of Banff and Jasper branches of "the Canadian Rocky Mountains Parks Motor Livery Operators Association" followed. Representations to the government continued and succeeded when an Order-in-Council, dated September 25, 1939, empowered the minister to negotiate an exclusive franchise for motor livery operations within the parks as soon as the organization was formalized with a constitution and by-laws. This would bring the motor transport business into line with procedures that had been in place in American parks for many years.

Jim, McLaurin and Ralph Harvey drafted a proposed constitution and by-laws and then called a meeting of all interested parties at the Mount Royal Hotel on November 12th. The well-attended meeting passed the constitution. Its major articles were that the association was for the betterment of motor livery services in Banff, Jasper, Kootenay and Yoho National Parks and that membership was open to all firms, persons and corporations which on March 30, 1939 were resident in and held motor livery licences for passenger transportation in any of those parks. By-laws enacted at the same meeting instructed that each member in good standing would have one vote plus one additional vote for every ten vehicles licensed over a basic ten and that members would be entitled to pay up to twenty-five percent commissions for business contracted outside the parks. While there were several other by-laws enacted, these two were the key ones from Brewster Transport's point-of-view. Its interests as the largest operator in the parks and its dependence on foreign and domestic tour agencies for its business were protected.

An election at the meeting chose an executive consisting of Jim as president, Jim McLeod as vice-president for Banff and Crosby as secretary-treasurer. Under their leadership the association turned its attention to negotiating the franchise and implementing new livery tariffs.

This latter item had become contentious since large companies, like Brewster Transport and Rocky Mountain Tours, favoured a uniform tariff while smaller companies regarded tariff rates as a maximum charge they were free to undercut. The issue required some urgency as there had been no revision in the livery tariff since 1925. Despite the differences, members of the Banff branch of the Motor Livery Operators' Association ultimately agreed on a proposal to the government that, with some notable changes and additions, left the 1925 rates intact. Changes were mainly decreases, reflecting the beliefs of the small operators and the government that rates were too high. Notable examples were a lessening in the round trip fare from Banff to Lake Louise from $8.25 to $6.25, round trip from Banff to Lake Minnewanka including launch trip from $3.25 to $2.50 and round trip from Lake Louise to Emerald Lake from $8.25 to $6.25. Additions included Banff to Emerald Lake continuous day trip via Lake Louise and Yoho Valley for $12.50, Banff to Mount Norquay for $1.00, Lariat Trail for $30.00, Lake Louise to Columbia Icefield for $12.50 return and Lake Louise to Jasper for $13.50 one way or $22.50 return. R. A. Gibson, Director of the National Parks Branch, agreed to these rates for the 1940 season but pointed out that final rates would depend on the franchise.

The association had been hoping to pay about two percent of each member's operating revenues for the franchise but the department held out for five percent. Negotiations dragged on through the winter and it became obvious that if the association did not give in it would be denied an agreement for the summer of 1940. This was particularly ominous, given that Greyhound and some smaller stage lines had submitted a brief to Gibson opposing any franchise. At the last possible moment, on July 3rd, a meeting at the Columbia Icefield Chalet accepted the five percent figure. The government, in turn, agreed to grant the franchise for one year when all members had signified their acceptance.

Brewster Transport had been eager to have the franchise matter settled quickly so it could take advantage of an opportunity the impending opening of the Big Bend Highway offered. George Brewster had fortuitously acquired a licence from the British Columbia government to operate from the eastern boundary of the province through to Vancouver via the Big Bend, which, combined with his Calgary-Banff run, was a powerful instrument. Jim worked out an arrangement with him that allowed Brewster Transport to provide service from Waterton Lakes through Calgary and Banff to Revelstoke where, by agreement with B.C. Coach Lines, passengers could connect for Vancouver. Passengers would

**BREWSTER'S NEW BIG BEND**

**MOTOR SERVICE**

**BANFF TO VANCOUVER**

**To the Pacific via new TRANS-CANADA EVERGREEN HIGHWAY—725 miles across the beautiful Selkirks and rugged Canadian Rockies—a seemingly never-ending panorama of unsurpassed scenic grandeur.**

The rushing torrents of the Fraser ,Columbia, Kicking Horse and Bow Rivers—innumerable canyons, waterfalls, snow-capped peaks and glaciers.

See this all by daylight, with overnight stops at Kamloops and Revelstoke. The route is via the newly opened BIG BEND HIGHWAY, through Yoho, and Banff National Parks. Short stops at outstanding beauty spots such as Lake Louise Kicking Horse Canyon, Natural Bridge, Surprise Rapids, Kinbasket Lake, Silver Tip Falls, etc.

Many species of Big Game are frequently seen. Cool forests of Maple, Cedar, Pine and Spruce tower above the highway. Countless varieties of wild flowers in the valley and upon the mountain side, fill the air with their fragrance.

**Visit this wonderland of refreshing contenment via new Deluxe Motor Coach Service. Convertible tops assure maximum in sight-seeing while traveling through the Park area. There is nothing comparable in America**

**See Us Today For Rates and Schedules**

Our reputation for courtesy assures every comfort on this romantic voyage by land on which you re-discover the trails of the Fur Traders and the Indians.

**Not just another trip—it is an unforgettable experience**

**Brewsters Transport Company Ltd.**

**BANFF ALBERTA**

leave Waterton Lakes and Revelstoke each morning at 7:30 and would reach the other end of the route the following evening after an overnight stop in Banff. During the park portion of the trip they would be carried in open sightseeing buses and short stops would be made at points of interest like Lake Louise, the Natural Bridge on the Kicking Horse, Surprise Rapids and Kinbasket Lake. After the official opening of the Big Bend on June 29th, the first run on this route was made in early July.

By the time the new service began, Jim's hope the association's franchise would forestall Greyhound from competing with Brewster Transport for any business in the park had been dashed. Fay, a tenacious opponent, through his own influence had succeeded in gaining secondary running rights from the provincial government between Calgary and the park gate. These rights were for non-stop service only, but an agreement with the Parks Branch, opposed by Brewster Transport and others, allowed Greyhound into the park as far as Banff townsite. Restrictions on the size of the buses allowed on park roads prevented its being granted the privilege of running through the parks. Similar agreements allowed Greyhound access to townsites in other parks, namely Jasper and Field.

Spurred by these successes, Fay found a way to circumvent the problem of access to the parks beyond these townsites. Through an agreement with one of the Banff members of the association, R. F. Colebrook, Greyhound transferred its passengers to vehicles meeting all criteria in terms of ownership and size for their tours in or passage through the parks. Since these trips originated outside the parks, the fares were not governed by the government tariff schedule and Fay, intent on showing park operators and particularly Brewster Transport in a bad light, kept them extremely low. He was willing to subsidize them from more lucrative runs so that, for example, it was cheaper for a passenger to take a trip from Calgary to Lake Louise on Greyhound and Colebrook buses than it was to take a trip from Banff to Lake Louise on a Brewster bus. Similarly the Greyhound-Cole-

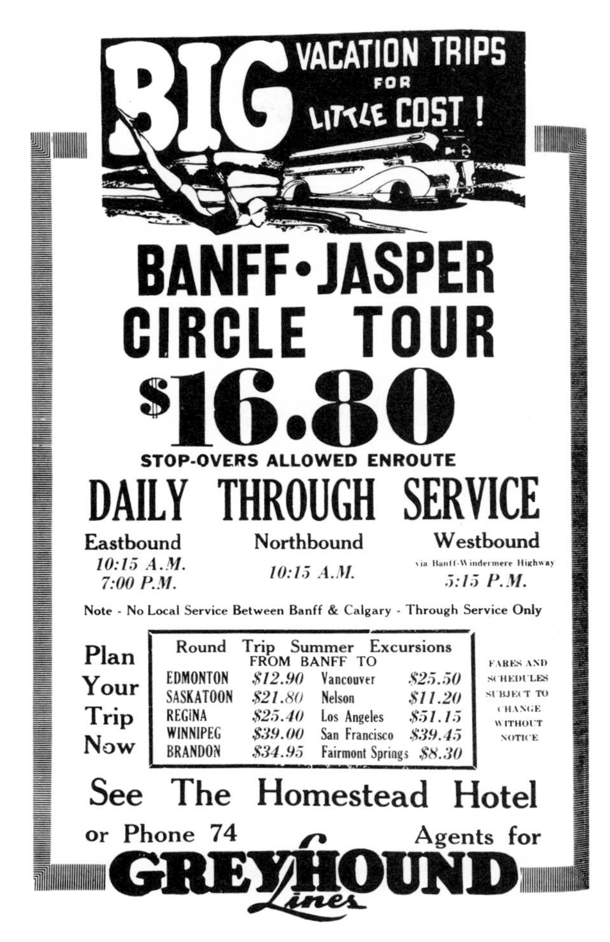


brook "Grand Circle Tour" which included Banff, Jasper, Edmonton and Calgary cost only $16.80 while a one-way ticket from Lake Louise to Jasper by Brewster Transport cost $13.50. Greyhound could also compete with Brewster Transport on its new service to Vancouver, although not by the Big Bend route. Using Colebrook vehicles and operating out of a bus depot at the Homestead Hotel, Greyhound provided transportation between Banff and Radium while it and B.C. carriers with which it had agreements completed the rest of the route.

Clearly Fay and his company had won the first round of the battle and had delivered a setback to Brewster Transport's hopes. But now that he could see the full extent of the opposition's intentions, Jim resolved to use every means to deter it.

Jim relaxing in his home, ca. 1940

# XIII: Death of the Mountain King

When Brewster Transport joined battle against Greyhound, Jim felt that he and the company were in a strong position to fight. Years of association with the CPR and his close personal friendship with Sir Edward Beatty were, he felt, valuable weapons. His political influence seemed as strong as ever with Mackenzie King firmly ensconced as Prime Minister in Ottawa and, for the first time in over twenty-five years, a Liberal sitting in the Calgary West federal seat. His personal fame was riding high, largely a result of his attendance on King George VI and Queen Elizabeth during their visit to Banff in 1939. Yet these factors weighed very little in the contest and not at all when the effects of the world war made themselves devastatingly felt in the tourist transport business.

Jim's part in the Royal Visit of 1939 was unquestionably the high point of his career. During a trip to Ottawa in 1938 he had pressed the government on behalf of the Banff Board of Trade to make money available to bring 100 Indians to Banff to greet the royal couple on its arrival. Other details of the visit were also discussed and he was apparently chosen to escort them in the Rockies. That he was the best qualified person to do so was unquestioned since his association with royalty and nobility went back to 1901 when the Duke of Cornwall and York, later King George V, stopped off in Banff as part of a Canadian tour and the nineteen-year-old Jim had acted as his interpreter in his conversations with the Stoneys. Numerous other encounters had followed. During the visit to Banff of the Duke of Connaught, Governor-General of Canada, in 1914 Jim offered his services as a guide for a canoe trip down the Bow River from Lake Louise. Greeted by a contingent of Mounted Police when their canoe docked at Banff, His Excellency learned the First World War had been declared. When Edward, Prince of Wales, first visited the Rockies in 1919, Jim was introduced to him and later accompanied him and his brother, the Duke of Kent, in games of golf and other activities during subsequent visits. In fact, the King was the only male member of the British Royal House whom Jim had not met when he arrived at Banff on May 26, 1939.

On the morning following their arrival Jim drove a shining new red Packard, purchased specially for the occasion, up to the Banff Springs Hotel and was presented to the King and Queen by Prime Minister King. The party then embarked for a drive through the town to Tunnel Mountain, where he accompanied them for a walk up the path to the summit, answering their queries about tourism, wild animals and his own involvement in the Rockies. Delivering them back to the hotel for lunch, he went to fetch a democrat for an afternoon ride around the Loop.

When the Queen had requested such an outing for their itinerary, Jim had found himself in an embarrassing position for the owner of a company that had once depended on horse-drawn vehicles. Brewster Transport had long since disposed of its last democrat and he had scoured the area for one before being successful at the Sarcee Indian Reserve near Calgary. Unfortunately the specimen was old and rickety, with wobbly wheels and springs sticking up through the seats, requiring the employees in the Brewster garage to spend a week getting it back in shape. The upholstery problem they solved by supplying two buffalo robes for Their Majesties to sit on, but the wheels were more difficult to repair. According to Jim's later account, as they were jolting around the Loop the Queen piped up, "Brewster, do you think this wheel's going to come off?" Jim replied, "No, ma'am, this buggy's good for a thousand miles." Laughing, the Queen replied, "I'm afraid we won't be with you quite that far." Happily the wheel did hold up and they were able to spend an enjoyable afternoon walking and being driven around the scenic golf course.

That evening Jim again drove the royal couple, first to the Green Spot on Stoney Squaw Mountain for a view up the valley and then along the shore of Vermilion Lakes to look for wildlife. Good fortune was with them and they saw both game and fowl, an occurrence that led the Queen to question Jim about his renowned collection of big game trophies. On the spur of the moment she asked if they could see the collection and he

"Brewster, do you think this wheel's going to come off?"

quickly agreed, even though his wife Dell would have no forewarning of their coming. As Jim put it, "I may forget a lot of things about the royal visit but never my wife's face when we walked in the door. She was so excited she nearly fainted, and her face was white as a sheet. However, it wasn't two minutes till the Queen and she were chatting away like old friends." The visit lasted more than half an hour, Jim explaining about trophy heads, Indian beadwork and other curiosities he had gathered in his travels. The King took an interest in the Simpson blaze which Jim had recovered in 1904 and he related its history and the discovery of it.

The following morning Jim drove the King and Queen to services at the Anglican Church and then took them up to Lake Louise for a visit to the Chateau. Afterwards they continued along to the Yoho Valley viewpoint and then to Field. There, before boarding their train, the King and Queen bade him farewell and thanked him for making their stay so enjoyable. So ended Jim's involvement in the visit, but not the notoriety it sparked. Reporters clamoured for interviews, and many lengthy newspaper reports were published about the man who had met Their Majesties on such informal terms. However, a rather blasé *Crag and Canyon,* familiar with Jim's former association with royalty, regarded it as only fitting that their "Jim" should be so honoured:

> Their Majesties conferred on Mr. J. I. Brewster the honour of being their chosen guide and companion for a day and a half. In so honouring Mr. Brewster, Their Majesties equally honoured Banff, for at no other place did other than officials drive or accompany them around, and with no other citizens did they allow official protective barriers to be lowered as they were lowered here.
>
> That they should so do was to be expected. More than once has "Jim" Brewster

driven and travelled as a companion with the present Duke of Windsor, when as Prince of Wales he visited these parts. . . .

With his knowledge of the Park, and of its development and history and his association with the former Prince of Wales, it was both logical and fitting that he should receive Their Majesties' invitation.

Unhappily, when it came to the nuts and bolts of business such plaudits did not count for much. Jim first had this brought home to him in his opposition to Greyhound in 1940 and it was even further exemplified in 1941. Late in the fall of 1940 he had heard two very interesting pieces of information. The first was that the majority of shares in Central Canadian Greyhound Lines, as the company was now known, had been sold to the American company whose name Fay had originally borrowed, Greyhound Lines of Chicago. The second was that Fay, now managing director of the company, had applied to the B.C. Public Utilities Commission to run scheduled service over the Big Bend route. Greyhound had made an initial bid to gain running rights on the Big Bend in 1940, shortly after Brewster Transport had begun its service, but Jim, in Vancouver for a hearing on the application, had successfully opposed it. He was not so sure he would succeed a second time and began marshalling all available forces to back him up.

Jim felt that his and the association's trump cards in the situation were the railroads, and he personally appealed both to Sir Edward Beatty and to S. J. Hungerford, Chairman and President of the CNR, for their support. His ploy was to place before them the bogey that the granting of running rights to Greyhound would be just a prelude to its carrying freight, or, even worse, obtaining trucking privileges through the mountains. It was effective: both men wrote to the Minister of Mines and Resources expressing their concerns. He responded that trucking rights were not contemplated through the parks but that the regulations respecting buses were to remain unchanged. This did nothing to help Brewster Transport's position, and McLaurin pointed out to Jim the railways would have to make much stronger representations on the operators' behalf. Neither man knew that Central Canadian Greyhound Lines, before being sold to Greyhound of Chicago, had been offered to the CPR and had been turned down. Obviously the CPR did not take the threat posed by Greyhound very seriously from its own point-of-view, much less Brewster Transport's.

Jim then communicated directly with R. A. Gibson to convince him of the soundness of his arguments opposing Greyhound. He bluntly asked that the Parks Branch prevent Greyhound from travelling in Yoho Park, using the approach that it was an American-controlled company siphoning off revenue that should go to Canadians and that its buses would be forerunners of transport trucks on park roads. Jim also let it slip that he felt the Liberal member in Calgary West, Manley Edwards, was in the camp of Greyhound and the Truck Operators' Association of Alberta and that he had "certainly lost a tremendous amount of prestige among the people who elected him such a short time ago." Gibson's reply is unrecorded but he likely informed Jim that the matter was already at the ministerial level and out of his hands.

The minister's decision was, of course, the same one that had been given to Beatty and Hungerford — to allow Greyhound the same privileges as the year previously. Jim's last ditch appeal to a war-preoccupied Mackenzie King brought no more than a referral back to the minister. With no alternative left, he accepted the decision he had feared from the B.C. Public Utilities Commission. Greyhound would receive through rights but not be allowed to run local service over the Big Bend route. It became apparent that Greyhound would cut fares were Brewster Transport to compete head-on. As the profit on the run was not spectacular, Jim felt that his company could not compete and discontinued its service.

Greyhound had a further surprise in store for the 1941 season. During the early months of the year, Jim, as president of the Motor Livery Operators' Association, was discussing renewing the franchise with the government. The government insisted on lowering some tariffs for 1941, a maximum concession of fifteen percent on all business contracted outside the park boundaries and members' agreement to make financial records available to a Board of Transport Commissioners economist so that he might determine a suitable long-term tariff for 1942. If the association didn't accept the conditions the government threatened to allow outside competitors to operate in the parks and perhaps to allow Greyhound even more privileges than it already enjoyed. The association members, with a few exceptions, signed the agreement.

One who didn't sign was the Madsen Sightseeing Company, a small Banff business owned by R. K. Madsen that had enjoyed indifferent success over the years. In March, 1941 Jim learned that Madsen had acquired several new buses. Their source soon became obvious — Greyhound was purchasing the vehicles for Madsen with the intent of running them on its through routes and over the Banff-Jasper Highway as it had done with Colebrook the year before. Jim again fired off complaints to the Department of Mines and Resources pointing out that this was a "smart practice" on Greyhound's part, that the department was "allowing an American outfit to edge in on everything that had cash in sight" and that the Motor Livery Operators' Association now felt that their organization "is of no value to them at all, either in protection or Government word." Despite Jim's threats that "the question should be brought to the floor of the house," department officials remained unmoved. Actually they could do little since Greyhound was buying Madsen out, thereby becoming through its subsidiary a member of the Motor Livery Operators' Association.

Although Jim continued his fulminations against the Greyhound threat to both his own company and the association, he had not received the most telling blow. Armed with new American capital, Fay was determined to get the coveted rights to the Banff-Calgary local run. The approach he used was to purchase five new deluxe convertible Cadillacs for the Madsen Sightseeing Company's use. Along with their two 12-passenger International buses they became bargaining points in his discussions with George Brewster concerning a possible Greyhound acquisition of the run. George had recently become associated with his brother Bill in the Brewster Auto Service, the location he was using for his bus terminal, and was already running a few vehicles for sightseeing purposes as a member of the Motor Livery Operators' Association. Fay offered him the Cadillacs and the buses Madsen operated in return for the rights to the run. Included in the package would be an agreement whereby George would carry all Greyhound passengers brought into the park on any sightseeing trips they desired and would overload for Greyhound on the Banff-Calgary run. The offer was too tempting to refuse and in February, 1942 Greyhound announced it was taking over the local run. For George it was the beginning of a new career as the owner of a venture to be known as Brewster's Skyline Tours, but for Jim it must have been a bitter pill to swallow.

Within a month Brewster Transport had to face a far more serious threat. The Second World War in two-and-a-half years had not detrimentally affected tourism in the Canadian Rockies. Armed forces personnel on leave from Commonwealth training programs taking place in Western Canada had largely replaced visitors from abroad. The threat to tourism was not a lack of tourists but rationing. Gas rationing, announced in November, 1941, required tourist transportation companies to carefully plan their 1942 campaigns. It was going to be difficult but they accepted it given the gravity of the situation. The next orders from Ottawa were devastating. In mid-March, 1942 the government's transit controller announced that as a measure to conserve gas and rubber no further sightseeing trips were to be taken by bus or car. Despite the transportation companies' pleas that they could run on existing tires and that their gas consumption was only a drop in the bucket, the transit controller made it plain that there were to be no exceptions.

The effect on Brewster Transport was immediate and severe. At the time of the announcement the garage staff was repairing, painting and refurbishing company vehicles for a normal summer season. All work halted and some employees were laid off, even though a substantial amount of money had already been spent in getting some machines partially prepared. By the time the season arrived the full extent of the ban was being felt. CPR officials announced that the Chateau Lake Louise would not open, thereby leaving Crosby's Deer Lodge as the ony major hostelry to handle those coming to the world-famous beauty spot. A good portion of the Brewster vehicles, particularly buses, were stored in Brewster Hall and in the old upper stables on Spray Avenue. The few vehicles remaining in service a later ruling allowed to take sightseeing trips to a maximum of fifteen miles. Runs to such points as Mount Norquay, Sundance Canyon and Lake Minnewanka that the relaxation allowed were not lucrative for a company the size of Brewster Transport, although some smaller operators, such as Skyline Tours, did well on them. As a result, gross operating revenue from transportation, which had stood at $166,000 two years previously, plunged to slightly over $25,000. Total wages decreased by two thirds from near $30,000 to about $10,000. A profit of $26,000 on all company interests in 1940 had turned into a loss of $20,000 by 1942.

If the company were to survive the crisis it would have to take drastic measures. Least difficult was an understanding with the CPR concerning the outstanding loan and payments of annual rents and commissions. The railway company readily agreed to charge no interest on the loan and waive all rents and commissions until business picked up. A decision as to what to do with excess equipment had to be dealt with . Not knowing exactly what the future held, Jim and Crosby decided to sell off some of the older, depreciated vehicles a bit at a time. During 1942 seventeen buses were sold to buyers who for the most part intended to strip them down and use them for trucks. The $11,775 income arising from the disposal of these units the company put into a special surplus account, presumably intended for the purchase of new equipment when the war ended. A final and much more difficult measure the management had to take was to lay off more staff. Not only did this include summer staff but also permanent staff who, like James Forteath with twenty-five years to his credit, had been with the company for long periods of time. Office staff was not immune; transportation manager Ralph Harvey went to Edmonton as transit supervisor for the Wartime Transportation Board and others were let go. Only Bert Manley and secretary Kay Ward were left to assist Jim and Crosby.

Undoubtedly everyone hoped that the war would end soon, but when it didn't the company's 1942 measures had to be perpetuated. In 1943 the Banff Springs Hotel was also closed and the transportation picture looked bleak. Transportation gross revenue did not reach the $6000 level and more excess equipment was sold off, this time twenty-two buses for a meagre $6500. In spite of it all, the company reported a small profit of $700 on its total operations for the year, seemingly a contradiction in the circumstances. It was mainly due to the excellent returns received from two of its three accommodation enterprises, the Mount Royal Hotel and Sunshine Lodge.

Historically the Mount Royal did better during bad times than good and fortunately this tendency held true. Under McCallum's capable management the expanded facilities of 1940 allowed for an increase of room revenue from $30,900 to $42,500 between 1940 and 1942. Part of this success many have been attributable to a heightened advertising campaign which included a high quality brochure devoted to the hotel and its services. At the same time the reputation of the dining room was also growing and its net revenue doubled to $7300 in the same period. In 1942 total profits from the hotel, $16,400, were by far the largest single item in Brewster Transport's profit and loss account. Clearly if anything were to carry the company through the war it would be the Mount Royal. This was even more obvious in 1943 with the closing of the Banff Springs Hotel. Its largest competitor removed, the hotel faced enormous pressure during peak periods. Rooms were completely booked at such times, leading to another big jump in revenue to $60,000, and the dining room often could not accommodate all comers.

Profit from the hotel reached $34,900 that year, helping to offset the $7900 loss on transportation operations. Unable to increase revenue more from its existing facilites, Jim realized the hotel would have to add rooms as quickly as possible. Aware that the company could not afford another major addition to the structure, he opted in favour of an annex for the hotel in an addition to a building the company owned across Caribou Street. On a valuable corner lot the company had purchased from the Imperial Bank, the building had been erected in 1940 and rented out as retail space to the Hudson's Bay Company. Construction on the addition commenced in September, 1944 and sixteen rooms were ready for occupancy early in the new year. The $11,800 cost was vindicated in the 1945 year-end statement which showed a rise in room revenue to $88,600.

The annex helped the financial picture of the Mount Royal but failed to win acclaim from the hotel staff. Bellhops had to trundle luggage across the street and upstairs without the benefit of an elevator and embarassed management had to assign rooms to prominent customers in the less than desirable surroundings of the annex. Jack Oakie, the actor, balked at being given a room not in the main hotel but, told that his room would have a nice view and was over "the bay," he relented. The poor bellhop who took him to the room was the one who had to explain that "the bay" was a department store and not a beautiful body of water.

Meanwhile, skiing at Banff continued its growth in popularity during the war with the facilities improving. In December, 1939 a group which included Calgary businessmen Eric Harvie and J. B. Cross formed Canadian Rockies Winter Sports Ltd. and built a new clubhouse at Mount Norquay in time for the Dominion Ski Championships hosted in late February and early March, 1940. The following winter Lou Crosby became president and managing director of the company in time to oversee the installation of the first permanent ski tow in the Canadian Rockies. Such developments attracted more skiers, as did improved access to the other major ski area at Sunshine. There Jim was finding that increasing use, particularly by soldiers on leave, meant growth in revenue from the mediocre levels at the beginning of the war to the point where it too was becoming a factor in the company's wartime survival. In 1942 gross revenue reached $19,500, and for the first time Sunshine was treated as an entity separate from the Mount Royal Hotel.

With this rise in popularity skiers pressed for better facilities. At the time there were two major ski runs at Sunshine, Brewster Rock, so named because it was as far as Jim would go on his skis, and Twin Cairns Peak, described in company advertising as "long swift mountain runs down thrilling changes of gradient unbroken by any obstacle." But there were no ski tows, which growing numbers of downhill skiers regarded as a necessity. Never slow to respond to patrons' demands, Jim had a small portable rope tow installed on Strawberry, the hill south of the lodge, for the spring season of 1942. The action immediately brought him into conflict with the government since it had not approved the tow's installation and his superiors in Ottawa were criticizing the local superintendent for not knowing what was going on. An application for a permanent 1200 foot tow made of one inch rope and powered by a Mercury V8 engine remedied the matter. In return for the government's approval for the tow, which it finally granted in September, 1942, the company agreed to pay five percent of the gross receipts received from its operation as a concession fee.

In 1944, after a visit of the Controller of the National Parks Bureau to Sunshine, Jim again locked horns with the government when he was criticized for the crude carpentry work on some of the buildings and for crowding his guests in the available space. The attack made him furious and he responded in his typical outspoken fashion:

> You will have to keep in mind that this was a pioneer effort, and had it not been for our efforts as a private enterprise, the Canadian Rockies would still be in the same old position it was years ago. Nobody knew there was any skiing in this part of the country. Now a great many people from all over the American continent, in fact all over the world, realize that we have the finest ski grounds possible. I note that other ski lodges throughout this district have made little or no effort to try accommodate people. Nor do they give the service in their lodges or transportation. While we are on the question of transportation, the road to Sunshine, as you know if you looked at it as carefully as you did the property, is not much better than a good pack trail

First permanent ski tow at Sunshine, ca. 1945

yet. . . . I have spent possibly $30,000 or $40,000 up there and still believe that little better facilities for getting in there is not unreasonable.

Despite the dispute with the government, patronage at Sunshine continued to grow after the erection of the tow. Under the management of Jack Brewster and his wife Merle, and then Jim's daughter, Fern, profits grew to $5900 by 1944. About $1300 in gross revenue came directly from the new tow. Significantly, the profit figure represented the third most lucrative aspect of Brewster Transport's 1944 balance sheet, only about $1000 less than rents on company properties, and it was an important part of the company's total profit of $18,900 that year.

While two of the three accommodation enterprises of the company performed so admirably, the Columbia Icefield Chalet lacked the opportunity to do likewise. With the sightseeing restrictions in force, the Chalet, which had turned a profit of $5700 in 1940, closed down for the 1942 season. The gas station and dining room remained open on a limited basis, keeping the loss to $750 for the year. In 1943 the loss amounted to $1600. In 1944, through an agreement with Jack Brewster, which included an allowance for profit sharing, the company opened the Chalet for armed forces personnel training on the Columbia Icefield. In November, 1943 eighty officers and men on a three week pilot training course used it, followed by officers of the Lovat Scouts who remained for the rest of the winter. This resulted in a $1200 profit for 1944.

While his company was toughing it out through the difficult years from 1942 onwards, Jim devoted his energy to promoting the war effort and preparing for the post-war period. Patriotic fervour led to the company's involvement in many fund-raising campaigns, including the "Spitfire Fund" organized by his sister Pearl Moore, and the various Victory Bond campaigns organized by Colonel Phil Moore. The company purchased $10,000 worth of three percent Victory Bonds in the first drive alone and continued to be a strong supporter thereafter, purchasing $5000 worth annually in each of the last three years of the war. Jim also saw to it that Brewster Transport provided facilities and staff for any war-oriented activities when they were needed. For example, in 1943 Brewster Transport's office became the official headquarters for a Canadian Red Cross fund-raising drive with Bert Manley and Kay Ward as its managers.

Preparations for the day when the war would be over led Jim into organizing tourist associations on both a national and regional level. In November, 1943 a meeting of the National Tourist Association in Quebec appointed him a director representing the Rocky Mountain area. He came away convinced of the advisability of forming a local branch of the organization and set about to do so. To get the movement underway he provided an interview for the *Crag and Canyon* in which he expounded his belief that Banff had to participate in nation-wide promotion of tourism to meet the post-war challenge: "Banff, one of, if not the most important tourist centre in Canada, has got to move fast if it is going to keep up with this move to prepare for the post war trade. This is our opportunity and that is why I am interested in seeing this Tourist Association Branch formed." His appeal proved effective. By April, 1944 the Canadian Rocky Mountain Tourist Association had formed, with Jim as honourary president and a strong board of directors, among whom were Crosby, McLeod and George Brewster. That fall he attended the National Tourist Association Advisory Council meetings in Windsor, Ontario and on returning reported that the rehabilitation of veterans into tourist work was one of the main objectives of the years ahead.

Within a short time he helped put this objective into practice. Travel restrictions on sightseeing transportation were partially lifted in June, 1945 allowing trips as far as Lake Louise from Banff. The end of the war meant the imminent removal of all restrictions and Brewster Transport anticipated the 1946 season optimistically since the CPR would reopen its hotels and passenger departments in the Rockies. Even though recovery did not come as quickly as hoped, the company did return a respectable profit of $31,800 that year and signs of a major post-war boom were apparent. Jim therefore looked forward enthusiastically to rebuilding Brewster Transport's transportation department so it could profit from the improved situation when it occurred. He was not to survive to see that day.

At the celebration of Banff Indian Days in July, 1946 Jim received the last and one of the most fitting tributes of his life. A friend of the Stoney tribe since his first acquaintance with William Twin fifty years previously, it conferred on him a chieftainship in a ceremony only seven white men had been honoured by. His knowledge of the Indians' language and his generosity in helping them through difficult times led to a relationship humourously summed up in a story in the *Crag and Canyon:*

> The only true weather prophets of this country, we have discovered to date, are the Stoney Indians. Last summer, at the Calgary Stampede, an American tourist visiting one of the Stoney tepees asked his Indian host if the trait they had for forecasting weather was inherited, or were the Indians taught a particular science?
>
> "Ugh," replied the Indian, "Jim Brewster, Banff, he tell us what come."

Jim, in accepting the chieftainship, paid tribute to the Stoneys, stating that he had always found them "hard working, honest and loyal" in his long association with them. They, in turn, named him "Chief Mountain Child," recognizing in him "a great pioneer of the Canadian Rockies and a friend of the tribe in time of famine and plenty."

Preparations for the official opening of the Banff Winter Carnival in February, 1947, thirty years after he had participated in its original organization, called for the new "chief" to deliver the opening address. On the eve of the event word spread through Banff that "Mr. Jim" was dead. "Canada's Mountain King," as a profile in *Liberty* magazine called him, had celebrated his sixty-fifth birthday on February 4th, seemingly in excellent health. Suddenly, shortly after midnight on February 12th, he was struck down by what was apparently a stroke. It came as a shock to everyone since he had always appeared so hale and hearty, but undoubtedly his drinking, which in no way had abated in later years, had done its damage.

The funeral was held in his residence on Bow Avenue at 2:30 p.m. on February 17th, the largest event of its kind ever witnessed in the town. Stores, offices and schools were closed at 1:00 p.m. and hundreds of mourners, each of

Liberty Profile:

JIM BREWSTER

Canada's Mountain King has a secret pact with the Rockies; neither traveler nor scenery will come to any harm if he can help it

BY ROLAND WILD

whom had in some way been touched by the man, lined the route to the cemetery. His five brothers, Bill, Fred, George, Jack and Pat and his nephew Claude were pallbearers and a long list of dignitaries, including many from the CPR, was in attendance. Fittingly, the committal service included not only Masonic rites but also an Indian ceremony carried out by some of the sixty-five Stoneys present. It was a day that everyone who was present would long remember, the end of an era in the history of the Canadian Rockies.

Tributes poured in to the family from home and abroad, and major newspapers carried extensive obituaries. Many of the tributes pointed out the vacant spot his passing created, comments such as "he was as much a part of the Canadian Rockies as the Bow River" being common. Even the National Parks Bureau, with whom he had locked horns on so many occasions, in its tribute sent by R. A. Gibson noted "he made a worthwhile contribution to the development and enjoyment of our Parks." The obituary that Jim himself might best have appreciated appeared in the Vancouver *Province*. It summed up his character in a few words: "Kings, captains and cowhands will mourn the passing of their friend Jim. He was equally at home with each and treated them all with the same offhand friendliness."

Lou Crosby, the fifty year man

# XIV: The Fifty Year Man

Jim had fortunately taken steps to ensure the transition after his death would go as smoothly as possible. His will, dated March 24, 1944, stated that his wife Dell and his daughter Fern, now Mrs. George Clarkson, were his two beneficiaries. Apart from his house and property, which many years before he had placed in trust for Fern, each woman was to receive certain personal effects and share equally in the income from his estate during her lifetime. The residual beneficiaries were his brother George's sons, Joe and Jim Brewster. Appointed as executors and trustees for the estate were the two women and Crosby. As for the company, he requested that his beneficiaries keep his shares with a view to continuing the business as long as it was "reasonably profitable." To ensure that it was "reasonably profitable" the last item in the will stated:"*It Is My Wish* that my Trustee Louis S. Crosby remain in the active management of Brewster Transport Company Limited so long as practical, since he has been associated with me for many years in the management of such Company and in my opinion his supervision and control of the affairs of said Company will be in the interests of my Estate."

Although he had forty years of experience with the company, stepping into Jim's shoes was no easy matter for Crosby. Over the years he had built up his reputation in both the community of Banff and transportation circles. Extremely sports-minded, he had since he arrived in Banff been actively involved in speedskating, first as a competitor and later as a coach and supporter of his three sons, Doug, Fred and Rob. In time his interests expanded into golf, and, becoming a charter member of the Banff Springs Golf Club, he quickly established himself as the man to beat in town. He consistently won the Birks Trophy, emblematic of the club championship, and other high calibre tournaments. On the quieter side of his life he was an avid horticulturalist, his flower garden being one of the show places in town, and a keen philatelist, his collection of Prince Edward Island stamps rated as the finest on the continent. In community service he had never spared himself, serving on the Advisory Council, Board of Trade and, beginning in 1925, on the School Board for what would eventually be twenty-three consecutive years. His transportation involvements were numerous and in the early forties the Associated Gray Line Sightseeing Companies of North America elected him vice-president. In spite of his accomplishments, Crosby lacked Jim's easygoing charm and affability, and his rather abrupt manner put some people off. But as inevitably as he would be compared with his former boss, it was equally inevitable that, given his determination and competitive drive, he would redouble his already considerable efforts to overcome this shortcoming. To the company's benefit the beneficiaries allowed him the opportunity to do so, electing him president and general manager at a salary of $9500 per annum plus commission.

On taking over his new responsibilities, Crosby was determined to tighten up the way the company was run. Foremost on his plate were decisions concerning the restaffing and reorganization of key positions as it emerged from its drastically reduced wartime operations. Some personnel too old to serve had, of course, remained with the company throughout the conflict — Frank Hayes, Fred Styles, Ernie von Kuschka, Bert McCallum, Lyle Currie and Bert Manley for example. Others such as Ralph Harvey, Jack Hayes, Lloyd Hunter and John McConville, who had left to serve their country, he took back into the fold. Although some of these men would soon disappear from the ranks of Brewster Transport, others would form the nucleus around which Crosby would build for the coming years.

Among those who quickly departed were Ralph Harvey, who remained less than two years before moving on to Calgary, Bert McCallum, who purchased Braemar Lodge in Calgary in 1948, and Lyle Currie, who passed away in 1950 after thirty-five years of service as the company's representative at Field. Those who remained Crosby soon gave new assignments. The key position of treasurer, which he himself had long held, he gave to his steadfast assistant of twenty-seven years, Bert Manley, with the new title of comptroller. Frank Hayes who had served many years as despatcher at the Banff Springs garage he appointed general superintendent of traffic with summer headquarters at Lake Louise, a position he retained until his death in 1955 after thirty-one years with the company. Lloyd Hunter, on returning from overseas, took on Hayes' former position of despatcher. Ernie von Kuschka, a former First World War airplane mechanic for the famous Red Baron and an employee of Brewster Transport since 1935, succeeded Fred Styles as fleet maintenance supervisor in 1948. In 1951 he left to join Brewster Auto Service and Bill Bunn replaced him. Styles, upon leaving his mechanical position, became the new manager of the Columbia Icefield Chalet, remaining there until his death in 1953. Don Hayes, the younger son of Frank Hayes, who had joined the company during the war and had replaced Lloyd Hunter as the driver to Sunshine, replaced Currie at Field despite the fact that he was only in his mid-twenties.

At the Mount Royal Hotel James Kelly, who joined the company in 1928, having worked previously at the King Edward Hotel, succeeded McCallum and remained in the manager's position until his death in 1951. His replacement, Mel Welsh, lasted only until 1953 at which point Crosby offered the manager's position to John McConville, a former driver who had gone to work in the hotel as a clerk in 1940. McConville felt that he was not yet ready for such responsibility and declined, thereafter serving as assistant manager under Don Smillie until 1963. When Smillie retired, McConville did become manager and remained in the job until his retirement in 1979, almost forty years after his first having joined the staff.

Crosby, astute enough to realize his own limitations, immediately began to look for a right hand man whom he could depend on for the present and groom as an eventual replacement for himself. His gaze soon fell on the eldest of Frank Hayes' two sons, Jack, who had recently returned from overseas after an air force career in which he had won a DFC.

Jack Hayes had grown up with the company in his blood. Born in England in 1921, he had come to Banff as a child of five and as a young lad spent much of his free time "hanging around" the Banff Springs Hotel garage with his father, learning all there was to know about the company and its equipment. Because the drivers often let him park the cars he was an accomplished driver himself by the age of fourteen, but was too young to obtain a licence. Thus his first paying position with the company was as a pony boy at the Banff Springs Hotel stable in 1936 and in following summers he bellhopped at the Mount Royal and Banff Springs Hotels. In 1939, as soon as he was of age, he finally achieved his dream of becoming a driver, joining about thirty university students who were working for the company that summer. After the war he talked with Jim about his future and was told that if he chose to remain in Banff the opportunity to work his way up in the company would be available. He first became transportation agent in the Mount Royal Hotel, but by the fall of 1946 he had become Ralph Harvey's assistant, accompanying Crosby east to visit the various tour agencies that winter. When Harvey left, Crosby appointed Jack to his position, but with a title change to "traffic manager" in respect for the feelings of some of the older company employees, including his father.

**Young Jack Hayes in a Packard, 1935**

Still expected to work seven days a week in the high season, permanent staff members did

**Brewster Transport post-war fleet with skyview roofs, 1946**

receive more compensation in the post-war years. The company increased salaries to a degree and added some new wrinkles. By 1950 Jack Hayes was receiving $225 per month, his father $200 per month and his brother $170 per month. Maintenance foreman von Kuschka received $225 per month and his assistants Al Semochuck and Cliff Petybridge $1.20 per hour. Chalet manager Styles, who worked in the garage in the winter, received $225 per month, Mount Royal manager Kelly $250 per month and clerk John McConville $170 per month. In addition to their regular salaries all these employees received monthly increases varying from $10 to $25 during the summer and an annual bonus of $150 to $400. Also, immediately after the war the company initiated an employee pension plan on which it generally paid between $100 and $200 per employee in premiums annually.

Equally important as the staff situation to Crosby was the need for the company's transportation department to continue the re-equipping that had begun in 1945 with the purchase of new Ford 25-passenger buses. Over the course of the war it had sold off fifty-six vehicles and converted several more into trucks for its own purposes. With the fleet reduced by over half, the purchase of new equipment was pressing. Technological and design advances in buses and government relaxation of size restrictions on buses travelling over certain park roads caused the cost of units to rise dramatically over the next few years. But their efficiency increased correspondingly.

Wisely the company had always kept proper reserves for depreciation, depreciating trucks and buses at fifteen percent and cars at ten percent annually. A small amount of funding was also in the special surplus account arising from the wartime disposal of vehicles. For its first major post-war purchase the company also borrowed $60,000 from the Imperial Bank, bringing total indebtedness to that institution to $150,000. With these funds in 1946 it purchased eight additional Ford 25-passenger buses, two GMC 25-passenger buses and two Dodge 25-passenger buses, each costing between $7900 and $8800. Crosby continued his preference for these models the following year, purchasing one more each of the Fords and Dodges and two of the GMCs. But these were not the entire shopping list in the immediate post-war period; for the first time in its history the company purchased custom-made vehicles.

A feature that quickly became a prerequisite of the post-war sightseeing bus was the skyview roof, plexiglas panels placed in the curved part of a coach ceiling, allowing an enhanced view. Ralph Harvey had read something about them in a European transportation publication and felt they would be perfect for viewing the precipitous scenery of the Rockies. They would also eliminate the need for convertible buses, an essential in the past. Brewster Transport turned to two Winnipeg suppliers of custom-built bus bodies to have these and other special features included in their new vehicles. They were Western Auto and

Truck Body Works, manufacturer of the "Western Flyer," and Motor Coach Industries, manufacturer of the "Courier." Both would play a significant role in providing units for the company, Motor Coach Industries maintaining that role to the present day.

The first purchase from Western in 1946 was in the form of two 25-passenger bus bodies built on Dodge DD7S truck chassis that Brewster Transport purchased from a Calgary Dodge dealer and delivered to the Western plant in Winnipeg. Over the winter of 1947-48 two more units were built on DE6 five ton truck chassis, essentially on the design of the "Western Flyer" coach but more luxurious with the skyview roof and reclining seats. They were larger, having a 29-passenger capacity, a modification made possible because the company had appealed to the government that it be allowed to run buses on the Banff-Jasper Highway larger than the twenty-six feet in length and seven feet six inches in width the regulations allowed. A ruling received from the government in January, 1948 allowed for a maximum width of eight feet and a maximum length of thirty feet. The units came in at $10,800 each and went into service with another purchase, a 1947 Dodge Power Wagon to be used at Sunshine. The new regulations also made the purchase of larger Motor Coach Industries "Courier" coaches feasible. These vehicles, which had a revolutionary new integral tubular steel alloy construction and an aluminum alloy body shell which kept the weight down, were considerably more expensive. Therefore not until 1950 did the company purchase its first two 33-passenger Model 50-33 "Courier Skyviews" at a cost of $17,635 each.

Of constant concern while the re-equipping was going on was the changing competition as the post-war recovery gained in momentum. Crosby, as the Banff secretary, had been very active in the Motor Livery Operators' Association and knew both the positive and negative aspects of the franchise situation. Immediately after the war he had been at the centre of a controversy surrounding the issuing of livery operators' licences to returned veterans. Attempting to protect the gains of the association, the few remaining active members had taken the position that, while it was a priority to hire veterans as drivers, they should not be issued their own livery licences unless they had been charter members. Vociferous protests against this stand by the

**Don Hayes and his wife Georgina with first Courier Skyview, 1950**

local secretary of the Canadian Legion, supported by the national executive, got a quick reaction from the government. Arguing that some members of the association had never accepted the franchise agreement and that it had not developed as originally intended, the government announced in April, 1946 that the franchise was cancelled. New procedures stipulated that "licences may be issued to all those heretofore holding licences in the Park and to any returned soldiers who are Parks residents with satisfactory equipment." The same directive pointed out that no livery tariff changes would be made and that the present tariff was a maximum with the right to undercut allowed "in keeping with our desire to encourage the liverymen to reduce fares where possible so that all Parks visitors so desiring may have an opportunity to enjoy the drives through the Park."

Crosby, in his capacity of secretary, fought this ruling but could do little about it. The return to the pre-franchise situation with its concomitants of frozen tariffs and the encouragement of tariff cutting was bound to hurt Brewster

Transport. Seven new operators, all veterans, received licences in 1946 alone. Crosby now had to focus his attention on offering a service superior to the competition's in the best equipment available, a factor which would keep Brewster Transport's profit margin low for several years despite growing gross revenue. Another alternative, of course, was to eliminate the competition, an approach that was also given some attention.

Brewster Transport's fastest growing competitor during the war years had been George Brewster's Skyline Tours, a fact that had not really bothered Jim since he felt it might better be his brother than someone else. With his new equipment and seven year Greyhound agreement in hand, George had done very well and acquired additional interests, purchasing the Saskatchewan River Bungalow Camp on the Banff-Jasper Highway in 1943, and in 1944 buying the Triangle Inn at Lake Louise. After the war further developments were also in store for another of his interests, Brewster Auto Service. Bill Brewster had purchased three lots on the corner of Bear and Caribou Streets in August, 1945 and in 1946 he began constructing a new building for his company, now known as Brewster Industries Limited, which was to house a new Ford showroom, offices of the company, and new offices for Brewster Auto Service. But George, like his brother Jim, was to be denied the opportunity to reap the benefits of an apparently bright future, as he died on January 16, 1948 at the age of sixty. By the terms of his will his brother-in-law Elmer Charlton became general manager of both the Brewster Auto Service and Skyline Tours.

Charlton operated Skyline Tours for one season but found the going rather difficult. The right to use the Texaco station on Banff Avenue had been withdrawn with George's death and Charlton had to find a new location at the Imperial Oil station on the corner of Caribou and Bear Streets. Since Skyline Tours depended on off-the-street business for its existence, the relocation of its headquarters proved detrimental. Consequently the executors of George's estate felt that it would be best to sell and therefore approached Crosby about a possible purchase. He jumped at the opportunity and made an offer which the estate accepted. Brewster Transport received not only Skyline Tours' equipment but also the valuable rights to handle Greyhound passengers coming into the park. In a turn of events that would have seemed impossible after the Greyhound-Brewster battle in the earlier part of the decade, the newly constructed Greyhound bus depot on the corner of Beaver and Caribou Streets officially opened on June 25, 1949 with a Gray Line Tours desk operated by Brewster Transport. The entire deal was a feather in Crosby's cap for it eliminated a potentially strong competitor and healed a dispute that had undeniably hurt the company for a number of years.

Brewster Transport's largest and longest standing competitor, Rocky Mountain Tours, continued to remain a thorn in the side. At the beginning of the war this company had achieved a long sought objective when it obtained the right to build a garage and headquarters at Lake Louise, thereby strengthening its ability to operate from that point. This it achieved through the influence of the CNR with which it had a reciprocal transportation agreement, Jasper Park Lodge carrying passengers from Jasper to the Icefield and then transferring them to Rocky Mountain Tours' vehicles and vice versa. Like its competitor, Rocky Mountain had been all but forced to cease business during the war with the onset of sightseeing restrictions. The Royal Canadian Air Force had approached Jim McLeod in 1941 offering to purchase all of his buses for use in the Commonwealth Air Training Plan. He agreed and immediately put the money into Victory Bonds, thereby easily boosting Banff over its quota in its first drive. At the end of the war he cashed in the bonds and supplemented the funds obtained by adding to them proceeds from the sale of his recently obtained interest in the Homestead Hotel. He used the money to purchase new equipment, mainly "Wester Flyer" units built on Dodge and Ford chassis, and by 1949 the company had about fifteen of them.

Meanwhile, McLeod's company had undergone a considerable shake-up in 1946 when he decided to retire. He offered to sell the company to his two sons and two sons-in-law and when they accepted it was reincorporated. The new general manager was Hal Waterhouse, the husband of Jean McLeod, who herself had worked in the company's office for many years beginning in the depression. Waterhouse resigned his commission in the RCMP to take on the position and he proved to be an extremely capable manager. He was ably assisted by another recent addition to the company's ranks, his brother-in-law, Bob

Rocky Mountain Tours' new garage, ca. 1949

Bray, who took over the financial end as secretary-treasurer, and by Allan and Jim McLeod jr. The management's major concern apart from re-equipping was to replace the dilapidated wooden garage it operated out of at 207 Banff Avenue. It was torn down in 1946 and replaced with an attractive stone structure which housed both a garage and an office that would meet its needs well into the future.

Although not nearly so large as Brewster Transport, its new fleet, management and facilities made Rocky Mountain Tours a force Crosby had to reckon with and he undoubtedly wished to eliminate or neutralize it. In 1950 Jack Hayes informed him that he and Allan McLeod had talked about the possibility of amalgamating the two companies when they had met on the road while visiting tour agencies in the east. McLeod had indicated he would bring the idea to the attention of the principals in his company and Hayes agreed to do the same. Crosby was interested and invited the shareholders of Rocky Mountain Tours to meet with the shareholders of his company to discuss the possibilities in December, 1950. An agreement was proposed that was very similar to the one Rocky Mountain Tours had turned down twenty-three years earlier — the formation of a new company strictly involved in transportation to which each existing company would contribute its equipment. Crosby pointed out the two most important advantages: a standardization of commissions paid to tour companies would save some $20,000 a year for the two companies, and elimination of duplicate services, such as two half-empty buses running between Banff and Lake Louise or Lake Louise and the Columbia Icefield. Rocky Mountain Tours initially reacted positively to the formation of a new company, to be known as "Gray Line of the Canadian Rockies," but consideration of Brewster Transport's having two-thirds of the voting power likely made them nervous and at their annual meeting they turned the proposition down. Although he attempted to change their minds, Crosby soon let the matter drop as other pressing matters were demanding his attention.

Second to rebuilding Brewster Transport's transportation business, his main concern was to sustain the excellent wartime revenue performance of its properties and developments. This was to prove difficult. In 1946, before Jim's death, the company had built a building with retail space on the main floor and an annex for the Mount Royal above at 223 and 225 Banff Avenue (Lots 12 and 13, Block 6). Approached by local realtor J. D. Hansen about a client interested in building on one of these lots, Jenkin's Groceteria Ltd., operators of a chain of grocery stores in Alberta, and by Unwin's Ltd., owner of a building on Lot 11, about building an addition to their hardware business on Lot 12, Crosby proposed that the two parties construct one building on the two lots which they would jointly share. Brewster Transport would own the building but the tenants would pay a nominal rent for two years. Jenkin's and Unwin's agreed and the architect was drawing plans when it occurred to management that a second storey could be easily added to provide overflow space for the Mount Royal. A new arrangement in April, 1946 saw the company agreeing to reimburse the two lower floor tenants for any structural upgrading required and to pay for the second storey itself. In the addition were twenty-six hotel style rooms that cost the company about $53,000 by the time they were furnished. The Brewster Block, as it became known, was not ready for occupancy until the spring of 1947 and it did not prove as profitable as expected. In 1947 and 1948 it registered small losses, but by 1949 it began to creep into the black.

The Mount Royal Hotel tended to languish somewhat as competition in the hotel business again picked up. Even with the addition of a curio shop to the premises, profits gradually began to erode. Net revenue fell consistently from $113,-500 to $88,000 in the five years after 1945, due largely to increasing operating costs. In 1948 the old Mount Royal Garage, one of the company's historic landmarks, was torn down to make room for future expansion, but the hotel's poor performance and the annex space in the Brewster Block led management to postpone further construction. In 1953, for the first time in many years, there was an increase in profits. Crosby then proposed an addition to the hotel to fill the space the demolition of the garage had provided. Construction on the addition, to include twenty-eight new rooms with baths, a full basement and room for four retail stores on the main floor, commenced in the fall of 1954. Plans to renovate and enlarge the hotel lobby and a new elevator required eliminating the beer parlour to provide the space. Profits from the beer parlour had been small and static for a number of years and management decided it wasn't worth the trouble it caused. The enlarged and upgraded hotel's resurgence in patronage made it possible to pay the $38,000 renovation costs out of its gross revenue for 1955 and still finish the year with only a $5000 loss. The following year it registered a profit of $50,800. Total cost of the 1955 addition and renovation was $216,000 compared with $131,600 spent on the hotel over all the years previously, effectively illustrating the expense of post-war construction.

The Columbia Icefield Chalet had failed to live up to even the rather lacklustre performance of its sister business over the same period. Profits were difficult to increase in the face of growing operating expenses. In a brief resurgence in 1947 it managed a profit of $11,400, largely on the revenue from the dining room. Unhappily the profit decreased to $3900 in 1948, despite Fred Styles' attempts to increase revenue by participating in a new venture, snowmobile tours on the Athabasca Glacier. Since 1940 tours of the glacier had been provided on horseback by Jack Brewster, a service by its nature restricted to a very few patrons. In 1948 Allan Watt, a former company driver, and now the owner of a business known as Snowline Transport, reached agreement with the company to operate half-track vehicles on the glacier on a commission basis, utilizing the Chalet as his headquarters. Initially his equipment consisted of one of the converted '29 Fords Brewster Transport had used at Sunshine but which had lain idle for a number of years. Watt's resurrection of it proved successful and he continued to build up his equipment through the 1951 season when he operated five Bombardier snowmobiles. The next year the government, recognizing the value of the proposition, decided to tender it out, the successful bidder being Bill Ruddy of Jasper. Brewster Transport thereafter lost the commission it had been receiving, although the $800 to $900 a year involved was not a significant amount, The Chalet's profit had sunk to $520 by 1950 and, with the exception of 1953, the new decade's first years saw losses varying from $600 to $6700 annually. In 1956 the situation began to turn around after the construction of a new coffee shop and increased revenue from the service station after the company began running it instead of leasing it out.

Given these difficulties in two of its accommodation interests, it is not surprising the company divested itself of its third. Sunshine, like the Mount Royal and the Columbia Icefield Chalet, did not perform well in the immediate post-war period. Despite this, while Jim was alive he was committed to promoting it. Under his daughter Fern's management Sunshine continued to expand, with work commencing on a new $4000 wing on the lodge in November, 1946. In addition to improvements at Sunshine proper Jim also contemplated expanding the development across the Great Divide to nearby Rock Isle Lake. As early as January, 1945 he requested a lease on two 160 acre plots at Rock Isle and Eohippus Lakes from the B.C. Lands Department, but the land was under reserve. Its reserve status withdrawn in January, 1947, he reapplied for 152 acres at Rock Isle Lake with an idea for a fishing and ski lodge at the site. The B.C. cabinet reviewed the request and informed Jim a few days before he died that it was being recommended.

Even though the Rock Isle development was one of Jim's fondest hopes, Crosby thought it would never be profitable and could not bring himself to go ahead with it. The lease itself cost the company some $760 annually, a high figure for undeveloped alpine land. Correspondingly, the profit with which Sunshine had ended the war was fast diminishing. Such services as ski lessons and ski rentals had increased revenue slightly but it was insufficient to overcome the rapidly rising cost of supplies, wages, repairs and maintenance. By 1947 Sunshine experienced a $2600 loss and within two years this had jumped to $10,000. This was particularly disheartening because at the same time an attempt was being made to improve services with Allan Watt utilizing his snowmobiles to ferry skiers to the top of the Brewster Rock and Standish Hump runs.

Another discouraging factor was the difficulty over the concession fee the company had to pay the government. A new five year licence of occupation, issued in 1944, required Brewster Transport to pay $30 per annum land rental plus what amounted to, using a very complicated formula, a five percent concession fee on Sunshine's net profits. In the 1949 renewal of the licence a flat fee replaced the percentage, obliging a cost to the company even in the years the business experienced a loss. This irked Crosby to no end.

About 1950 a search began for a possible buyer of Sunshine. The search became even more intense in 1951 when the winter housecount fell some eighteen percent, due largely to the cancellation of many special ski trains. Extensive losses in the previous four summer seasons led management to keep the lodge closed in the summer of 1951. That fall negotiations for sale began with George Encil, a native of Austria who earlier had purchased the Mount Norquay ski development. A price of $70,000 payable over a two year period was agreed on and on January 29, 1952 the purchase was made, although there were some slight subsequent amendments and Encil did not take possession until June, 1952. It was not the end of Brewster Transport's association with the ski area, for in December, 1952 it announced a new schedule of buses to carry skiers to what Encil had renamed Sunshine Village. This service was to remain a key part of the company's winter activities, for, despite the fact it usually lost money, it provided a means for keeping a nucleus of staff on the payroll year round. In 1980 a new gondola system at Sunshine transporting skiers from the Bourgeau Parking Lot to the lodge finally replaced the buses.

Crosby, often criticized for his disposal of Sunshine since it later proved to be a viable ski operation, had regarded it only as a bottomless pit into which the company could pour large amounts of money with little or no return. Conversely, a sale which netted a profit of $22,000 over its $48,000 book value looked extremely attractive. As it turned out, the Sunshine sale became a turnaround point for an improvement in the company's fortunes after its seven year struggle with rising costs and investments in equipment.

In the post-war period the company had been experiencing a deficiency in working capital (difference between liquid assets and current liabilities), a problem which plagued it throughout its existence. Any contemplated major purchase or development always hinged on an ability to borrow the entire sum of capital required. For the first time the Sunshine sale changed these circumstances, giving the company a bit of breathing space in the form of a capital surplus. This seemed to herald a change in attitude towards expansion. It is significant that Crosby's argument that convinced his board to take the company's biggest and most costly post-war gamble, the Mount Royal Hotel addition, was that the company need borrow only $100,000 if the Sunshine funds were poured in.

In the same vein, equipment purchases were thought more practical, given the company's improved financial situation, even though most required additional loans from the bank. These Crosby attempted to repay as quickly as possible, usually by the end of the summer when revenue had built up, thereby keeping the credit rating high and interest payments low. In 1952 the company purchased a 37-passenger "Courier Skyview" and in 1953 two more of the same model and four new Dodge sedans. Later the same year, because of additional business resulting from several motion picture companies working in the mountains that summer, it purchased six additional sedans.

Finally, with some of the pressure off, Crosby suggested some much needed adjustments in both his own salary and those of some of the other key personnel. Because of declining profits his salary had actually been decreasing instead of increasing, and a board meeting held on September 10, 1952 offered him the option of a straight $12,000 per annum or $7500 plus ten percent of profits. He chose the former and safer option. In addition he secured agreement on a salary of $4200 for Jack Hayes, whom he had appointed to the new position of assistant general manager, $4500 for comptroller Bert Manley and $3300 for recently hired accountant Norman Campbell.

Having turned the corner in 1952, Crosby began to look toward increasing the annual profit, which had stood at a lowly $4500 for 1951. Since the two major beneficiaries of Jim's estate depended on annual dividends for their income this was extremely important, although less so for Fern who, having divorced her first husband, had married Harry Dooley, president of Gray Line.

Since Jim's death the shareholders of the company had included Dell, Fern, Crosby and Lloyd Fenerty, McLaurin's successor as legal counsel after his appointment to the Supreme Court of Alberta. Each of them held one share with the remaining 596 standing in the name of Jim's estate with dividends accruing equally to the two women. In addition to being shareholders the ladies both served on the board of directors, Dell as vice-president and treasurer and Fern as vice-president and secretary. In attendance at most board meetings was George Steer, an Edmonton lawyer who represented the interests of the two ladies. Between Jim's death and 1952 total profits earned had been $176,400 while total dividends were $116,600, leaving little profit to plough back into the business.

Crosby realized an obvious way to increase profits was to keep operating expenses down while building up gross revenue in transportation operations, where he chose to direct much of the company's energies. Aware that existing operations could increase revenue only a bit despite the growing numbers of tourists, by the mid-fifties he was keeping his eyes open for expansion into new areas. Jack Hayes brought one to his attention in 1955 after conversations he had held with George Ross, the son-in-law of Paul Andrew, owner of Athabasca Motor Tours in Jasper. Ross, who was managing the business, told Hayes they were interested in selling out the transportation end of their hotel business since they could see no way of expanding it. Crosby knew the company since Brewster Transport had a reciprocal agreement with it and made Andrew an offer. It was accepted and all Athabasca Motor Tours' equipment, consisting of eight Ford and Dodge buses and three "snakes" (elongated touring cars on one ton chassis), Brewster Transport purchased outright for $40,000 payable over a ten year period. In addition the company received an exclusive motor livery franchise at the Athabasca and Pyramid Hotels for a ten year period at a flat concession fee of $10,000 per annum.

As a result of the purchase and a general increase in business, Crosby expected the company to achieve an all time record in volume of business handled, and he was not to be disappointed. Gross operating revenue jumped to $490,000 from $364,000 in 1954. Probably this affected his interest in another Jasper opportunity which Don Hayes, the company's new manager at the location, pointed out. C. E. Davignon, owner of Mountain Motors, was interested in selling off his considerable property at a reasonable price. An agreement, signed on November 25, 1955, provided for a purchase price of $132,000 payable over ten years and gave the company a secure base in Jasper from which to operate and expand. The major item in the purchase was the Mountain Motors garage located on three lots (Lots 13-15, Block 3) on Connaught Drive, the town's major thoroughfare. The 100 by 150 foot stone and concrete structure, complete with hoists and other equipment, housed a bowling alley in one part and was the area's franchised General Motors dealership. Less valuable initally, but ultimately more important profit producers, were two service stations dealing in Imperial Oil products. Totem Service stood on Lots 14-15, Block 9 while a smaller station stood on a lot across the street. A small cafe adjacent to the garage was soon moved and made into a staff quarters. Unfortunately, shortly after the purchase, Mountain Motors' roof collapsed under the weight of snow; after long negotiations an adjustment reduced the purchase price to $117,200.

Because of the acquisitions at Jasper and the addition and renovation of the Mount Royal

Hotel in Banff, the company's capital expenditures of $357,300 for 1955 proved to be a record. Similarly, liabilities reached an all time high at $346,200. In his annual report to the shareholders Crosby pointed out that the company was operating 95 pieces of equipment — 52 buses, 29 cars and 14 baggage trucks — with a total seating capacity of 1500. Net assets had reached $1,316,500, more than double what they had been in 1945, and this even before the Mountain Motors assets were included. Therefore he could forthrightly assure them that he was "not at all apprehensive as to our ability to take care of all these obligations, so long as business continues at its present level," but he cautioned against further developments for a year or two until the company could substantially reduce its obligations.

This warning probably guided the shareholders' decision to turn down another interesting proposition in Jasper. Fred Brewster, who had been in business there over forty years, was at the time running a few buses, launches on Maligne Lake, and Fred Brewster's Rocky Mountain Camps, a system of camps and chalets, the major one at Maligne Lake. In 1955 he repaid Brewster Transport $5700 it had loaned him when he was starting the camps. Once this matter was settled, he suggested to Crosby that Brewster Transport should acquire controlling interest in his company as he was getting on in years and felt that it should in some way remain in the Brewster family. However, Crosby's warning, coupled with an asking price in the neighbourhood of $100,000 and the fact that the CNR owned a fifty percent interest in the Maligne Lake Chalet, made the proposition untenable to the directors.

The confidence Crosby expressed in his 1955 report that "tourist traffic will grow beyond our fondest hopes" proved not to be misplaced. The following year the company's gross income reached $1,067,900, the first time it had broken the million dollar mark. The increase of $237,-800 over the previous year was almost wholly accounted for by the Jasper operations which grossed $233,500. Brewster Transport's profit of $23,500 for the year allowed a dividend of $21,300 to be paid, bringing total post-war dividends to $183,000. This figure, Crosby proudly pointed out, was over $7000 in excess of total dividends paid in the company's entire history prior to 1945. Everything seemed to be going quite smoothly except for an alarming and uncharacteristic rash of accidents the transportation department was experiencing.

Over its long history Brewster Transport had compiled an impressive safety record, considering the number of passenger miles it had logged over treacherous mountain trails and roads. Nothing of a serious nature had occurred until a freak accident resulted in its first recorded fatality in the summer of 1942. On that occasion Lloyd Hunter, driving to Sunshine, stopped to help another company car which had developed a vapour lock. Attempting an old trick to get it going again, he had taken some gas from the tank and was in the process of pouring it in the carburetor while the other driver, Syd Sanderson, turned the engine over when it backfired. This set fire to the gasoline and carburetor and Hunter reacted by flinging the flaming gas can into the road. Unknown to him an elderly passenger, Charles Paul, who was standing directly behind him, was immediately doused with burning gasoline. Clothes aflame, Paul began running down the road. Hunter quickly overtook him and put out the flames by rolling him in a blanket, but Paul died a few days later in hospital. The police report did not call for an inquest, since there had been no negligence, but the accident caused the company to review its safety procedures.

Nothing serious occurred again until August, 1955 when a bus driven by William Selby, a University of Alberta law student and a veteran of seven summers' driving for the company, was hit by a gravel truck near Herbert Lake on the Banff-Jasper Highway. Luckily both vehicles had turned towards the side of the road prior to impact, avoiding a head-on collision, and the injuries the passengers sustained were the result of flying glass broken by the gravel. Passengers' claims against the company amounted to $300,000 but Fenerty's office managed to settle them for $58,000, all of which was covered by insurance. Of the $14,000 in damages to the bus, $5000 was also covered by insurance leaving the company with a $9000 loss as a result of the accident.

Another and much more serious accident followed in July the next year when driver Herb Gascoigne at the wheel of a Courier bus carrying eleven passengers missed a shift and then experienced a brake failure while descending the hill near Panther Falls on the Banff-Jasper Highway.

Gascoigne wisely drove the bus into a rock wall before it got going too fast, but the gas tank ruptured and caught fire. All the passengers managed to escape before the vehicle was completely burned but one passenger, fifty-five year old Miss M. Guest, later died of a heart attack and several others were admitted to hospital. The jury at the ensuing inquest in August, 1956 gave the company an indirect slap on the wrist by recommending that more rigid control be exercised concerning the abilities of drivers working in the national parks and more rigid and frequent inspections be made on public passenger carrying vehicles. No claim against the company was ever pressed by Miss Guest's relatives; accident and liability insurance covered the injured passengers' claims and the replacement cost of the bus, but premiums rose forty percent the next year.

Troubling as these accidents were, they in no way detracted from Crosby's sense of accomplishment. On August 10, 1957, fifty years had passed since the day in 1907 when he had got off the train from Calgary and Bill Brewster had hired him. Since that day, as he pointed out in his annual report, the company's gross earnings had increased fourteen times and its assets over ten times. At a banquet tendered in his honour at the Mount Royal, the directors presented him with a gift of $2000 and a gold watch engraved "L. S. Crosby, 50th Anniversary with B.T.C., August 10th 1957." He was deeply moved and in his response to the presentation attempted to sum up what the occasion meant to him:

> I look back over the past fifty years with satisfaction and pride in our organization which has progressed along with the Tourist Industry and which has a good name throughout the length and breadth of this Continent and other parts of the world. Few people are so fortunate as I in being able to boast of continuous service with one organization for half a century. It has been a wonderful experience. My memories are all happy ones and to have been privileged to have spent most of one's life with a wonderful wife and family, in such beautiful surroundings, is ample reward for whatever effort I have put forward to do a good job for my Associates and render some small service to our Community.

**Gertrude and Lou Crosby at his 50th anniversary**

BANFF CRAG & CANYON

An independent newspaper serving Banff National Park

Sixty-Fifth Year — No. 28 Wednesday, July 14, 1965 10c Copy — $3.00 per Year

# Hint Brewster Empire Sale Greyhound Offer Studied

Greyhound Bus Lines have made an offer of an undisclosed sum for all the holdings of Brewster Transport and Brewster Rocky Mountain Gray Line Ltd.

It has been hinted the offer exceeds $2,000,000.

Spokesmen for both organizations confirmed negotiations were taking place but no agreements have been reached.

Brewster president Jack Hayes said Greyhound has been interested in the company's holdings for some time.

The negotiations concern Brewster's Hotel, transportation and real estate interests in Banff, Yoho and Jasper National Parks.

Included are: about 135 vehicles, buses, lease cars and taxis; Banff's 100-room Mount Royal Hotel, The Emerald Lake Chalet, The Columbia Icefields Chalet and other pieces of real estate in the parks.

One big factor in present negotiations is believed to be the attitude of the Canadian Pacific Railway to any proposed sell-out. CP is Brewster Rocky Mountain Gray Line's biggest customer and a large scale promoter of travel business in the national parks.

The railway operates three major hotels in the Banff-Lake Louise area and through its vast transport network generates a big share of all internal passenger traffic for the local firm.

Any opposition by CP to the proposal could seriously effect its outcome says a reliable source, especially if CP cancelled its present transportation contracts with the company.

Brewster interests are believed to be next in size to the CP and Canadian National Railway holdings in the parks. Their association with CP began in the 1890's when horse drawn wagons and saddle trains packed supplies to railway workers from the farm of the late John Brewster.

Since 1945 the Brewster interests have bought out five other transport companies in the parks to become sole operators of public transport in Banff, Kootenay, Yoho and Jasper parks.

The firms hires about 100 year-round employees with a summer peak of 400 on its payroll.

Heirs to the estate of the late James Brewster are his widow, Mrs. Dell Brewster, of Banff, and a daughter, Mrs. Fern Dooley of Chicago and Banff.

The estate holds all shares in trust except for a director's share held by Calgary lawyer Lloyd Fenerty, QC, chairman of the Brewster firm.

# XV: The Family Bows Out

When Crosby celebrated his fiftieth anniversary with the company he had reason to be doubly proud. By happy circumstance it coincided with the long sought merger of the transportation operations of Brewster Transport and Rocky Mountain Tours. The new company which the merger created could concentrate on increasing revenue and profits from what had essentially become a marginal business for both, and Brewster Transport could concentrate on the growth of some of its non-transportation aspects.

After the unsuccessful merger attempt of 1950, circumstances at Rocky Mountain Tours changed rapidly. In November, 1951, the company's manager, Hal Waterhouse, passed away at the young age of forty. Jim McLeod jr. became the new president. Operating in opposition to Brewster Transport became increasingly difficult and the remaining principals became more amenable to joining forces with it, particularly after the death of Jim McLeod sr. in 1955. Jack Hayes and Allan McLeod had kept their original plan alive in periodic discussions and in the summer of 1957 serious negotiations began. Each company would contribute its transportation assets to the formation of a new company and would receive shares in it proportionate to the assets contributed. At the time Rocky Mountain's fleet consisted of twenty-one buses, eleven of which were 33-passenger Couriers, and thirteen cars giving it a total carrying capacity of 712. In comparison, Brewster Transport owned fifty-eight buses, twenty-one of which were Couriers, and twenty-nine cars, providing it with a total capacity of 1658. However, Rocky Mountain's equipment was somewhat newer and its assessed value of $309,000, compared to Brewster Transport's $600,000, would give it a third of the shares in the new company. Fenerty drew up an agreement on this basis and on July 31st the official press release announced that a tentative agreement had been reached. The new company would take the name Brewster-Rocky Mountain-Gray Line, Limited, incorporating the names of the two parent companies as well as Brewster Transport's Gray Line connection. The announcement also pointed out that the two parent companies would operate their non-transportation interests separately. Other details were to be worked out during the summer since the company would not formally come into existence until the end of the current season.

One matter to be settled was the status of the CPR livery concession. A renewal agreement of October 1, 1949 had continued to stipulate that Brewster Transport would pay ten percent commission on all "unorganized" business. To protect its interest the railway had insisted on a new clause which gave it an option to purchase fifty-one percent of the company's shares at its discretion. The CPR had been willing to agree to the proposed 1950 merger only if Brewster Transport and Rocky Mountain Tours would each give the railway a similar option. In 1957 the CPR modified its position in regard to the merger proposals. It still required the option but the new company would pay five percent commission on *all* business, a stipulation which would benefit the railway, and the term of the contract was to be ten years rather than five, providing more security for the company. Brewster-Rocky Mountain-Gray Line would not be responsible for providing saddle horses. Claude Brewster's purchase of all Brewster Transport's horses, saddlery and packing equipment in 1954 for $7500 had marked a final break with the company's historical roots; in 1957 he entered into a separate agreement with the CPR.

With the CPR concession matter in hand, the formal incorporation of Brewster-Rocky Mountain-Gray Line took place on September 20, 1957. The authorized capital was $250,000, made up of 40,000 five percent noncumulative redeemable preferred shares of $5.00 each and 50,000 common shares of $1.00 each. Two thirds of the shares were assigned to Brewster Transport and the remaining third went to Rocky Mountain Tours, all shares purchased by contributing fixed assets at cost less depreciation, accounts receivable, goodwill and inventories of accessories, parts, gas, oil and other supplies. Brewster Transport's total contribution was $251,668 less assumed bank loans of $85,000.

Immediately the shareholders of the new company met to work out procedures and to elect officers. All permanent transportation employees of both companies, numbering about twenty, would become employees of the new firm, although there would be some reassignment of duties. Brewster Transport would carry out accounting services and reservations, and despatching and related services would be handled in the Rocky Mountain Tours building. The new company would rent that building and the Lake Louise garage from Rocky Mountain Tours, the Banff Springs Hotel garage from the CPR, and one-third of the Brewster garage at Jasper. The new officers included Crosby as president and chairman of the board, Jack Hayes as vice-president and general manager, Jim McLeod as vice-president, Allan McLeod as assistant general manager, and Bob Bray as secretary-treasurer. All the foregoing were also directors of the company along with Dell Brewster, Fern Dooley, Lloyd Fenerty and Bert Manley. At a subsequent meeting further appointments included Norman Campbell as comptroller, Bob Bray as office manager, Jim McLeod as manager of Banff operations and Joe Brewster, who had joined Brewster Transport in 1953, as traffic manager. The upper management level of the company, it soon became apparent, was top-heavy and Allan McLeod decided to leave within a year.

At lower management levels there was a similar melding of the two parent companies' employees. Rod Adams, who had gone to school in Banff and worked as a driver for Brewster Transport both before and after serving in the navy, had replaced Lloyd Hunter as despatcher after Hunter became manager of the Columbia Icefield Chalet in 1953. Adams initially remained despatcher in the new company but later became operations manager, where he was assisted by Bill Hope, a local lad who had originally worked for Skyline Tours during the war and Rocky Mountain Tours after it. George Murray, another long time employee of Rocky Mountain Tours, became head ticket agent for Brewster-Rocky Mountain-Gray Line. At Jasper, Don Hayes retained responsibility for both Brewster Transport's and the new company's interests.

Meanwhile, all the vehicles were being painted in the new red, white and gray colour scheme of the company and the former Rocky Mountain Tours vehicles were having Gray Line crests affixed to them. When Brewster-Rocky Mountain-Gray Line began operations on November 1, 1957 it could muster 121 passenger vehicles with a total seating capacity of 2370. Its incredibly strong position vis-à-vis tourist transport in the mountain parks augured well for the future of both it and Brewster Transport. As Crosby put it in his annual report: "With the present set-up which approaches a virtual monopoly of the Motor Livery business in the three National Parks: Banff, Jasper and Yoho [and] by virtue of the fact that practically 100% of the available hotel room space is controlled by our new company, as most of the smaller hotels are also under contract for livery privileges, it may confidently be anticipated that for the ensuing few years, barring an Atomic War, or some other unforeseen calamity, the future of your company seems to be approaching an era of unprecedented prosperity."

Brewster-Rocky Mountain-Gray Line immediately warranted the faith which had been placed in it. About $200,000 in loans owed by the company, some assumed in the merger agreement and some made for the purchase of new equipment, had been reduced to $70,000 by July, 1958. Tourist traffic was down somewhat, a result of a business recession in the United States, but eliminating duplicate services and streamlining operations allowed profits to go up. The net profit for the first year was $30,200, with Brewster Transport's share amounting to $20,100 or twelve percent on investment. This compared favourably with a profit of $15,200 for Brewster Transport's overall operations, including transportation, the year previously. Contributing to this respectable first year profit picture were commissions from two new aspects of its business that Brewster Transport had brought into the company, parking lots and car rentals.

After the war tourism by car continued to grow and the CPR had to build extensive parking lots for its hotels and offer a valet parking service. In a 1954 agreement with Brewster Transport, the railway contracted the parking lots and the parking service in return for a commission of forty percent. The resulting income amounted to only $1200 by 1957, but in 1958 the new company approached the CPR, which was then enlarging its parking lots, with a request for a larger share of the gross income. This the hotel

**Brewster-Rocky Mountain-Gray Line fleet at the Banff Springs Hotel garage, ca. 1960**

department agreed to, reducing the commission rate to thirty percent. Profits on the service increased immediately and by 1959 had doubled from their 1957 level.

The government had called for tenders for car rental service in August, 1956 despite opposition to the idea by Brewster Transport and Rocky Mountain Tours. When the government first broached the subject in 1951 Crosby and Waterhouse had both protested vociferously, stating they needed to protect their small margin of transportation profit from such competition, and that rental cars were a public danger. However, since the government had decided to proceed, both companies tendered, although neither was successful because of the high rates they intended to charge and the low percentage they offered the government. The successful tenderer was Dominion Drive-Ur-Self System Ltd., operator of Hertz-Rent-A-Car. In the fall of 1957 Jack Hayes and Dominion entered into negotiations and in November reached an agreement. Brewster-Rocky Mountain-Gray Line would rent out thirty vehicles from an office in the Rocky Mountain Tours building on a commission basis. Operating profits were $1250 in 1958 and increased to $2300 in 1959 after Hertz increased its daily rates from $6.00 to $10.00.

Another new aspect of the company that held potential for the future was The Calgary Gray Line, Ltd., a joint creation with Cardinal Coach Lines, Ltd. of Calgary. Involving the outlay of only $3500 by each parent company, the 1959 agreement called for the new company to acquire from the United Taxi Company the Gray Line sightseeing franchise for Calgary and to purchase one bus from Cardinal. Brewster-Rocky Mountain-Gray Line expected no great immediate return from the venture but felt it would protect the Gray Line name in the Calgary area. More popular than expected, it required the Banff company to lend some of its skyview sightseeing buses on several occasions.

As a result of growing revenue, Brewster-Rocky Mountain-Gray Line's profit picture improved in 1959, reaching $53,500. Of the dividend of $30,000, $20,000 went to Brewster Transport, an amount which tended to be the

**Emerald Lake Chalet**

norm for the next few years, providing a base amount on which Brewster Transport could depend. Unfortunately, the parent company failed to live up to the same level of performance.

Brewster Transport's problem in the late fifties and into the early sixties was its continuing deficiency in working capital. Of course, a substantial decrease in the deficiency had occurred in 1958 with the removal of transportation operations to the new company, but this situation was shortlived. Dividends still had to be paid and the company was acquiring new interests, some of which were none too profitable. Crosby would have liked to float an issue of debentures to increase capital but the fact that Brewster Transport was now a private company prevented it.

One acquisition which seemed a welcome addition to the company's interests but which soon proved itself a liability was the Emerald Lake Chalet. The CPR in 1959 wished to divest itself of its lodges at Emerald and Moraine Lakes, and the directors of Brewster Transport, always looking towards controlling more hotel rooms for tour bookings, felt they would complement the company's other hotel interests. Crosby, given the go ahead to attempt the purchase, negotiated an agreement that took effect on November 1, 1959. The selling price was $185,000, split on the basis of $150,000 for Emerald Lake and $35,000 for Moraine Lake. Crosby then immediately sold Moraine Lake Lodge for $50,000. Effectively the company had already shown a profit of $15,000 and its own down payment was only $10,000. It looked like the beginning of a lucrative venture which, like the Mount Royal Hotel and Columbia Icefield Chalet, would make substantial contributions to the company coffers. The hope was quickly dashed.

The Emerald Lake Chalet required considerable funds to put it in proper condition. The twenty-eight old bungalows had to be equipped with propane heaters at an outlay of $7500. In the 1960 season patronage proved disappointing with net revenue from room rental, the dining room and the curio shop amounting to only $20,400. Operating expenses proved high and the business experienced a shocking loss of $32,300 its first year, the worst performance ever of any Brewster interest. The company's chartered accountants observed that the staff was too large for the amount of business and direct costs were high throughout the operation compared to the Columbia Icefield Chalet. Crosby himself felt the meals in the dining room were much too lavish for the price charged. Measures to tighten up the business included hiring a new manager. The results were dramatic. Net revenue increased in all phases of the chalet operation by over $8000, room rental making the most significant strides, and expenses dropped by some $7000. However, Emerald Lake still ended the year with a $6000 loss.

In Jasper, Mountain Motors was another drain on the company. Overall the Jasper operation, despite a gross income of $233,500, lost $14,500 in 1956. Athabasca Tours had held its own, but Mountain Motors' sales of new and used cars, parts and accessories and billings to customers on labour resulted in a gross of $28,200 against expenses of $44,300. The two service stations' profits of approximately $10,000 offset the loss somewhat. Since Crosby and Hayes both favoured further diversification into service stations, the company entered into an agreement with the Imperial Oil Company, and by its terms Imperial loaned $12,000 of the total of $18,000 needed to construct a new service station on the two lots adjacent to Mountain Motors, with the hope it would increase profits. Unhappily it didn't; service station profits remained static.

Ominously, Mountain Motors' gross income almost doubled in 1957, but its loss remained about the same. On receiving these figures Crosby immediately called a meeting of management to analyze the whole Jasper situation. The analysis confirmed the findings of the company's auditors; overhead costs were too high and labour charges for both customers and company cars were at too low a rate per hour. Steps to rectify the problems in 1958 succeeded in halving the loss, but the following year it was worse than ever, reaching $18,700 and frustrating Crosby immensely.

With the disheartening performance of the Emerald Lake Chalet, the situation at Mountain Motors resulted in Brewster Transport's first loss position in many years. The company had gone into the red on its own operations the year before, 1959, but a $20,000 dividend from Brewster-Rocky Mountain-Gray Line redeemed it. In 1960, despite the dividend and increases in profit from the Mount Royal Hotel and the Columbia Icefield Chalet, losses on the Emerald Lake Chalet and on Jasper operations resulted in a net loss of $10,800. The predicament was very serious considering the extensive liabilities the company had incurred in acquiring these assets.

In 1959 some $9100 from the surplus account provided the normal dividend of $21,300. The following year the whole of the dividend came from the same source. Crosby again pointed out to the directors that the company's working capital position would not improve so long as it continued to maintain its dividend rate. He presented a study that showed ten of Canada's most successful companies retained an average of thirty percent of their profit for operation and expansion and suggested that the directors should consider a similar policy for Brewster Transport.

Actually the company had restrained itself from making new investments after the purchase of Emerald Lake. Taking a cue from its Jasper operations, it excepted service stations. In 1958 it started a small service station just over the Kicking Horse River from Field on a site the Brewster outfitting business once occupied. When construction of the new Trans-Canada Highway through Rogers Pass made it apparent that greatly increased traffic would soon be passing the site, upgrading the facility at a considerable sum seemed justified. In 1962 the company borrowed $90,000 from the British-American Oil Company, repayable over twenty-five years, to build a larger four pump service station and manager's cottage. Its first year operating profit of $15,900 led to the company's involvement in another service station, Highway Service, which it opened in Banff at 302 Lynx Street, on the site Brewster Hall originally occupied. In this case Brewster Transport rented the building from B-A Oil for about $2000 per annum. The company put some $4000 worth of furnishings and equipment into it and achieved an operating profit of $3700 its first year in business.

Apart from the service stations, the only new additions to the company's holdings were buildings constructed on agreements similar to those for the Banff Cafe and the Brewster Block. In 1959 Leagh Kendal constructed a one-storey fireproof building on the east half of Lot 1, Block

7 and a two-storey building on the west half of Lot 2, Block 7, immediately adjacent to the company offices on Caribou Street. Kendal was to have the use of the buildings for ten years, after which they were to become the sole property of Brewster Transport. The one-storey building replaced the old Brewster Hall, which had finally met its demise after over fifty years of service as a hall, community center, Masonic Lodge, armoury, bowling alley, garage, storage area, and dormitory. After World War II it first served as a dining hall for summer students at the Banff School of Fine Arts, then housing in the summer for university students driving for the company, and finally it stood vacant for eight years.

A similar agreement in 1962 allowed Len Kamenka, the lessee of the old Brewster Trading Company premises on Lot 16, Block 1, to replace the building with a modern, fire-proof one, costing some $40,000, in return for twelve years of free occupation. At the end of that time a new lease for five years was to be negotiated on mutually agreeable terms.

Brewster Transport's existing properties also required some renovations: a refurnishing of the Mount Royal Hotel dining room, costing $30,000, and a remodelling of the second floor of the hotel annex. The intent of the latter was to consolidate the administrative offices of Brewster Transport and Brewster-Rocky Mountain-Gray Line, thereby increasing efficiency since the two companies jointly employed several officers. By simply removing some partitions and rearranging some plumbing from the old guest rooms a nice suite of offices was created and the old office spaces of both Brewster Transport and Brewster-Rocky Mountain-Gray Line were opened up for rental. Later, in 1961, Brewster-Rocky Mountain-Gray Line's ticket office vacated the Rocky Mountain Tours building for relocation in the Greyhound Bus Depot, which the company was then managing through an agreement negotiated with Greyhound in 1959. This office, under the management of Gerry Evans, handled all sightseeing ticketing and car rentals and gradually began to supply a few airline tickets as well. Eventually it was managed by Arnold Potter, a former company driver, who developed it into a full scale travel agency, Brewster Travel.

Brewster Transport's restraint on new investments after 1959 improved its financial position somewhat, as did better performance on its Jasper interests and at Emerald Lake beginning in 1961, and the growing revenue of Brewster-Rocky Mountain-Gray Line. This company had proved an unqualified success after some ups and downs. For example, in 1960 its revenues had decreased sharply from previous years while administrative costs increased and its profit for the year fell to $37,000 from $86,800 in 1959. The company's amending its policy on depreciation of vehicles allowed for a reduction of $79,900 in accumulated allowances for depreciation which was then added to the surplus account, permitting the usual dividend of $30,000 to be declared. A complete turnaround in the transportation situation followed in 1961 and the operating profit before income tax increased by $77,400, an increase of almost 200 percent. The trend continued the next year bringing total profits to $161,300 and allowing a dividend of $85,000. Significantly, assets of Brewster-Rocky Mountain-Gray Line topped the million dollar mark for the first time, $980,000 of them in the automobile and bus fleet. Sightseeing transportation had finally come of age in the mountain national parks.

As if to accentuate the reaching of a turning point in the development of the business, the early sixties saw a changing of the guard at Brewster Transport. In April, 1961 Bert Manley, the company's second most senior employee, passed away at seventy-three, four days after returning from a trip to Hawaii. Crosby, approaching his mid-seventies, showed no signs of slowing down or wishing to retire. But time was also catching up with him and on February 28, 1964, after fifty-seven consecutive years with the company, he succumbed to a heart attack at his home at age seventy-six. With his passing, the last link with the early days of the company was severed. It was a great loss to both Brewster Transport and the community, for he had given his very best to both. As his obituary very accurately phrased it, he was one individual of whom it could be truthfully said "he left his town a better place than he found it." The same could have been said for his dedication to Brewster Transport.

No one was more aware of what Crosby's passing meant than the two major shareholders of the company, Dell Brewster and Fern Dooley. The ladies had always felt obliged to retain ownership of the company, as Jim had requested in his will, so long as Crosby remained at the helm. Now, not sure what action to take, they were willing to follow the advice of their lawyer, George Steer. His advice was not long in coming. At the board meeting held in mid-April to determine the future of the company, Lloyd Fenerty suggested himself as president and Jack Hayes as vice-president and general manager. The strong-willed Steer said he saw no reason why Hayes should not be president and, having been made a director a few minutes before, so moved. The ladies supported the motion and Jack Hayes immediately became the fifth chief executive officer in the company's history, succeeding Jim and Bill Brewster, Fred Hussey and Lou Crosby. Steer next suggested that selling the company should be investigated since his two clients could then be guaranteed an income that was not subject to the vagaries of annual dividends. That motion was also passed, and Hayes was designated to pursue the matter.

Jack Hayes

Since the CPR held options to purchase both Brewster Transport and Brewster-Rocky Mountain-Gray Line, Hayes first contacted the railway to see if it were interested. Marathon Realty, a recently created branch of the corporation, was responsible for negotiating CPR contracts of this type. Rod Sykes, the Western Canadian general manager for Marathon at the time, was lukewarm on the idea of a purchase. He took the matter to a board meeting for a decision but so many other items on the agenda preceded it, it was never discussed. Sykes soon afterwards made the decision himself, sending a letter to the Brewster Transport board informing it the CPR would not exercise its option. Hayes then initiated discussions with the next most likely interested party, Greyhound Lines of Canada.

At an earlier time George Fay had hoped to eliminate Brewster Transport as a competitor in the national parks, allowing him to forge another link for his dreamed of Toronto-to-Vancouver bus service. His securing the Calgary-Banff run from

George Brewster had accomplished his objective, and thereafter relations between Greyhound and Brewster Transport had improved. Fay's successor at Greyhound was Robert L. "Bob" Borden, a man who had joined the company from the ranks of the unemployed in 1935 and who, under Fay's tutelage, became his executive assistant in 1943 and, ultimately, president after Fay retired in 1957. Borden operated in much the same style as his mentor, developing plans and making decisions himself before presenting them for approval to the board of the American parent company. Hayes' proposal surprised Borden but, after thinking the matter over, he informed the Brewster president that Greyhound was interested in making an offer.

The Brewster Transport board had put a price tag on the company including its share in Brewster-Rocky Mountain-Gray Line in excess of $2 million. Borden examined the 1964 financial statement which, with real estate and Brewster-Rocky Mountain-Gray Line stock valued at cost, showed the assets of the company at $1,036,-139.98. Realizing that a reevaluation would raise the figure substantially, he made an offer,and began the lengthy negotiations which involved only Hayes and himself. The principals of Rocky Mountain Tours had an interest in these negotiations as owners of a third of the shares in Brewster-Rocky Mountain-Gray Line, but took no direct part. Jim McLeod had resigned from the company in May, 1964 and moved to the Okanagan, leaving Bob Bray as the only family member actively involved in the company, and Hayes kept him informed of the progress of negotiations. In early July, 1965 it was announced that Greyhound had made an offer but that several stumbling blocks were yet to be overcome.

The stumbling blocks included the CPR's assent to any deal, and the approval of the Department of Northern Affairs for the transfer of leases. To overcome the first hurdle Hayes arranged for CPR Hotel Department head Roy Mackie to meet Borden to receive assurances the service would continue to be up to the same standard. A new concession agreement would see Brewster Transport's paying concession fees based on ten percent of the average of the past five years' gross income from transportation after deducting travel agents' commissions. The second hurdle was more difficult: many people were expressing publicly their concern about the control of what was essentially a monopoly situation passing to an American-dominated company. It was a genuine concern since the federal government had announced it would take steps to limit the amount of foreign capital invested in Canadian companies, with the aim of retaining Canadian control. But once Hayes and Borden had presented all the information concerning the sale to federal officials, approval of the lease transfers came immediately. However, the government did require the company to surrender its perpetual leases and renegotiate them on the basis of forty-two year agreements.

With all impediments removed, on July 31, 1965 Greyhound Lines of Canada purchased all issued and outstanding shares of company stock. Thus ended family ownership of Brewster Transport, the largest and longest-lived family-controlled enterprise in the Canadian Rockies and, according to some reports, the largest privately owned sightseeing company in the world. For seventy-three years some member of the Brewster family had been involved in the transportation business as a part of Brewster Transport or one of its predecessors. An interview with family members in the Calgary *Albertan* quoted Bill Brewster as stating that "it hurts to see it crumble," and an outspoken Pat Brewster said "I don't want to see it happen and I don't give a hoot who knows what I think."

All sentimentality aside, most observors realized the sale was inevitable since Brewster Transport had gone as far as it could as a private company. It was failing to take advantage of new opportunities because of its continually poor working capital position. The company that had made its way with colour and verve through the ups and downs of the tourist business now had to come to grips with a more complex modern age. An editorial in the *Albertan* entitled "Of Benefit To All" put the matter in its proper perspective. It said that while it would have been preferable to see the company remain in Canadian hands, the fact of the matter was that no Canadian-controlled company had made an offer to purchase it. It went on to point out that the sale could be extremely beneficial since the CPR seemed to be no longer interested in providing efficient passenger service while Greyhound was and it envisioned Greyhound's pouring the kind of promotional money into Banff that the family operated enterprise never could. It summed up by stating: "Sentimentally, the cutting of the Brewster link with Banff may be an emotional loss. Practically, however, the transfer could be of immense benefit to both Banff and the Alberta economy."

Columbia Icefield Snowmobile Tours Foremost snowmobile on Athabasca Glacier

# Epilogue: The Greyhound Years

Bob Borden, the new chairman of the board of Brewster Transport, intended the conclusions of the Calgary *Albertan's* editorial prove correct. The policy of the parent company in Chicago was not to interfere in the affairs of Greyhound Lines of Canada so long as it was profitable, and Borden's policy was essentially the same with regard to the new subsidiary. This left the ball in the hands of Jack Hayes and the management team that had come with him from pre-sale days. They were to show themselves worthy of the trust placed in them.

The first board meeting held after the purchase, on January 7, 1966, elected Bob Black, Q.C., of Calgary as secretary, John S. Frew, comptroller of Greyhound Lines of Canada, as treasurer, and Bob Bray as comptroller and assistant secretary, in addition to Borden as chairman and Hayes as president. The 600 shares of issued stock, valued at $100 per share, were assigned, Greyhound Lines of Canada receiving 599 shares and Borden 1 share. Balance sheets, dated October 31, 1965, were introduced showing reevaluated assets of $1,191,657 for Brewster Transport and $879,534 for Brewster-Rocky Mountain-Gray Line.

Two situations Hayes had to face immediately proved to be of constant concern. Directly after the purchase, the Amalgamated Transit Union began to try organizing Brewster Transport workers. In the transportation branch those in the management category included Rod Adams, now operations manager for the Banff area, Bill Hope, transportation supervisor at Lake Louise and Don Hayes, operations manager for the Jasper area. The remainder of the twenty-five permanent employees were the target of the union organizers. Pre-sale Brewster Transport wages varied from $1 per hour for parking lot attendants to between $1.25 and $1.50 per hour for junior drivers, not nearly so attractive as those Greyhound employees received. About fifteen of the permanent employees immediately joined the union and bargaining began on their behalf with no immediate results. In early August, 1966 the unionized employees decided to walk off for a fifty percent wage increase. Some 100 of the 130 student drivers, many of whom were studying law, met and decided to back them in their demands, sending the company into its first strike in its long history. The strike lasted for eight days, completely shutting down sightseeing operations, before the mediation efforts of Father Paul O'Bryne, the local Catholic priest, succeeded in reaching a compromise.

The two-year contract, not ratified until May 4, 1967, clearly defined employees' rights and procedures, such as bidding for routes and time off, seniority, fringe benefits and holiday pay, as well as wage rates. It defined categories for drivers, mechanical staff and terminal employees and established a two-stage wage increase. The rates provided a junior or "Class A" driver $2.00 per hour and a senior or "Class A 4" driver $2.68 per hour in the latter part of the contract. Likewise, a junior mechanic would receive $2.70 per hour and a senior mechanic $2.80 per hour; a junior ticket agent $285 per month and a senior ticket agent $305 per month. These wages were not equivalent to those paid Greyhound employees but they went a long way toward narrowing the gap, and it continued to close in the years ahead.

A second problem that took equally long to solve was the age and suitability of the Brewster Transport fleet. The equipment which had been added during the Brewster-Rocky Mountain-Gray Line period consisted mostly of second-hand reconditioned units. In the immediate post-sale period Brewster Transport purchased additional used coaches from the parent Greyhound company and had them reconditioned as sightseeing buses. As Motor Coach Industries was now a wholly-owned subsidiary of Greyhound, it was a foregone conclusion that all these vehicles would be MCIs. In November, 1966 seven used 41-passenger MCI 1956 Model 96 coaches were purchased from Greyhound for $2323 each and $8000 per unit was reserved to convert them to sightseeing use, including the installation of skyview roofs. A Winnipeg company, Beverley Bus and Truck Body Company,

**Minister of Highways Gordon Taylor and Jack Hayes presenting Walter Ashdown with his Million Mile Safe Driving Award, 1970**

did the actual conversions and the vehicles were ready for the 1967 season. That year a further purchase of ten used MCI 1958 Model 96 coaches was approved.

The seventeen additional vehicles were a welcome supplement to the fleet, but they barely kept pace with units being taken out of service because of age. The company could add few more vehicles because of its limited service facilities. The Banff Springs Hotel garage, built in 1926, had been inadequate for many years, so in November, 1971 the board approved building a service garage in the Banff Industrial Compound allowing for expansion of the Banff fleet. Contemplating new purchases after its completion, the company examined its policy of acquiring only rebuilt older units. Sightseeing buses were inadequate for the growing winter operations of the company, particulary for ascending the steep grade to Sunshine Village. Consequently, 1973 equipment purchases included seven new Taylor school buses and five used Model MC-3 coaches from Greyhound. The Taylor buses, which cost $14,200 each, performed better on steep grades, had lower fuel costs and had greater carrying capacities, making them useful in summer for short distance, high volume transfer trips.

Even though these purchases helped modernize the fleet, half the company's vehicles were still over fifteen years old, making fleet maintenance costs abnormally high. The parent company's board recognized the state of affairs and in 1974 its investment committee authorized the purchase of the first new sightseeing buses in many years. These were three MC-5Bs costing $65,000 each, and they were supplemented by five new school buses at $15,000 each, two used MC-7s with glass top conversions, costing $46,000 each, and three MC-5As also with glass top conversions, costing $18,200 each. Following this investment of $416,600 was a further investment of $491,000 in 1975, including two new MC-8 coaches with glass roofs, now costing $90,000 each. Even with the upgrading the fleet's average age was a rather high 14.3 years and it was not until several more major purchases were made, the last being five new 41-passenger MC-5C coaches with glass roofs at $114,000 each in 1979, that the average age was brought down to a respectable 10.6 years.

The company needed the increasingly sophisticated sightseeing buses to keep pace with the demands of tourists for the maximum in comfort and convenience while sightseeing, and while riding between Calgary and Banff, a result of a fundamental change in tourism which began in the fifties. Instead of arriving by train, by the late fifties some tourists were arriving by airplane and needed transportation between the airport and Banff. Brewster-Rocky Mountain-Gray Line had reached an agreement with Yellow Cab, the concessionaire at the Calgary Airport, which allowed them to run an 11-passenger bus to pick up such people. Over the years Brewster Transport had become heavily involved with two large tour companies, Cartan and U.T.L., and when their groups began to arrive by plane the company had to provide large numbers of units to pick them up at the airport. By 1967 virtually all tour groups were arriving by plane and were handled in this way.

While the company was upgrading its conventional sightseeing equipment in the early seventies, it was also paying attention to some new and rather exotic machinery, a result of Brewster Transport's creating a subsidiary company in 1969. Bill Ruddy, who had obtained the government concession to operate snowmobiles on the Columbia Icefield in 1952,had built up the business to the point where he had about fourteen Bombardier snowmobiles, auxiliary equipment, and a staff camp for approximately seventy-five employees. In 1968 he gave Brewster Transport an option to purchase and Hayes set about convincing the board to exercise it, arguing that the business would fit in well with the company's existing hotel facilities at the Columbia Icefield Chalet and could easily share some staff. The board agreed and created a new company, Columbia Icefield Snowmobile Tours, Limited, in March, 1969. Initially it operated with the Bombardiers but as business grew they were inadequate for the demand. The company approached Foremost, a Calgary-based maker of tracked vehicles for oilfield use, and asked it to design a high capacity passenger body that could be fit on their chassis. The prototype, capable of handling 28 passengers, went into service in 1970, followed by a 40-passenger model in 1971. In 1976 Brewster Transport provided the body shells of two Model 96 MCI buses for Foremost to convert into two additional 40-passenger snowmobiles. These steps increased the total carrying capacity to 308 passengers, making the business

**Brewster Transport fleet, 1978**

**Columbia Icefield Chalet with its new wing**

a very profitable one. Particularly gratifying was the fact that the Columbia Icefield Chalet and the snowmobile tours required no more staff than the tours alone previously had.

The board, which very quickly after the sale had several American directors appointed to it, was also interested in developing Brewster Transport's non-transportational concerns. In November, 1966 they began by approving an addition to the Columbia Icefield Chalet. The Chalet had been performing exceedingly well in the early sixties, particularly on its dining facilities, a result of both the increasing number of bus tours the company was bringing to it and a growth in traffic on the Banff-Jasper Highway. The proposal, pointing out the restaurants in the Chalet were handling up to 500 people a day in June and September and up to 1000 a day in July and August, called for 100 seats to be added to the coffee shop, bringing its total capacity to 153. In the addition there were also to be thirteen twin-bedded rooms, doubling their number to twenty-six. According to financial projections this would bring operating profits before taxes up to $50,000 per annum from the current $34,000 per annum.

Another development concerning the Icefield property occurred in May, 1968 when British-American Oil agreed to build and equip a new service station and then lease it back to the company. The lease would be nominal on the understanding that the company would buy all its petroleum products from B-A at delivered prices. At the end of twenty years all the improvements were to revert to Brewster Transport.

Shortly after committing themselves to an expansion of the Columbia Icefield Chalet, the directors had to make a major decision regarding the Mount Royal Hotel because of a disastrous fire that destroyed the old wing of the building on March 31, 1967. The fire, starting in the garbage storage area of the kitchen in the late evening, got into some grease and quickly spread up through the artificial asphalt brick on its rear exterior. Before the alarm sounded the old wooden structure was ablaze and the town's volunteer fire department could do little to save it. The author Arthur Hailey happened to be staying in the hotel that night and earlier in the evening had given manager John McConville an autographed copy of his latest novel, *Hotel.* Hailey and the other guests safely escaped from the inferno and the next day he provided an exclusive front-page story to the Calgary *Albertan* in which he summed up the feelings of many people about the sad end of the original building: "The Mount Royal Hotel had been a good hotel. Despite its age, it was well run, clean, efficient. It had something of that elusive thing called character."

The fire destroyed fifty-two guest rooms and the dining room but a firewall saved some fifty additional rooms and the retail stores in the newer part of the building. In the fire's aftermath the directors met on May 15, 1967 to look into a rebuilding program. The company expected to receive slightly over $600,000 from insurance but Hayes requested the directors to put up $720,000 for the rebuilding. For this investment he promised the most modern hotel in Banff with thirty-five new rooms, a dining room, a coffee shop, a cocktail lounge and banquet rooms. Approval was given and later the same year a further

The old Mount Royal Hotel consumed by fire

$50,000 was allocated to increase the length and add five more rooms. The new structure, with its Rundle stone, brick and cedar shingle exterior, designed by Calgary architect W. C. Milne, was hailed as "a building that through its natural appearance belonged to Banff."

The confidence which Greyhound expressed in the Columbia Icefield Chalet and the Mount Royal Hotel it had not extended to the company's other accommodation interest, the Emerald Lake Chalet. This business continued to experience financial problems and the directors and management determined it was just too small an operation for a large company like Brewster Transport to run efficiently. Consequently, in the spring of 1966 it was sold to Mr. and Mrs. Bill Smyth, the same couple who had purchased Moraine Lake Lodge from the company in 1959.

The Jasper operations of the company, which had also had their share of fiscal woes but which had been slowly improving since the early sixties, were completely reorganized in 1970. The government needed the company's property in Jasper in order to widen Connaught Drive so, in return for the company's 20,000 square foot site and a further 4000 square foot lot on Patricia Street on which it held an option, the government provided a 60,000 square foot site on Connaught Drive in a new development area. The company immediately sold the site to Imperial Oil, which agreed to build a new service station on it and then lease it back to the company on very attractive terms. At the same time, the company built a new service garage on a lot acquired in Jasper's industrial area. The whole undertaking provided a shot in the arm for the Jasper business.

Because of Greyhound's willingness to support the well-planned programs of Brewster Transport in both the transportation and property development fields, the company fared well in the post-sale period. Dividends rose from the $85,000 level they had been in 1962 to almost $290,000 for the combined businesses of Brewster Transport and Columbia Icefield Snowmobile Tours a decade later. Virtually all the profits went back into equipment and development, but with them the company proved to its American directors it could hold its own.

Jack Hayes, the man responsible for many of these successes, remained in the president's chair until May 31, 1977 when he resigned to pursue his own business interests. Replacing him as general manager was David Morrison, a twenty-nine year old native of Sydney, Nova Scotia and graduate from Dalhousie University in Commerce. He had first driven for the company in the summer of 1968 while attending university and had continued to work part-time after he became an accountant at the Banff Springs Hotel. In March, 1973 he joined Brewster Transport full-time as an accountant and then quickly moved through the ranks as chief accountant, controller and vice-president of administration respectively. On February 1, 1980 he was officially confirmed as president.

As of 1981 Morrison is responsible for a fleet of 62 sightseeing buses with a total capacity of 2659, 24 school buses with a total capacity of 1056, 10 minibuses with a total capacity of 140, 17 cars with a total capacity of 78, 24 snowmobiles with a total capacity of 308 and numerous trucks, tractors and snowplows, and his staff in summer reaches almost 400. During the 1980-81 fiscal year his company will purchase ten new MC-9 47-passenger buses at a total cost of $1.6 million and the following year ten more, making it the most modern sightseeing fleet of its type in Canada. Morrison's aim, like that of Bill and Jim Brewster when they took out that fishing party of 1892, is unvarying — to provide visitors from many lands the opportunity to experience and enjoy one of the world's great treasures, the Canadian Rockies.

Dave Morrison with a new MC-9, 1981

# A Note on Sources

The primary source of material for this history was the papers of the Brewster Transport Company, to which I was given free and complete access. Coinciding with the publication of this work the company has deposited these papers (up to 1964) in the Archives of the Canadian Rockies (The Whyte Foundation) Banff. Other collections in the Archives of the Canadian Rockies, particularly those of Brewster family members, were also useful. A third major source of material was the early Parks Branch records on deposit in the Public Archives of Canada in Ottawa. In addition to the Parks records in the public domain and available for research, I was given permission by Parks Canada to view several restricted files, including the lease files for the various Brewster properties.

Filling in the gaps in the written record were numerous oral interviews which I conducted. These included interviews with: Mrs. J. I. (Dell) Brewster; F. O. (Pat) Brewster; Jack Brewster; Elmer Charlton; Fred Crosby; Mrs. Basil Gardom; Ralph Harvey; Jack Hayes; Bill Hope; T. W. Kirkham; John McConville; Campbell McLaurin; Dave Morrison; and Jean (McLeod) Walls. Another useful source for filling in gaps were newspapers, including the *Crag and Canyon,* and *Rocky Mountain Courier* and various Calgary papers.

Most of the photographs in the book are drawn from the rich collections of the Archives of the Canadian Rockies. The exceptions are: p. 6 courtesy of Pat Brewster; p. 21 courtesy of the Public Archives of British Columbia; pp. 39, 132, 143 courtesy of the Crosby family; pp. 40, 100 courtesy of the McLeod family; pp. 61, 62 courtesy of Glenbow Museum Archives; p. 107 courtesy Bud and Annette Brewster; pp. 134, 136 courtesy Don Hayes; pp. 152, 154, 157, 158, 161 courtesy Brewster Transport.